Education and the Labour Gov

This book presents a valuable and authoritative evaluation of the real impact Labour's two terms have had on the British education system.

On the 1st May 1997 the British Electorate witnessed a watershed moment. After an eighteen year Conservative rule, a New Labour Government took office. When asked what his top three priorities were for the first term, Tony Blair stated that they would be 'Education, education, education.' This book questions the extent to which the policy has met the rhetoric, by examining Labour's education policy, practice, and achievements during Blair's two terms in office.

This new selection of writings by highly respected academics in this field charts and evaluates the effects of policy changes on the various sectors of the educational system and on the major indicators of inequality.

This book was previously published as a special issue of the *Oxford Review of Education*.

Geoffrey Walford is professor of education policy at the Department of Educational Studies, University of Oxford

Education and the Labour Government

An Evaluation of Two Terms

Edited by Geoffrey Walford

Routledge
Taylor & Francis Group

LONDON AND NEW YORK

First published 2006 by Routledge
2 Park Square, Milton Park, Abingdon, Oxon, OX14 4RN

Simultaneously published in the USA and Canada
by Routledge
270 Madison Ave, New York NY 10016

Routledge is an imprint of the Taylor & Francis Group

Transferred to Digital Printing 2007

© 2006 Taylor and Francis Group Ltd

Typeset in Plantin by Genesis Typesetting Ltd, Rochester, Kent

British Library Cataloguing in Publication Data
A catalogue record for this book is available from the British Library

Library of Congress Cataloging in Publication Data
A catalog record for this book has been requested.

ISBN10: 0-415-36870-7 (hbk)
ISBN10: 0-415-46412-9 (pbk)

ISBN13: 978-0-415-36870-4 (hbk)
ISBN13: 978-0-415-46412-3 (pbk)

CONTENTS

Introduction: education and the Labour Government

Geoffrey Walford

Introduction

The United Kingdom General Election on 1 May 1997 gave a landslide victory to a re-vitalised Labour Party. Following 18 years of Conservative government, first under Prime Minister Margaret Thatcher and then John Major, Tony Blair became Prime Minister with a huge Commons majority of 179 over all other parties. Such a majority meant that extensive changes of policy could be implemented with little effective opposition.

During the election campaign Tony Blair had repeatedly claimed that the top three priorities of a New Labour government would be 'education, education, education', and on page two of the Labour Party's election manifesto (Labour Party, 1997) a smiling Blair is seen with Nelson Mandela—the unacknowledged originator of the oratorical education triplet.

In less rhetorical language, the manifesto outlined that education was the first of ten 'pledges' in the 'contract' that the Labour Party made with voters.

Over the five years of a Labour government:

1. Education will be our number one priority; and we will increase the share of national income spent on education as we decrease it on the bills of economic and social failure (p. 5).

Six bullet-points (p. 7) set out the framework for a raft of new policies:

- Cut class sizes to 30 or under for all 5, 6 and 7 year-olds
- Nursery places for all four-year-olds
- Attack low standards in schools
- Access to computer technology
- Lifelong learning through a new University for Industry
- More spending on education as the cost of unemployment falls.

There were to be changes in almost every area of education. Yet, there were also to be strong continuities with past Conservative policies—a feature made clear in almost all of the contributions that follow. Against the advice of most educationalists on the political left, choice and diversity were to be retained and even expanded at secondary level. A key aspect of this was that, while there was to be no return to (or, at least, expansion of) 11 plus examinations, comprehensive schools were to be 'modernised', and with the aim that each would develop its own strengths and ethos. Grammar schools would be allowed to continue where local parents wished it, and regular testing of children and published 'league tables' were to be retained. The rhetoric was of 'standards not structures', yet much of what was planned related to both.

In terms of the absolute number of policies that have come from the Department for Education and Employment and then, since 2001, the Department for Education and Skills, it is certainly true that education has been a first priority. The two terms of Labour government have seen a deluge of policies on education. There have been eight separate Education Acts, and hundreds of separate initiatives—some already defunct—all jostling for attention.

David Blunkett was appointed as Shadow Secretary of State for Education following Blair's election to Party Leader in 1994 and, for the next three years, they worked together and with such educationalists as Michael Barber (1996) to craft a series of education policies that they believed would make the Party more popular and electable. This meant that, with David Blunkett now Secretary of State for Education, the *Education (Schools) Act 1997*, which phased out the Assisted Places Scheme which had provided funding for academically able children to attend private schools, could be swiftly legislated. Further, just over two months after the election, the government published its first substantial White Paper, *Excellence in Schools* (DfEE, 1997), which incorporated many of the promises of the election manifesto. The White Paper led to the *School Standards and Framework Act 1998* (bulging with 145 Sections and 32 Schedules), which introduced: a new structure for the funding and organisation of schools, education action zones, new admissions and selection arrangements, and many other changes. A further short Act, the *Education (Student Loans) Act 1998*, allowed student loans to be transferred to the private sector, while the *Teaching and Higher Education Act 1998* introduced the General Teaching Councils, tightened Headship qualifications, gave OfSTED the power to inspect Initial Teacher Education and Training, and further legislated on student fees and loans in further and higher education.

Work on lifelong post-16 learning soon led to a Green Paper, *The Learning Age: a renaissance for a New Britain* (DfEE, 1998), followed by a White Paper, *Learning to Succeed: a New Framework for Post-16 Learning* (DfEE, 1999), finally leading to the *Learning and Skills Act 2000*. The major change brought about by this Act was a new regulatory and funding framework for all post-16 education and training other than higher education. The Learning and Skills Council replaced the Further Education Funding Council and the Training and Enterprise Councils and would have responsibility for another new initiative, Individual Learning Accounts, and close contact with a new University for Industry, both introduced in the same Act.

The final Education Act of Labour's first term of office was the *Special Educational Needs and Disability Act 2001* which extended the more general *Disabilities Discrimination Act 1995* to education. This made it unlawful to discriminate against students or any others with contacts with educational organisations, and used a definition of discrimination which demanded reasonable adjustments to be made to facilities, teaching processes and assessment procedures.

It is impossible and undesirable to list here all of the changes made in the first term of office (good discussions and analysis can be found in Fielding, 2001; Tomlinson, 2001 and Chitty, 2004), but most would agree that the most important events included the introduction of National Literacy and Numeracy Strategies to ensure that all primary children meet agreed targets, the establishment of a Social Exclusion Unit within the Cabinet Office, and the creation of the General Teaching Councils. The structure and funding of schooling and 14–19 education was greatly changed, new types of specialist schools were introduced, and some priority was given to the disadvantaged through anti-discrimination legislation and through what were called Education Action Zones and then, later, a programme labelled Excellence in Cities.

David Blunkett continued to develop and implement new educational policy throughout his time in office, and the publication of the 2001 Green Paper, *Schools: building on success: raising standards, promoting diversity, achieving results*, published just prior to calling a General Election, acted as a summary of what had been achieved and what he believed was still to be done. Many of the ideas were incorporated within Labour's Manifesto for a second term, *Ambitions for Britain* (Labour Party, 2001).

Within this new manifesto, education was still proclaimed as 'Labour's number one priority', but the first mention of this statement appears on page 18 (Labour Party, 2001, p. 18), and it is only to be found in small print in a wider section on 'World-class public services' following a somewhat contradictory statement on the previous page (in much larger print) that 'Labour will put education and healthcare first'. Numeracy is not a strong point of the manifesto as the 'Five pledges for the next five years' actually contain 10 points (two of which are '10,000 extra teachers and higher standards in secondary schools'), while the 'Ten goals for 2010' actually contain 15 points. Two of these ten goals, which contain three of the 15 points, are (Labour Party, 2001, p. 3):

● Expanded higher education as we raise standards in secondary schools
● Opportunity for all children, security for all pensioners.

It is not clear what exactly was meant by 'opportunities for all children', how success in achieving this would be measured, or why this should be linked to 'security for all pensioners'. A double-page spread in the manifesto (pp. 6/7) headed 'Investment and reform' also lists several other aims for education including:

● Increase education spending by more than five per cent in real terms each year for the next three years as we increase the share of national income for education in the next Parliament

- Ensure every secondary school develops a distinctive mission including the expansion of specialist schools
- Diversify state schools with new City Academies and more church schools
- Direct more money to headteachers, more freedom for successful schools
- Reform provision for 11- to 14-year-olds to ensure higher standards in English, maths, science and information technology
- Introduce new vocational options from 14 onwards, with expanded apprenticeship opportunities
- Ensure primary schools offer more chances to learn languages, music and sport, as well as higher standards in the basics
- Provide a good-quality nursery place for every three-year-old.

Overall, education had a less prominent place in this manifesto compared with the previous one. 'Economic stability' and 'Prosperity for all' had a more dominant position in the programme, and the discussion about the economy, while including several aspects of training and skills, only sees these as linked to employment and productivity. Incidentally, a picture of a smiling Tony Blair with Nelson Mandela is similarly reduced in scale in this manifesto and relegated to page 40 instead of page 2.

But, although reduced in emphasis, there were still some highly significant plans for education. While not neglecting primary and early years education (where the government was generally considered to have had considerable success during the first term of office), the focus of the plans for the second term were more on secondary, further and higher education—in particular, improving standards in secondary, encouraging more diversity of curriculum post-14 including more vocational routes, and moving towards 50% of all young people under 30 having a higher education experience. Greater diversity was to be encouraged for all schools with special encouragement being given to the growth of faith-based and other schools with non-state sponsors.

The Labour Party was returned to power in June 2001 with a reduced, but still substantial, majority. Estelle Morris (who had previously been Minister for Schools) took over as Secretary of State for Education, and the department was reformulated as the Department for Education and Skills. Again, the newly formed government acted quickly to introduce new legislation with a White Paper, *Schools Achieving Success* (DfES, 2001) being published in September 2001, followed by a new Education Bill in September 2001. The resulting *Education Act 2002* (with 217 Sections and 22 Schedules) introduced many changes and developments to policy, but the increased support for choice and diversity in schooling was one of the most central. The Act legislated for the formation of Academies and City Colleges and made it necessary for local education authorities to invite tenders from any potential external sponsors whenever it was necessary to open a new school. Amongst other changes, the Act made changes to teachers' pay and conditions, amended admissions and exclusions procedures, and diluted the National Curriculum at Key Stage 4 (after 14).

Estelle Morris was in office only for 16 months. Having seen the *Education Act 2002* through to the statute books, she ran into problems with the teacher unions following a casual comment about some comprehensive schools being so bad that, if she were still a teacher, she would not 'touch them with a bargepole'. She also emphasised a 'post-comprehensive' structure for schools, generated further problems with her handling of a marking crisis in A-level examinations, and failed to ensure that a new Criminal Records Bureau system of background checking new entrants to teaching was working on time (Chitty, 2004, p. 82). She resigned, candidly admitting that she felt she had been less successful at running the whole department than she had been as Minister for Schools. She was replaced by Charles Clarke in October 2002.

The first White Paper that Clarke put his name to was *The Future of Higher Education* published in January 2003. This presented further information on, amongst many other topics, the promised increased investment in higher education and the expansion to 50% of the proportion of people under 30 with a higher education experience. It also gave information on the government's desire for diversity of mission within the higher education sector, its greater emphasis on teaching quality, the raising of top-up fees for students to a maximum of £3000, and the introduction of an independent Access Regulator to negotiate contracts with universities to ensure greater social equality in access. Parts of this programme were highly controversial, but the government's majority ensured most of the plans remained unchanged in the resulting *Higher Education Act 2004*.

The above description has merely outlined some of the major elements of the eight separate Education Acts. Beyond these specific Acts, other non-education Acts have had significant effects on children and learners and not all of the changes that have been made have actually required primary legislation. Indeed, there have been so many different new policies during the period that many have complained of 'initiative fatigue'.

But the number of separate initiatives is little guide to the direction or overall effectiveness of government policy. There has been considerable academic debate and controversy over what have been seen as contradictions between the various element of policy. For example, while many of these policies (such as Education Action Zones) have been directly aimed at reducing inequality and providing better educational opportunities for the disadvantaged, many commentators (e.g. Walford, 2001; Chitty, 2004) have argued that other policies (such as encouraging greater diversity at secondary level) have acted in the opposite direction. There have been policies that have led to both centralisation and localisation, and it has been frequently argued that the sheer number and variety of separate initiatives have led to a lack of overall coherence.

Although it is self-evident that no collection of comment and analysis can be comprehensive, the contributions that follow attempt to give a preliminary and timely evaluation of the main features of Labour's educational policy during two terms of office. The contributions are arranged in two broad sections. The first section is structured in order of the stages of schooling. Thus Kathy Sylva and Gillian Pugh explore the early years; Kevin Brehony investigates primary; Chris Taylor, Stephen Gorard and John Fitz examine secondary; Richard Pring looks at 14 to 19; and Alan Ryan writes on higher education. The second, smaller, section brings together one article on lifelong learning by Dick Taylor, another on teachers and teacher education by John Furlong, and three broadly-based papers on special education (by Derrick Armstrong), ethnicity (by Sally Tomlinson) and gender (by Madeleine Arnot and Philip Miles). Rather than attempt complete coverage of all the issues, purposive selection has been made throughout. In terms of complete coverage there are thus some omissions both in the selection of broad areas of concern and within each article. The collection as a whole does not attempt a complete evaluation, but the individual authors have selected specific areas for discussion that they believe are the most significant.

At the macro level, the most important omission is probably the fact that all of the articles mainly focus on England and not Wales, Scotland or Northern Ireland. But it is incontrovertible that political devolution to a National Assembly for Wales and a Scottish Parliament have been amongst the most significant educational policies that the Labour government has implemented (Paterson, 2003). For those living in Wales and Scotland, devolution has had highly significant educational implications. While Scotland has always had a separate educational system, devolution has allowed the Labour Parties in those separate administrations to develop and implement distinctly different educational policies—often in direct contrast and conflict to those of the central UK government. For example, in 2001 when the UK Labour government was extolling the benefits of diversity in secondary schooling, the Labour-controlled National Assembly for Wales made it clear that it would strongly support comprehensive schools, that there would be no specialist schools or academies in Wales and that the private sector would not be permitted to establish new state-maintained schools. Similar, diametrically opposed policies can be found in Scotland, where top-up fees for students in higher education have not been introduced. The differences are so great that separate contributions would be necessary to cover each of the non-English areas of the United Kingdom.

A further problem is that a definitive evaluation cannot, of course, be made so close to the events themselves. A longer perspective would be needed to generate a fuller judgement and to provide the necessary data for such an evaluation. Nevertheless, the contributions that follow provide much of the information and many of the insights that should inform any rigorous analysis of how much, or how little, has been achieved. The various authors seek to test the extent to which the reality has matched the rhetoric, and provide an early assessment of some of Labour's educational policies, practices and achievements during these two terms of office. As another General Election is expected within a few months of publication, such an assessment is highly desirable.

Notes on contributor

Geoffrey Walford is Professor of Education Policy at the Department of Educational Studies, University of Oxford, and Fellow of Green College Oxford. His new books *Private Schools: tradition and diversity* and *Markets and Equity in Education* are both to be published by Continuum in 2005.

References

Barber, M. (1996) *The learning game. Arguments for an education revolution* (London, Victor Gollancz).

Chitty, C. (2004) *Education policy in Britain* (Basingstoke, Palgrave Macmillan).

Department for Education and Employment (1997) *Excellence in Schools*. White Paper (London, The Stationery Office).

Department for Education and Employment (1998) *The learning age: a renaissance for a new Britain*. Green Paper (London, The Stationery Office).

Department for Education and Employment (1998) *Teachers*. Green Paper (London, The Stationery Office).

Department for Education and Employment (1999) *Learning to succeed: a new framework for post-16 learning*. White Paper (London, The Stationery Office).

Department for Education and Employment (2001) *Schools: building on success: raising standards, promoting diversity, achieving results*. Green Paper (London, The Stationery Office).

Department for Education and Skills (2001) *Schools achieving success*. White Paper (London, The Stationery Office).

Department for Education and Skills (2003) *The future of higher education*. White Paper (London, The Stationery Office).

Fielding, M. (2001) (Ed.) *Taking education really seriously. Four years' hard Labour* (London, RoutledgeFalmer).

Labour Party (1997) *New Labour. Because Britain deserves better*. Election Manifesto (London, Labour Party).

Labour Party (2001) *Ambitions for Britain*. Labour's Manifesto 2001 (London, Labour Party).

Paterson, L. (2003) The three educational ideologies of the British Labour Party 1997–2001, *Oxford Review of Education*, 29(2), 165–186.

Tomlinson, S. (2001) *Education in a post-welfare society* (Buckingham, Open University Press).

Walford, G. (2001) From common schooling to selection? Affirming and contesting the comprehensive ideal, 1976–2001, in: R. Phillips & J. Furlong (Eds) *Education, reform and the state: politics, policy and practice 1976–2001* (London & New York, RoutledgeFalmer).

Transforming the early years in England

Kathy Sylva and Gillian Pugh

Part 1: The promise

> While the nineteenth century was distinguished by the introduction of primary education for all and the twentieth century by the introduction of secondary education for all, so the early part of the twenty first century should be marked by the introduction of pre-school provision for the under fives and childcare available to all. (Rt Hon Gordon Brown, MP, Chancellor of the Exchequer, 2004 Comprehensive Spending Review)

With its resounding electoral victory in 1997, Labour set about increasing services and support for young children and their families. Not only did they plan to increase spending on early years provision, they intended to alter its nature and the way services were delivered. In 1998 the 'National Childcare Strategy' was unveiled and this went far beyond education. It called for: free nursery education places for all four year olds whose parents wished it, Ofsted (Office for Standards in Education) inspections to assure quality of provision of free nursery education places, and 25 Early Excellence Centres to be set up across the country which would serve as 'models' for high quality practice integrating early education with childcare. Labour's vision was to meet the educational needs of young children but also the needs of their families for childcare and parent support or education.

The new government put early years high on its agenda of reform. They were not working from a blank slate, for during their years in opposition there had been a series of influential reports recommending an expansion in early education and an integrated approach to services for young children and their parents (see DES, 1990; Ball, 1994; Audit Commission, 1996, for example). The model for early excellence centres had been articulated by Pugh (1994), drawing on developments which went back to the earliest days of nursery education, but more specifically on the small number of 'combined nursery centres' which had been established since the 1970s.

In 1998 the Green Paper *Meeting the Childcare Challenge* was published. It went far beyond extending a half-day free educational place to three year olds. Some 1.6 million places were promised by 2004, and child care and early education were to become one experience for children and a seamless service for families. Responsibility for all 'day care' services for children under eight was transferred from the Department of Health to the Department of Education and Employment, which was to take a lead in 'joining up' the provision and funding of services for young children and their families. With its concern for expanding child care to support parents' return to work, the Department of Work and Pensions also had a stake in these services. Within months of coming into office, the government also established a Treasury-led cross-departmental review of services for children under eight, which led to proposals for the establishment of the Sure Start initiative, whereby some 250 (and later 500) local Sure Start programmes were to be set up in disadvantaged neighbourhoods, providing community-based support for parents and children under four. Financial support was offered to families on low incomes through the Working Families Tax Credit. The Foundation Stage was established for children from three until the end of reception year (aged five/six), a curriculum framework entitled *Curricular Guidance for the Foundation Stage* (DFEE/QCA, 2000). This was followed by *Birth to Three Matters*, a complementary framework for practitioners working with the growing number of children under three in early years services (DfES/Sure Start, 2003). All were part of an explosion of initiatives, programmes and funding streams.

The goal of this paper is to explore this recent history in terms of innovation in policy (i.e. the promise), the grounds for change (i.e. the research), delivery of new services (i.e. the achievement), and the tensions and gaps which remain (i.e. the shortfall). The paper will focus heavily on research evidence in terms of the effects of early years provision on children. Will the new policies make a difference for children and their families?

Part II: The research

Why are the early years important?

From its very first days Labour promised policies which would be 'informed by evidence'. Their speeches and reports on the early years were infused with research findings, all providing the rationale for policy initiatives.

Two lines of research explain why early learning is important. First are the many studies on the development of the brain, suggesting that early learning contributes to the brain's developing architecture. Scientists made clear that early learning stimulates optimal brain development (Blakemore & Frith, in press). Although the brain research is beguiling (Bruer, 1997; House of Commons, 2000a), the more powerful research comes from developmental psychology (see Gopnik *et al.*, 1999) which shows how the earliest interactions between child and carers provide the cultural structure that underpins the development of intellectual schemas. In essence, the neurological research confirmed the importance of learning in the early years whereas the psychological studies suggested which kind of learning was best (Sylva, 1994a; Melhuish, 2004). Children learn from conversations with adults and older peers, and it is through these conversations that young children acquire the cultural 'tools' to aid them in setting and achieving goals and in becoming part of communities (Bruner, 1986). Sylva extended the argument by showing that early learning experiences shape children towards a 'mastery' orientation in learning or a 'performance' one. Well before entering school the young child has acquired learning dispositions as well as key cognitive skills (Sylva, 1994b).

Finally there were scores of studies, especially from the USA, which demonstrated the powerful effects of early education on children's readiness for school and for their attainment throughout education and even employment. Melhuish (2004) reviewed the international literature on the effects of early education and care, concluding 'for provision for three years onwards the evidence is consistent that pre-school provision is beneficial to educational and social development for the whole population ... the evidence on childcare in the first three years for disadvantaged children indicates that high quality childcare can produce benefits for cognitive, language and social development. Low quality childcare produces either no benefit or negative effects'. Note that the word 'quality' has entered the debate.

Most striking in the international literature are the Perry Pre-school study (Schweinhart *et al.*, 1993) and the Abercedarian study (Ramey & Ramey, 1998). Both used randomised control designs and both demonstrated the lasting effects of early education and care, especially for children from disadvantaged backgrounds. The Perry studies were especially persuasive because they showed that early education (half day, ages three to five years) improved high school grades, decreased delinquency and adult crime, and improved employment status and earnings. Even more important, early education saved the taxpayer money because for each $1 of investment in the service, $7.16 was saved in social, health and justice systems later on (Barnett, 1996).

Research in the early years has been substantial in the UK. Throughout the Labour government a large-scale longitudinal research study on effective education in the early years has been carried out by the EPPE team (Sylva *et al.*, 1999), commissioned by the government in 1997. This has been influential in guiding the development of policy and has been used by ministers and the Treasury as the 'evidential base' for expanding universal services and targeting enhanced provision for the poor.

The Effective Provision of Pre-School Education (EPPE) project is the first major European longitudinal study of a national sample of young children's development between the ages of three and seven years. To investigate the effects of pre-school education, the EPPE team collected a wide range of information on 3,000 children. They also studied their parents, home environments and the pre-school settings children attended. Settings (141) were drawn from a range of providers (local authority day nursery, integrated centres, playgroups, private day nurseries, nursery schools and nursery classes). A sample of 'home' children (who had no or minimal pre-school experience) were recruited to the study at entry to school for comparison with the pre-school group. In addition to investigating the effects of pre-school provision, EPPE explored the characteristics of effective practice (and the pedagogy which underpins it) through twelve intensive case studies of settings with positive child outcomes. EPPE has demonstrated the beneficial effects of high quality provision on children's intellectual and social/behavioural developmental measured at school entry as well at the end of Years 1 and 2 (Sammons *et al.*, 2002, 2003; Sylva *et al.*, 2004).

Key findings on the effects of pre-school at age five and also at age seven

- *Impact of attending a pre-school—lasting effects* (Sammons *et al.*, in press)
  - Pre-school experience, compared to none, enhances all-round development in children.
  - The duration of attendance is important, with an earlier start being related to better intellectual development.
  - Full time attendance led to no better gains for children than part-time provision.
  - Disadvantaged children in particular can benefit significantly from quality pre-school experiences, especially where they are with a mixture of children from different social backgrounds.
  - The beneficial effects of pre-school remained evident throughout Key Stage 1, although some outcomes were not as strong as they had been at school entry.
- *Does type of pre-school matter?*
  - There are significant differences between individual pre-school settings and their impact on children; some settings are more effective than others in promoting positive child outcomes.
  - Good quality can be found across all types of early years settings; however even after taking account of a child's background and prior intellectual skills, the type of pre-school a child attends has an important effect on developmental progress. EPPE found that integrated centres (these are centres that fully combine education with care and have a high proportion of trained teachers) and nursery schools tend to promote the strongest intellectual outcomes for children. Similarly, fully integrated settings and nursery classes tend to promote better social development even after taking account of children's backgrounds and prior social behaviour.
- *Effects of duration*
  - The number of months a child attended pre-school continued to have an effect on their progress throughout Key Stage 1, although this effect was stronger for academic skills than for social behavioural development.

- *Effects of quality*
  - Pre-school quality was significantly related to children's scores on standardised tests of reading and mathematics at age six. At age seven the relationship between quality and academic attainment was somewhat weaker and the effect of quality on social behavioural development was no longer significant.
  - Settings that have staff with higher qualifications have higher quality scores and their children make more progress.
  - Effective pedagogy includes interaction traditionally associated with the term 'teaching', the provision of instructive learning environments and 'sustained shared thinking' to extend children's learning (Siraj-Blatchford *et al.*, 2002).
- *The importance of home learning*
  - For all children, the quality of the home learning environment promotes more intellectual and social development than parental occupation or qualification.

The EPPE study has demonstrated the positive effects of high quality pre-school provision on children's intellectual and social behavioural development up to the end of Key Stage 1 in primary school. The EPPE research indicates that pre-school can play an important part in combating social exclusion and promoting inclusion by offering disadvantaged children, in particular, a better start to primary school. Figure 1 shows clearly that disadvantaged children fail to meet the 'expected level' (level 2) in reading and writing if they do not attend pre-school education. The EPPE findings indicate that pre-school has a positive impact on children's progress over and above important family influences. The quality of the pre-school setting as well as the quantity (more terms but not necessarily more hours/day) are both influential.

EPPE has also shown that individual pre-school centres vary in their effectiveness in promoting intellectual progress over the pre-school period, and indicate that better outcomes are associated with some forms of provision. Likewise, the research points to the separate and significant influence of the home learning environment. These aspects (quality and quantity of pre-school and home learning environment) are more susceptible to change through policy initiatives than family characteristics such as SES. Early childhood services are a powerful lever in reducing inequalities and government used this message in 1999–2004 as a rationale for policy (House of Commons, 2000b, 2004; Inter-departmental Childcare Review, 2002).

EPPE results were replicated in a study in Northern Ireland (Melhuish, 2002, 2003) suggesting that the benefits of early education were to be found throughout the UK. Moreover EPPE findings were supplemented by small-scale studies, such as Bertram *et al.* (2002), suggesting that integrating services and focusing on families were the 'best' ways to promote child development and family capacity to support their children.

Part III: The achievement

In the period since 1997 there has been substantial investment in services for young children and their families, some of it universal and some targeted at the most

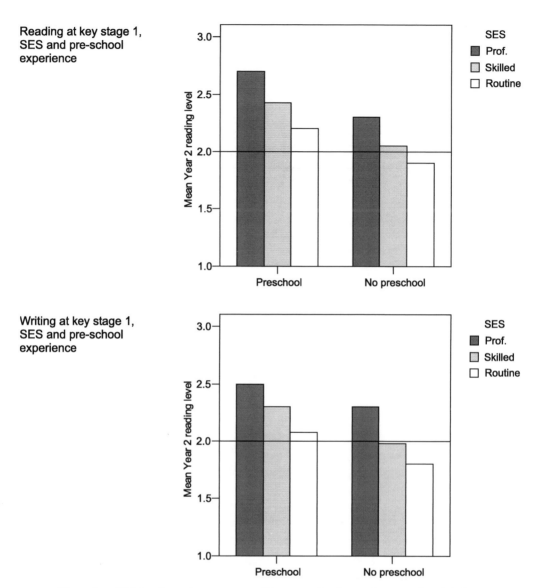

Reading at key stage 1, SES and pre-school experience

Writing at key stage 1, SES and pre-school experience

Figure 1.   Children's attainment at age 7 by pre-school attendance and social class
Source: Sammons *et al.* (2004)

disadvantaged communities (for further details of programmes and expenditure see http://www.nao.org.uk/publications/nao_reports/03-04/0304268.pdf, p. 22). The £2 billion annual government expenditure in 1997 had soared by 75% to £3.5 billion by 2003 (see Figure 2). Indeed, some £14 billion has been spent on early years services since 1998 (National Audit Office, 2004). However, as is evident in Figure 3, parents still make the major financial contribution to the cost of care— around 45% of the national childcare bill in 2002–2003, although part-time early education is free for three and four year olds.

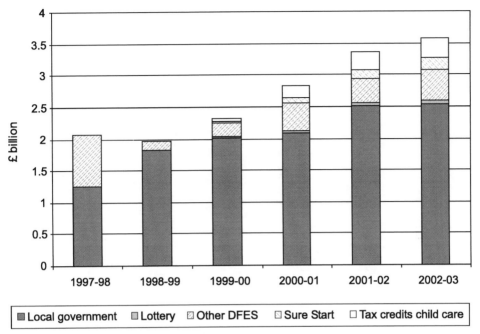

Figure 2.   Government expenditure on early years since 1997
Source: National Audit Office (2004)

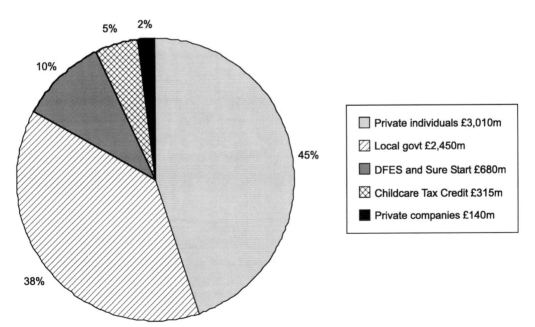

Figure 3.   How early years provision is paid for 2002–2003
Source: National Audit Office (2004)

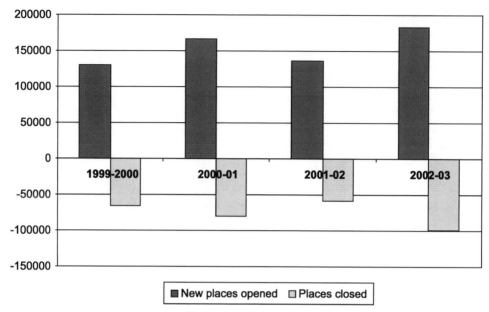

Figure 4.   Annual changes in childcare places 1999–2003
Source: National Audit Office (2004)

With this level of investment, the sector has experienced some dramatic changes in the landscape, with a considerable number of centres both opening and closing, as nurseries in the private and voluntary sectors struggle to make ends meet. As can be seen from Figure 4, in the childcare sector each year there are nearly half as many closures as there are new places. The most rapid expansion has been in full day care places and in out-of-school clubs (some of which include places for children under five) (Table 1), along with expansion of part-time early education. Nursery education is the only universal service for all three and four year olds whose parents wish to take advantage of it. The numbers of children using these free places has risen by over 40% since 1998, from around 800,000 to 1,150,000 (Figure 5). The public funding to provide 12.5 hours a week in term time for children of three and four is available to nursery and primary schools in the statutory sector and to private and voluntary sector nurseries and pre-school groups, provided they meet nationally approved standards. For parents who wish to use more than this two and a half hours a day, and also to find provision during the holidays, there is a commitment to increase the amount of 'joined up' provision through children's centres and 'wrap around care' (see below) but parents will probably have to pay, unless they are eligible for working tax credit, or live in an area in which the local authority has subsidised the cost of the provision.

Working tax credit, introduced in 1998 as Childcare Tax Credit, was intended to assist low income families with up to 70% of their childcare costs. However, the take-up has been low. Only 15% of eligible couples and 24% of lone parent families receive

Table 1.   Number of childcare places in England (excluding nursery education or sessional pre-school places)

	Places for children (registered)	
	1997	2004
Childminders	365,200	322,100
Full Daycare	193,800	483,600
Out of school clubs	78,700	332,400
Total	637,700	1,138,100

Source: Daycare Trust (2004)

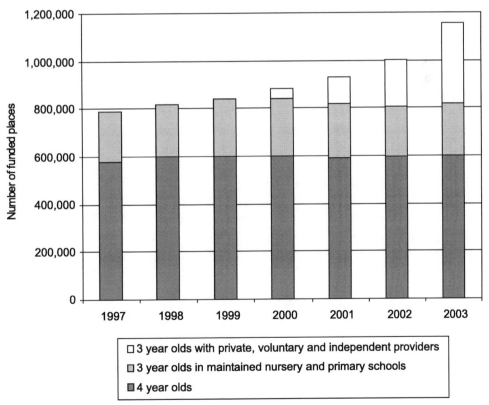

Figure 5.   Number of children in early years (nursery education) 1997–2003
Source: National Audit Office (2004)

the child care element and according to the National Audit Office 20% of low income parents still pay all costs themselves (National Audit Office, 2004).

Much of the expansion in service provision has been targeted on those areas with the highest level of need. The initiative that has reached the greatest number of children is Sure Start, where some 520 local programmes have been set up with a catchment area of between 500 and 900 children under four and their families. With a focus on the emotional, social and intellectual development and health of young children, and support for their parents, the programmes are managed by a local partnership board involving parents and professionals from health, education and social services. There is an extensive evaluation underway, but there are as yet few published reports on outcomes; those that are available from the very early programmes show 'a positive but limited effect' (National Evaluation of Sure Start, 2004).

The flagship of integrated services, providing seamless care and education for children from a few months old until five were 'Early Excellence Centres', some 107 'one stop shops' providing all day all year care and education for children, support for parents and often access to adult education as well. Few of these were new centres: most were built on existing centres or networks of services, with the provision of a little additional funding to extend the service and encourage the centre to take on a training and dissemination role. The initial evaluation of these centres (Bertram *et al.*, 2002) suggested substantial benefits for children, families and the wider community through the bringing together of a range of services that met families' needs without the stigma associated with specialist provision.

A further plank of the expansion of early years provision has been the Neighbourhood Nurseries Initiative, which has aimed to meet the needs of children and parents in disadvantaged areas with a 'mixed economy' approach within the private, voluntary and statutory sectors. Some 1400 neighbourhood nurseries are planned by March 2005 but some have closed already, and many are now becoming children's centres.

In 2003 the government launched its 'children's centre' programme, building on early excellence centres and neighbourhood nurseries through a promise of a centre in the 20% most disadvantaged communities. Children's centres are less generously funded than early excellence centres, but they do have an additional emphasis on health, being required to provide a base for midwives, health visitors and speech and language therapists, as well information and support for parents, and training and support for childcare workers (see Pugh, 2003). From 2006 local Sure Start programmes will be integrated into children's centres, and the forthcoming Ten Year Strategy is likely to promise children's centres in every community by the end of the next parliament (Prime Minister's speech, November 2004).

The Foundation Stage curriculum has been well received and enthusiastically adopted by early years professionals (Aubrey, 2004). The *Foundation Stage Guidance* (DfEE QCA, 2000) and, more recently, *Birth to Three Matters* (DfES/Sure Start, 2003) provide a clear framework for all years practitioners working with children up to the age of six. Both are based on clear principles and on the central importance of learning through play, but within a structure in which there are opportunities for children to engage in activities planned by adults as well as those they plan or initiate themselves. Both the three to six and the birth to three frameworks also recognise the centrality of social, emotional and creative development, as well as literacy and numeracy. The government has made the radical step of specifying developmental objectives and pathways for its youngest children.

The EPPE research cited above found that a key to the quality of the provision and good outcomes for children was the level of qualification of the staff working in early years settings. Table 2 outlines the qualifications and age of the workforce, illustrating not only the discrepancy between teaching and non-teaching staff in qualifications and levels of pay, but also how little many staff are paid. It is not surprising that the Equal Opportunities Commission recommended to the Select Committee on Childcare (2004) that government should 'invest in the workforce. Staff should be better paid and receive good quality training ...'

The EPPE researchers (Taggart *et al.*, 2000) showed a hierarchy in staff qualifications across the sectors: 'Nursery classes and nursery schools ... could be viewed as the most highly qualified, followed by combined centres, then private day nurseries and local authority centres together, and finally, playgroups that have the lowest proportion of qualified staff'. Qualifications in the workforce and equity of pay and conditions remains a major problem as will be discussed below.

Government has clearly seen both quality and integration of provision as a key to transforming early years provision, and in this it has been supported by findings from the EPPE study and by the evaluation of the early excellence centres. But how good is the quality of our early years provision? The 2003 Ofsted Early Years report concluded that 'on the whole, childcare providers have reached the level set out in the national standards'. But as the final section of this paper shows, whilst the promise was clear and the delivery swift, problems remain in realising the longer term vision.

Table 2. Characteristics of the childcare workforce

	Women	Under 25	NVQ3	Hourly pay
Childcare workers	98%	41%	52%	£5.50
Childminders	99%	6% *	15%	N/A
Nursery Workers	99%	16%	76%	£7.10
Playgroup Workers	99%	7%	44%	£5.40
Teachers (for comparison)	72%	5%	97%	*£11.07*

*20–29 years
Adapted from Daycare Trust (2004) and Moss (2004)

Part IV: Tensions remaining—the shortfall

The authors of this paper are not alone in applauding the government's achievements. 'Tremendous progress has been made in children's services in England since the first OECD review took place in December 1999. Most noteworthy are the significant increase in investment, the expansion of (local) Sure Start schemes and new moves towards children's centres and extended schools' (private communication from John Bennett, author of the forthcoming OECD report on early years, 2004).

While the past seven years have seen considerable increases in the level of provision, and a commitment to ensuring high quality, even more is promised. The DfES ten strategy for early years and childcare, to be published at the end of 2004 and heralded in a speech given by the Prime Minister in November 2004, promises 2,500 children's centres by 2008 and a universal offer by 2010, some to be developed out of existing provision, including primary schools. In addition every school is to offer extended opening hours in order to support parents' working patterns. Given the challenges in sustaining the quality and quantity of existing services these are extraordinarily ambitious targets. Let us examine briefly some of the issues that are raised—the integration of care and education, whether services are sustainable, and the quality of the services, including the calibre of the workforce.

The concept of children's centres assumes, from the child and family's perspective, an integrated service, offering high quality education and care, available all the year round and for a long working day, providing support for parents, access to training and employment, and with health care and outreach into local communities. This is the vision at the centre of the government's Change for Children agenda, as embodied in the Green Paper *Every Child Matters* and the Children Act 2004. Within this, children's centres are the key to joined-up service delivery, as are extended primary and secondary schools for children and young people aged 5–16. But it is a far cry from the current maze of different providers and services that parents must navigate. There are currently only 71 children's centres—a long way for one in every community. The universal vision is an excellent one—but can we travel this far so fast, given the reluctance of professionals to work in integrated teams and the challenges of bringing together different professional cultures, patterns of training, working practices and salaries, and conditions of service?

Whilst joining up services is a challenge, it is nothing to the size of the expansion required, nor the challenges of sustaining the growth already experienced, at a price that parents can afford. The government's 'offer' to parents for children before the age of five is for two and a half hours of free nursery education a day for three and four year olds in term time only. Anything beyond this (including provision for children under three) is paid for by parents, with some subsidy provided for some parents through working tax credit. As has been shown, working tax credit reaches only a relatively small number of parents (parents are either earning too much or not earning at all) and even for those who claim, the amount received is far from the actual cost of a place. In one London borough, for example, it costs on average £250 per week for a child care place. In order for parents to be able to afford this, the borough has to subsidise all places by £80 per week to help parents to bridge the gap (London Borough of Camden, 2004). In areas in which there is no subsidy, many parents cannot afford the fees.

Those providing early education—whether in the statutory, voluntary or independent sector—are equally unable to meet the costs without subsidy and, as has been shown, the level of turnover amongst providers is rising. Government figures show that between April 1997 and March 2004 over one million childcare places were created, but there was only a net gain of 540,000 places (Hansard column 1050W, 17 June 2004). Any further increase in the number of places will therefore require substantially increased subsidies for both parents and providers.

A government with elections to win is likely to put increased quantity higher on its agenda than improved quality, and yet the research evidence cited in this paper shows that it is only early education of high quality, provided by staff who are well qualified, that is effective in the longer term. There is currently a very wide variety in the quality of children's experiences in early years services. Government inspectors rate 54% of childcare as satisfactory rather than good, and much of the workforce is poorly trained and under qualified, particularly in the voluntary and independent sectors, with high staff turnover. Only 50% of staff in day nurseries are qualified to NVQ level 3 (some way below graduate level) and there are significant differences in pay and conditions between those with a teaching qualification and those without. The new Children's Workforce Council is charged with improving the qualifications and training of all who work with children but it remains to be seen how closely they are able to work with the Teaching Training Agency to bring some cohesion to the early years workforce. Additional funding is urgently required to improve training and qualifications, and to pay the increased salaries that these better-qualified staff will be able to demand.

Even within nursery classes situated in primary schools, many children are in classes where teachers are not qualified to work with three and four year olds. A recent study of children's experiences in reception classes concluded: 'If the purpose of the Foundation Stage was to extend to four and five year olds in primary/infant schools the best practice in the education of three and four year olds, then it has not succeeded. There is a demonstrable gap between the quality of children's experiences in the reception classes (the year preceding Year 1) and the quality of their experiences earlier in the Foundation Stage...' (Adams *et al.*, 2004). There are huge implications here for the training and ongoing professional development of the early years workforce, all of which have considerable resource implications.

As this quotation illustrates, there is concern that the Foundation Stage curriculum, intended to guide the practice of those working with children aged three, four and five years up until the end of the reception year, is not being implemented as it was intended. The Foundation Stage guidance and *Birth to Three Matters*, have been widely welcomed across the early years sector. But a high priority for government now must be to extend the Foundation Stage to incorporate the birth to three phase, and to ensure that the foundation phase is seen as the first stage of education, for all children from birth to five/six years.

Another tension concerns the government's commitment to a mixed market. EPPE (Sylva *et al.*, 1999) and other research has shown that there is higher quality in the state sector than the voluntary and private sectors. Will further expansion of the non statutory sectors compromise quality? Further, Moss (1999) questions the over-arching 'preparation for school' rationale of early years education, and calls for a re-investigation of the very nature of childhood (see also Montgomery *et al.*, 2003). This, he believes, would result in fundamental changes to the way early years education is conceived and approached. Early years practitioners have long argued that this first phase of education must be seen as of value in its own right, and not as training for academic skills needed in school (DES, 1990).

And finally—is this expansion primarily focused on the needs of children for high quality early education in the first years of their lives, or is it driven by the wish to enable as many parents as possible to return to work? Can 'early education' be reconciled with 'childcare for working parents'? Much of the drive for additional places has come from a commitment, led by the Chancellor of the Exchequer, to dramatically reduce the number of children living in poverty. The most effective way of doing this, it is argued, is by enabling parents in workless households to return to work, which they could do if there were adequate childcare. The expansion of 'childcare' places is long overdue and welcomed by parents and early years professionals alike, but expansion cannot be at the expense of quality, and parents must feel that they have some choice. As the EPPE research has shown, the educational environment of the home and the support that parents give their children is key to all aspects of their future development, but many parents feel torn by the dual messages of 'work' and 'be better parents' and under some pressure to return to work before they are ready.

Much has been achieved, and the ten year strategy promises yet more. Yet the vision is still hazy. Over the past year the integrated education and care of young children has been referred to by government as nursery education, day care, childcare, early years services, the foundation stage/phase and early education. Is it to be high quality early education led by well trained staff, or edu-care offered by a poorly qualified and low-paid workforce? As the expansion continues, there are nettles to be grasped and adequate resources to be found if the quality of early education is to be central to all early years services, and if care and education are to be truly integrated.

Acknowledgements

The authors are grateful to James Walker-Hall for bibliographic assistance and help with figures and tables.

Notes on contributors

Gillian Pugh has been Chief Executive of Coram Family since 1997. Over the past 25 years she has advised governments in the UK and overseas on the development of policy for children and families and has published many books. Gillian was a founder member and is chair of the Parenting Education & Support Forum and a trustee of the National Family & Parenting Institute. She is chair of governors of the Thomas Coram Centre for Children and Families and an advisor to the Children, Young People and Families Directorate at the Department of Education & Skills. She was awarded the DBE for services to children and families in 2005.

Kathy Sylva is Professor of Educational Psychology at the University of Oxford, Department of Educational Studies. After earning a PhD at Harvard University she moved to Oxford. Her book *Childwatching at Playgroup and Nursery School* broke new ground by questioning an unbridled 'free play' ideology. She has also carried out research on early literacy in Reception and Year 1. She is one of the leaders of the DfES research on effective provision of pre-school education. In 2000/2001 and 2004 she served as specialist adviser to the House of Commons Select Committee on Education and Skills.

References

Adams, S., Alexander, E., Drummond, M. J. & Moyles, J. (2004) *Inside the foundation stage: recreating the reception year* (London, Association of Teachers and Lecturers).

Aubrey, C. (2004) Implementing the foundation stage in reception classes, *British Educational Research Journal*, 30(5), 633–656.

Audit Commission (1996) *Counting to five* (London, Audit Commission).

Ball, C. (1994) *Start right: the importance of early learning* (London, Royal Society of Arts).

Barnett, W. S. (1996) Lives in the balance: Age-27 Benefit-cost analysis of the high/scope perry preschool program, *Monographs of the high/scope educational research foundation*, 11 (Ypsilanti, High/Scope Press).

Bertram, T., Pascel, C., Bokhari, S., Gasper, M. & Holtermann, S. (2002) Early Excellence Centre pilot programme, DfES *Research brief RB 361*.

Blakemore, S. & Frith, U. (In press) *The learning brain* (Oxford, Blackwell Publishing).

Bruer, J. T. (1997) Education and the brain: a bridge too far, *Educational Researcher*, 26(8), 4–16.

Bruner, J. (1986) *Actual minds, possible words* (London, Harvard University Press).

Daycare Trust (2004) *A new era for universal childcare?* www.daycare.trust.org.uk.

Department for Education and Employment (1998) *Meeting the childcare challenge.* http://www.dfes.gov.uk/childcare/chldcare.doc.

Department of Education and Skills (1990) *Starting with quality: report of the committee of enquiry into the educational experience offered to 3 and 4 year olds* (Rumbold Report) (London, HMSO).

DfEE/QCA (2000) *Curriculum guidance for the foundation stage* (London, Qualifications and Curriculum Authority).

DfES/Sure Start (2003) *Birth to three matters, an introduction to the framework* (London, HMSO).

Gopnik, A., Meltzoff, A. & Kuhl, P. K. (1999) *Scientist and the crib: what early learning tells us about the mind* (New York, William Morrow).

Hansard written answers to questions (2004) *Attainment Gap.* Volume no 422, part no 103, column 1050W.

House of Commons (2000a) Early years learning. *Post*, 140 (London, Parliamentary Office of Science and Technology).

House of Commons (2000b) Education and employment committee. *Early years* (London, The Stationery Office).

House of Commons (2004) *Early years: progress in developing high quality childcare and early education accessible to all* (London, The Stationery Office).

Inter-Departmental Childcare Review (2002) *Delivering for children and families* (London, Department for Education and Skills/Department for Work and Pension/HM treasury/Women and Equality Unit).

London Borough of Camden (2004) *The shortage of under fives childcare in Camden.*

Melhuish, E. C. (2002). Prospects for research on the quality of the pre-school experience, in: W. W. Hartup & R. K. Silbereisen (Eds) *Growing points in Developmental Science* (Hove, Psychology Press).

Melhuish, E. C. (2003) Daycare, in: B. Hopkins *et al.* (Eds) *Cambridge encyclopaedia of child development* (Cambridge, Cambridge University Press).

Melhuish, E. (2004) *A literature review of the impact of early years provision on young children, with emphasis given to children from disadvantaged backgrounds* (London, National Audit Commission).

Montgomery, H., Burr, R., & Woodhead, M. (Eds) (2003) *Changing childhoods: local and global* (Wiley, The Open University).

Moss, P. (1999) Renewed hopes and lost opportunities: early childhood in the early years of the Labour Government, *Cambridge Journal of Education*, 29(2), 229–238.

Moss, P. (2004) *Why we need a well qualified early childhood workforce.* Powerpoint presentation.

National Audit Office (2004) *Early Years: progress in developing high quality childcare and early education accessible to all* (London, The Stationery Office) (http://www.nao.org.uk/publications/nao_reports/03-04/0304268.pdf).

National Evaluation of Sure Start (2004) *Towards understanding Sure Start local programmes* (London, DfES).

Office for Standards in Education (2003) *Early years: The first national picture* (London, Ofsted Publications Centre). (http://www.ofsted.gov.uk/publications/index.cfm?fuseaction=pubs.displayfile&id=3372&type=pdf).

Prime Minister (2004) Speech to the Daycare Trust conference, November 11.

Pugh, G. (1994) Born to learn, *Times Education Supplement* (http://www.tes.co.uk/search/story/?story_id=9504).

Pugh, G. (2003) Children's centres and social inclusion. *Education Review*, 17(1), 23–29.

Ramey, C. T. & Ramey, S. L. (1998) Early intervention and early experience, *American Psychologist*, 53, 109–120.

Sammons, P., Smees, R., Taggart, B., Sylva, K., Melhuish, E., Siraj-Blatchford, I., & Elliot, K. (2004) *The effective provision of pre-school education project (EPPE). Technical paper 2: Special educational needs in the early primary years: primary school entry up to the end of year 1* (London, DfES/Institute of Education, University of London).

Sammons, P., Sylva, K., Melhuish, E., Siraj-Blatchford, I., Taggart, B. & Elliot, K. (2002) *The Effective Provision of Pre-School Education Project (EPPE). Technical paper 8a: Measuring the impact of pre-school on children's cognitive progress over the pre-school period* (London, DfES/Institute of Education, University of London).

Sammons, P., Sylva, K., Melhuish, E., Siraj-Blatchford, I., Taggart, B. & Elliot, K. (2003) *The Effective Provision of Pre-School Education Project (EPPE). Technical paper 8b: Measuring the impact of pre-school on children's social/behavioural development over the pre-school period* (London, DfES/Institute of Education, University of London).

Sammons, P., Sylva, K., Melhuish, E., Siraj-Blatchford, I., Taggart, B., Elliot, K. & Marsh, A. (2004). *The effective provision of pre-school education project (EPPE). Technical paper 11: The continuing effects of pre-school education at age 7 years* (London, DfES/Institute of Education, University of London).

Schweinhart, L. J., Barnes, H. V. & Weikart, D. P. (1993) Significant benefits: the high/scope perry preschool study through age 27, *Monographs of the high/scope educational research foundation*, 10 (Ypsilanti, High/Scope Press).

Siraj-Blatchford, I., Sylva, K., Muttock, S., Gilden, R., & Bell, D. (2002) *Researching effective pedagogy in the early years* (Norwich, DfES/Queen's Printer).

Sylva, K. (1994a) The impact of early learning on children's later development, in: C. Ball *Start right: the importance of early learning* (London, RSA).

Sylva, K. (1994b) School influences on children's development, *Journal of Child Psychology and Psychiatry*, 35(1), 135–170.

Sylva, K., Melhuish, E., Sammons, P. and Siraj-Blatchford, I. (1999) *The effective provision of pre-school education project (EPPE). Technical paper 1: Introduction to the effective provision of pre-school education project (EPPE)* (London, Institute of Education, University of London).

Sylva, K., Melhuish, E., Sammons, P., Siraj-Blatchford, I. & Taggart, B. (2004) *The effective provision of pre-school education project (EPPE). Technical paper 12: Effective pre-school education* (London, DfES/Institute of Education, University of London).

Sylva, K., Siraj-Blatchford, I., Melhuish, E., Sammons, P., Taggart, B., Evans, E., Dobson, A., Jeavons, M., Lewis, K., Morahan, M. & Sadler, S. (1999). *The effective provision of pre-school education project (EPPE). Technical paper 6a: Characteristics of the pre-school: an introduction to the EPPE project* (London, DfES/Institute of Education, University of London).

Taggart, B., Sylva, K., Siraj-Blatchford, I., Melhuish, E., Sammons, P. & Walker-Hall, J. (2000) *The effective provision of pre-school education project (EPPE). Technical paper 5: Characteristics of the centres in the EPPE study: interviews* (London, DfES/Institute of Education, University of London).

The Treasury and Department of Education and Skills. (2003) *Every child matters* (London, The Stationery Office).

Primary schooling under New Labour: The irresolvable contradiction of excellence and enjoyment

Kevin J. Brehony

Introduction

This article aims to provide both an account and an assessment of the most significant policies adopted by New Labour on primary schooling since its victory in the election of 1997. A secondary intention is to determine what these policies reveal about New Labour and its political project. Whilst theorists close to New Labour, like Anthony Giddens, have discerned a Third Way in politics, neither social democratic nor neo-liberal (Giddens, 1998, 2000) others have observed that New Labour's policies on education, as in other fields, have combined an extension of neo-liberal measures inherited from the Conservatives with social democratic policies of a more traditional Labour variety (Brehony & Deem, 2003). Exactly how these two contrasting approaches to education policy have been configured has varied from sector to sector, but a key policy objective in New Labour's two terms of office since 1997 has been the retention of the electoral support it received from voters who had benefited from policies pursued by the Thatcher governments. Identified by Philip Gould, one of Prime Minister Tony Blair's close advisers, as the 'middle-class' who inhabit the suburbs of 'middle England' (Gould, 1998), they have been courted assiduously by New Labour. As Stuart Hall has argued, the New Labour government 'has adapted the fundamental neo-liberal programme to suit its conditions of governance—that of a social democratic government trying to govern in a neo-liberal direction while maintaining its traditional working-class and public-sector middle-class support with all the compromises and confusions that entail' (Hall, 2003). However, Hall suggests that within New Labour's ideological stances, the neo-liberal strand is dominant. A slightly more nuanced analysis of the elements composing New Labour's education policy that takes into account the divergent policies arising from devolution has been provided by Paterson who argues that there are not two strands but three. New Labourism is for him 'a renovated version of social liberalism, a form of weak developmentalism, and a type of new social democracy' (Paterson, 2003). Devolution, especially in Wales, has tipped the balance more towards the (new) social democratic end of the policy spectrum.

Here, for reasons of space, I shall only discuss New Labour's policies as they have affected primary schools in England, not in Scotland, Wales or Northern Ireland. As has been frequently noted, New Labour has been particularly active in the field of education policy (Ball, 1999, Tomlinson, 2001). A plethora of policy initiatives have impacted on primary schools such as the National Grid for Learning Programme commencing in 1998, which brought investment in infrastructure and training in information and communications technology (Selwyn & Fitz, 2001). Workforce remodelling has also begun to have an impact following the signing of a national agreement on workforce reform on 15 January 2003. This has occurred in spite of the National Union of Teachers, which represents the majority of primary teachers, not signing the agreement. Another significant policy is the extension of Excellence in Cities to primary schools. This is a series of policy measures aimed at raising educational achievement in deprived urban schools in the most economically disadvantaged areas of England. Although Excellence in Cities has been seen as consistent with endogenous growth theories in that these theories require social inclusion (Dolowitz, 2004), it is more common to view the initiative as being more characteristic of social democracy. Nevertheless, rather than discuss these policies, I shall focus mainly on policies impacting on curriculum and teaching, both of which, historically, have been key sites of ideological conflict within primary schooling (Cunningham, 1988; Selleck, 1972).

Regarded from the perspective of education in England as a whole, New Labour has adopted, and in some cases extended, both the neo-liberal privatising and the centralising policies it inherited from its Conservative predecessors. It has also fostered the adoption in the education service of new managerialism; the organisational forms, technologies, management practices and values more commonly found in the private business sector. More specifically, in the primary phase, it has continued the trend begun by the Conservatives towards the elimination of its distinctive character. Enunciated most powerfully in the Hadow Report of 1931 (Board of Education, 1931) and reiterated in the Plowden Report of 1967 (Central Advisory Council for Education, 1967), the belief that children in their primary years required an education that was specifically adapted to their stage of physical and intellectual development constituted the dominant discourse on primary schooling until the mid-1970s. After the Education Reform Act of 1988, this position was abandoned. The National Curriculum introduced by the Act envisaged a seamless experience from the age of 5 to 16. The National Curriculum also adopted, in opposition to the primary schools' adoption of projects, the time-hallowed conception of the organisation of school knowledge into subjects. In turn this led to a change in the training of primary teachers so that instead of aiming to produce generalists whose professional expertise lay in assisting children's learning, their training was orientated towards the production of subject specialists. In this shift of focus, from child-centred to society-centred education, an emphasis on learning was replaced by one on teaching. Furthermore, schooling, in all its phases, has become subordinated to the perceived requirements of the labour market, the latter characterised in two White Papers as operating within an ill-defined, 'knowledge economy' (Department for Culture Media and Sport, 1999; Department of Trade Industry and Department for Education Employment, 2001). Unusually, in the history of primary schooling, because of its distance from entry into the labour market, preparation for employment has become a key determinant of the curriculum in recent years.

Class size: placating middle England?

I shall begin not with the curriculum but with class size reduction, an issue New Labour promoted as a key policy before it came to power. This is a policy that unites the material dimensions of schooling such as demography, teacher supply and expenditure. The party promised to reduce class sizes for all five, six and seven-year-olds in England by September 2002. Writing in the *New Statesman*, Peter Wilby concluded that it could be argued that, 'the pledge was deliberately designed to benefit the middle-class floating voters that Labour targeted in the election campaign' as they would benefit disproportionately (Wilby, 1997). Szreter, on the other hand, pointed out that Britain's pupil–teacher ratio in state schools was among the highest in the high-income countries and referred to the White Paper, *Excellence in Schools* (Department for Education and Employment, 1997) in which the class size pledge was made wherein 'all the talk is of standards rather than resources' (Szreter, 1997). Policies on class sizes are always at the mercy of demographic trends. The number of full-time equivalent (FTE) maintained nursery and primary school pupils increased from the mid-1980s. It reached a peak of 4.33 million in 1997/98 but by 2002/03, numbers had fallen by about 2% and they are predicted to fall further. The widely reported school funding problems encountered in England in 2003 led to disagreement between the National Union of Teachers (NUT) and the government over whether or not, lower financial settlements for some schools were due to falling pupil numbers. A survey commissioned by the NUT showed that less than a third of primary schools experienced falling rolls (Curtis, 2003). Nevertheless, in 2003, primary schools in England lost 800 teachers due to falling rolls. Teacher numbers increased overall in primary schools but at Key Stage 1, class sizes for five to seven-year-olds rose, with more infants being taught in groups of more than 30 (Curtis, 2003). At the same time, average class sizes fell, from 26.3 to 26.2 pupils in primary schools overall, but worsened for five to seven-year-olds (infants), from 25.5 to 25.7. The percentage of infants in classes of 31 or more rose to 1.6% from 1.2% which meant that 5,810 more children were in classes of a size that Labour promised in 1997 to eliminate during its first term of office. Following a drop from 11% of infants in classes of more than 30 in 2000 to 0.6% in 2002, the percentage of classes with more than 30 has started to rise again (MacLeod, 2004).

In addition to missing the target it had set for class sizes, the government was also criticised because the evidence for the effectiveness of class size reduction in enhancing children's learning is contested and inconclusive. Like some other New Labour, 'Third Way' education policies, class size became a policy issue in the United States when the US President, Bill Clinton, in his 1999 State of the Union address also promised to reduce class sizes in the early grades (Clinton, 1999); another instance of policy borrowing (Phillips & Ochs, 2003) or policy transfer (Dolowitz, 2000; Dolowitz & Marsh, 2000).

The inconclusive nature of the research on the effects of a reduction in class size was noted in the review of research on class size conducted by Ehrenberg, Brewer, Gamoran and Willms in the United States (Ehrenberg *et al.*, 2001). On the other hand, prominence was given in the UK to the evidence of the positive effects of class size reduction produced by the Tennessee's Student Teacher Achievement Ratio (STAR) project (Ritter & Boruch, 1999). Drawing on further evidence from the US, Matthew Taylor, a former senior adviser to Tony Blair and director of the centre-left think tank, the Institute of Public Policy Research, told a conference of independent school head teachers in 2002 that New Labour's policy had been wrong as, 'reducing class sizes from 32 to 30 makes no difference' but that it was known from research in the United States that the provision of 'classes of 15 and 20 pupils in the inner-city areas would have made a difference' (Garner, 2002). Taylor's assertion is contradicted by recent research in England (Blatchford, 2003) but this was published several years after New Labour had embraced a policy of class size reduction. As Wilby maintained, the policy on class size reduction was more of a pragmatic electoral adjustment, a populist measure designed to appeal to middle-class parents, a view which Taylor reportedly confirmed (Garner, 2002).

Literacy and numeracy

The contention that under New Labour primary school teachers have lost control not only of what to teach but how to teach it and hence much of their professional autonomy and discretion, gains evidential support from the Literacy and Numeracy Strategies. Of all its policies in primary schools, New Labour claims that its greatest achievements have been in raising standards of literacy and numeracy.

Speaking in 2004 to headteachers in Cardiff, the Prime Minister, Tony Blair, claimed that, 'The proportion of 11 year-olds up to standard has risen by almost a fifth since 1997: which means 80,000 more children a year succeeding in each subject than before, each one of them a tribute to the skill and dedication of our primary teachers school by school' (Blair, 2004).

This emphasis on literacy and numeracy may be seen, in part, as exemplifying the supply-side, welfare to work policies (Cutler, 2001) associated with the Third Way advocated by the New Democrats in the United States and by Robert Reich, Clinton's former secretary of Labour, in particular. Reich, who constructed a version of endogenous growth theory, communicated regularly with the New Labour Chancellor of the Exchequer, Gordon Brown, and his adviser, Ed Balls, which has led to one analyst arguing that this is a case of policy transfer (Dolowitz, 2004). The level of intervention and prescription in the areas of pedagogy and curriculum under New Labour have been unprecedented, at least since the demise of Payment by Results and the withdrawal of the Elementary School Code in 1926. From the 1960s, freed from the requirements of the selective 11 plus examination, as the process of comprehensivisation advanced, primary school teachers attained a level of autonomy characteristic of the bureau professionals (Mintzberg, 1983) they had become. The Conservatives reversed this trend with the introduction of the National Curriculum, which removed a great deal of teachers' discretion over the curriculum. In 1992, the report of the 'Three wise men' (Alexander, Rose & Woodhead, 1992) indicated a willingness of the Conservatives not only to invade the secret garden of the curriculum but also that of pedagogy too, as whole class teaching became the officially advocated approach. Alongside whole class teaching, setting of pupils according to attainment was encouraged in the White Paper, *Excellence in Schools* (Department for Education and Employment, 1997) and also by OFSTED, the non-ministerial government department responsible for the inspection of schools in England. In its review of primary schools for the years 1994–1998, OFSTED commented on an increase in the practice of grouping pupils by ability especially in English and mathematics at Key Stage 2 (Office for Standards in Education, 1999). Recent research concludes that by itself, grouping by ability does not raise standards (Hallam *et al.*, 2003; Hallam, *et al.*, 2004).

With the National Literacy and National Numeracy Strategies, New Labour went much further in the direction of a 'teacher proof' curriculum that indicated that primary teachers could not be trusted to implement its top down, standards agenda. These strategies originated under the last Conservative government. In 1996, the Department for Education and Employment (DfEE) set up The National Literacy Project. It was funded through Grants for Education Support and Training at a cost of £12.5 million over five years. Initially 266 primary schools were involved in a sample of local education authorities and the project was led by John Stannard, a senior member of Her Majesty's Inspectorate (HMI) (Beard, 2003). The programme of objectives entitled, 'Framework for teaching' developed in the National Literacy Project appeared in modified form in the New Labour's National Literacy Strategy (NLS). Within the *Framework* there is a description given of the literacy hour designed, 'to provide a practical structure of time and class management which reflects the structure of teaching objectives in the NLS Framework'. Although it is non-statutory, the *Framework* states that, 'the Literacy Hour should be implemented throughout the school to provide a daily period of dedicated literacy teaching time for all pupils' (Department for Education and Employment and Unit, 1998). The explanation given in the *Framework* for why a period of an hour was chosen was the classically bureaucratic reason that English is allocated five hours per week in the National Curriculum and 'almost all schools' therefore provide at least an hour each day for literacy teaching.

While in opposition, the Labour Party established a Literacy Task Force chaired by Professor Michael Barber (later the head of the Department for Education and Skills (DfES) Standards Unit, and currently head of the Public Policy Delivery Unit), which developed the National Literacy Strategy. Wyse argues that elements of the National Literacy Strategy arose out of a combination of inspection evidence produced by OFSTED and school effectiveness research. An official account confirms the role of OFSTED and its report in 1996 on the teaching of reading in London primary schools. This identified poor teaching and low standards in this aspect of literacy (Office for Standards in Education, 2002). Wyse also identifies as significant in the formulation of the National Literacy Strategy, a shift in emphasis in the OFSTED reports for 1994 to 1998 from 'purpose and organisation' to 'the mechanics of writing, including phonics and grammar' (Wyse, 2003). Other analysts also cite the role of OFSTED and its leader, Chris Woodhead, an advocate of a 'back to basics' policy of clearly structured whole-class teaching and a vigorous opponent of child-centred approaches (Woodhead, 2002). In literacy this was associated with a stress on phonics (Rabinovitch, 2002) and in numeracy this was to be accompanied by an emphasis on calculation skills (Brown *et al.*, 2000).

The National Numeracy Task Force, out of which emerged the National Numeracy Strategy, was established just prior to the May 1997 election and it was chaired by Professor David Reynolds. He had recently co-authored a report for OFSTED in which he had speculated on the possible causes for the apparent superiority of Taiwanese methods of teaching science and mathematics over those used in England (Reynolds & Farrell, 1996). Announcing the formation of the National Numeracy Task Force, David Blunkett made clear what problem the task force needed to address. 'All the international indicators' he asserted, 'show we are too far behind our competitors in the three Rs'. This time-worn invocation of the international struggle for survival (Brehony, 1998) was conjoined to a New Labour claim that traditional teaching methods such as whole class teaching where every child takes part had 'delivered good results in countries like Taiwan' (Department for Education and Employment, 1997).

The National Numeracy Strategy, like its Literacy counterpart, also contained a strong back to basics prescription of lessons focusing on whole-class teaching and a strong emphasis on mental calculation. Readers of the *Daily Mail* and other right-wing newspapers that have campaigned against child-centred education for many years (CCCS, 1981) may also have been reassured by the tripartite structure of the daily mathematics lesson which starts with oral work and mental calculation, followed by the teaching of new topics or the consolidation of previous ones and ends with a plenary. In a move that may have been designed to further reassure its new middle England constituency that standards were being addressed, a national target for England was set which was that by the year 2002 80% of 11 year olds would reach the expected standard for their age in English and 75% would reach this level in mathematics. David Blunkett, the secretary of state for education and employment promised to resign if the targets were not met.

Given the subsequent commitment of the New Labour government to evidence based policy (Cabinet Office, 1999; National Audit Office, 2003) there is a certain irony in the fact that the role of research evidence in the development of the National Literacy Strategy and the National Numeracy Strategy that followed it in September 1999 has been challenged. Both the content of the strategies and their implementation were supposed to embrace evidence of 'what works', the pragmatic counter to ideology that was held to have dominated primary schools in the past. Arguably, it was a rather selective version of what works that was utilised. In particular, it was a partial reading of international comparisons in education, especially the TIMMS report (Harris *et al.*, 1997) which gave rise to the rhetoric of 'world class education' associated with Michael Barber (Barber & Sebba, 1999).

As part of a number of initiatives associated with the two strategies, such as training and support for teachers, the development of materials and the appointment of literacy and numeracy consultants in all Local Education Authorities in England, New Labour continued the development of a National Curriculum for initial teacher training (Teacher Training Agency, 1997) which commenced under the Conservatives (Graham, 1998). For intending primary teachers this top-down, OFSTED enforced National Curriculum emphasised the core subjects and the literacy and numeracy strategies. Some feared this concentration on standards would lower the levels of specialist subject knowledge of those achieving primary QTS (Emery, 1998). Prescription of methods in the strategies was extended to prescription of the programmes for student teachers. Under the new national curriculum for intending teachers, 'students are required to demonstrate both the required knowledge and skill in methods of teaching the strategies' (Burgess, 2000).

Curriculum imbalance

By 2000, evidence that the Literacy and Numeracy strategies were causing an imbalance in the curriculum of primary schools had begun to accumulate. The last review of the National Curriculum had taken place in 1997. One of the intentions behind the review was to introduce changes to the National Curriculum in order to support the drive to raise standards, particularly in areas such as literacy and numeracy, in order to help schools meet the national targets in 2002 (QCA, 1997). The main outcome of the review was that in 1998 the detailed statutory requirements in the programmes of study at key stages 1 and 2 in six foundation subjects were lifted in order to allow schools to concentrate more on the targets for literacy and numeracy. Primary schools were told in 2000 that they could cut back on subjects such as art, PE and music to concentrate on literacy and numeracy.

This was a significant departure from the broad balanced curriculum outlined in the original National Curriculum and in the annual report published in 2002. Her Majesty's Chief Inspector (HMCI) also referred to the pressures on the primary curriculum and their impact on breadth and balance. In what was a departure from OFSTED's previous commitment to the standards agenda, the report referred to the amount of time taken up by the drive to raise standards in English and mathematics and by the national tests. The report concluded that 'It is the aspects of subjects that bring them to life—enquiry, problem-solving and practical work—that have suffered most' (Office for Standards in Education, 2002).

In research on primary teachers' working lives commissioned by the NUT, and also published in 2002, Galton and Macbeath confirmed the view of HMCI that concentration on literacy and numeracy was squeezing out other areas of the curriculum. They highlighted a decline in creativity and wrote that 'art, drama, music and ICT are being squeezed and are only partially covered by lunchtime and after-school clubs' and added that the decline in the curriculum time available for these creative subjects is matched by a decline in teachers' 'own sense of creativity' (Galton & MacBeath, 2002).

The government responded to these criticisms by setting up a committee under the chairmanship of Baroness Ashton, the Schools Minister, to review the curriculum. The top-down nature of the review was illustrated by the absence of teachers on the committee (Ward, 2002). Further evidence of the distorting effect on the primary curriculum was provided in 2003 by a survey of 294 schools for the Qualifications and Curriculum Authority by the Centre for Formative Assessment Studies at Manchester University (CFAS, 2003). The survey found that the proportion of time spent in primary schools on subjects other than English and Maths had fallen by more than 10% since 1997. Half the week was now spent on these two subjects. In more than a quarter of primary schools surveyed, staff held the view that that the emphasis on English and Maths meant they were now unable to provide a balanced curriculum (CFAS, 2003). In his annual report for 2003, David Bell HMCI, the eventual successor to Chris Woodhead, claimed that the pressure on primary schools to improve literacy and numeracy is producing a two-tier curriculum. But at the same time, he identified the standstill in Key Stage 2 test scores in English as a cause for concern. He also said that primaries lacked the confidence to take control of the curriculum despite having the scope to do so. He suggested that a broader curriculum could help restart improvements in literacy and numeracy. This was also the message of an OFSTED report on successful primary schools (Office for Standards in Education, 2002) and the evidence was mounting that the standards agenda was having a distorting impact on the primary school curriculum.

Evaluating the strategies

The frequent citation of the work of the Canadian academic, Michael Fullan, by figures influential in the formulation of New Labour's policies, like Michael Barber, was characteristic of many of New Labour's policy texts but it was still somewhat surprising when a team from the University of Toronto, led by Fullan, was brought in by the Department for Education and Skills to evaluate the two strategies. The decision to employ the Canadian team caused some consternation among researchers in England. However, Michael Barber was reported as justifying the choice on the grounds that, 'no one caught up in the process of reform here could bring the perspective or detachment to the evaluation that experts from abroad could bring' (Budge, 1999). The strategies were evaluated over a four-year period and the team from the University of Toronto produced three reports (Earl *et al.*, 2000, 2001, 2003). In their final evaluation report, the Toronto team was generally upbeat in its assessment of the impact of the strategies declaring that they represented 'an approach to school change that is still not common among governments'. The report continued by stating that the 'investment in building school capacity, and especially in changing teaching practice, is an exciting and ambitious undertaking. The results to date suggest that it is possible to improve outcomes with a sustained and focused approach of this kind' (Earl *et al.*, 2003). Significantly, it was teaching that seemed to have changed the most. The main changes were listed as a: 'greater use of whole class teaching, greater attention to the pace of lessons, and planning based on objectives rather than activities' (Earl *et al.*, 2003). In some senses these might be seen as a shift away from child centred practices but while this might be seen as successful from the perspective of New Labour's ideological agenda, evaluators noted that, 'it is more difficult to draw conclusions about the effect of the Strategies on pupil learning than on teaching practice' (Earl *et al.*, 2003).

In addition, the limitations of New Labour's top down approach were identified. Initially, setting targets helped mobilise teachers but subsequently the high stakes testing and targets skewed teaching methods and narrowed the curriculum. In view of these negative impacts the team concluded that, 'setting ever-higher national targets may no longer serve to mobilise and motivate, particularly if schools and local education authorities see the targets as unrealistic' (Earl *et al.*, 2003).

Before the final report was published, OFSTED, which, under Chris Woodhead, had pushed for the back to basics elements in the strategies and therefore had a stake in their outcomes, produced its own report on the National Literacy and Numeracy Strategies (Office for Standards in Education, 2002). Regarding the Numeracy Strategy, OFSTED declared that, 'it has brought about substantial improvements in the teaching of literacy in English primary schools'. Nevertheless the criticisms of its functioning were many and substantial. Several of these criticisms were directed at teachers, as for example when too many headteachers were judged to see the strategy 'as a classroom initiative'. A consequence of this was that, 'their own knowledge of it was weak and they did not see it as a tool for whole-school improvement' (Office for Standards in Education, 2002). Moreover, teachers were identified who still followed, 'the framework and guidance with too little questioning and reflection.

In its report on the numeracy strategy, OFSTED concluded, as it had for the literacy strategy, that it, 'has brought about radical, much-needed change in the way mathematics is taught in English primary schools' but it also identified a number of what it described as weaknesses including weak leadership and management of the strategy which were, 'a significant barrier to progress in one in eight schools' (Office for Standards in Education, 2002).

Resistance

As has been indicated, New Labour's standards and testing agenda is very much at variance with the child-centred tradition that has been deeply embedded in primary education for a long time in England. In the light of this, it is surprising that resistance

by teachers and by parents has been so limited. The last school to resist the implementation of the Standard Assessment Tasks (SATs) was Rosslyn Junior School in
Nottingham, which finally agreed to set the tests in 1999. 'The chair of governors at
Rosslyn Junior, Gill Bainbridge, said the tests would be irrelevant to large numbers
of the school's pupil intake, which is drawn from some of Nottingham's most
deprived areas' (Anon, 1999). The OFSTED report on the school in 2003 noted that,
'the area around the school has substantial and extensive socio-economic disadvantages. Over 54 per cent of pupils are eligible for free school meals, which is well above
the national average for this type of school. Children joining the school have very low
attainment, significantly below that generally found in children of their age'
(OFSTED, 2003). More recently, Headteacher Carol Lyndon attracted national
publicity when Kings Rise Community primary school in Birmingham boycotted the
SATS (Collins, 2004). Like Rosslyn Junior, the school was, according to an
OFSTED report of an inspection carried out in 2000, found to be in 'an area of severe
deprivation' (OFSTED, 2000). These individual acts of resistance to new Labour's
testing regime have been accompanied by acts of cheating which have led to the
results being annulled and heads suspended. In one case in 2003, a headteacher was
jailed for three months for forging tests (Woodward, 2003). The chair of the governors at the school reportedly said that the school had been left at the bottom of the
league tables and the head was worried that fewer children would come to it (Woodward, 2003). These cases arising from the application of the standards agenda in areas
of social disadvantage and deprivation serve to highlight the contradiction between
New Labour's advocacy of social inclusion and the legitimation of exclusion granted
by the SATs (Hall *et al.*, 2004).

Collective resistance has been organised in the British Association for Early Child-
hood Education, which opposes the Key Stage 1 SATs. Another body opposed to the
SATs tests is the National Primary Alliance. This unites the National Primary Trust,
the National Primary Heads Association and the National Association of Primary
Education, which are all professional associations. In addition, 'an alliance of local
authority chief education officers, school governors and headteachers including the
Association of Chief Education Officers (ACEO), the National Association of Head
Teachers (NAHT), the Secondary Heads Association (SHA) and the National Governors' Council has called for a review of primary school league tables in England, to
make national tests less "high stakes" and the resulting data more reliable and mean-
ingful' (Smithers, 2003).

In 2003, the National Union of Teachers balloted its members on whether they
would refuse to conduct the work necessary to administer the tests, due to be taken
by pupils at Key Stages one and two. More than 86% of the 35,000 teachers who took
part in the ballot voted to refuse work necessary to administer the tests, due to be
taken in the following May by seven and 11-year-olds. More than 86% of the 35,000
teachers who took part in the ballot voted to support a boycott, but under NUT rules
more than two-thirds of the 103,000 infant, junior and primary teachers balloted had
to vote in favour; that proportion was not reached so the tests were administered
(Smithers, 2003).

Even though the action did not take place, the number voting in favour indicates that there is a considerable amount of resistance to the SATs among primary teachers, whose commitment is essential to the implementation of New Labour's policies in education.

The new turn and the future

In 2000 and 2001 it was becoming clear that the rate of improvement in the SATs results was slowing down and may have reached a plateau. The goal of continuous improvement, which was embraced by Michael Barber among other New Labour policy makers (Barber, 2002), began to appear elusive. Barber observed that, 'the framework for continuous improvement has been less successful in tackling low performance which results not from school failure but from a combination of factors such as low community aspirations, high pupil turnover, serious poverty and/or fractured communities' (Barber, 2002). The constraints imposed by social structures on educational outcomes that New Labour sought to disregard had proved intractable (Whitty, 2001). It was also predictable that at least some of the improvements in the Key Stage 1 and 2 SATs were due, in part, to a Hawthorne effect (Earl *et al.*, 2003).

If there was a growing sense that the standards agenda had failed in relation to the targets that had been set for it, pressure for a new policy direction was coming from another quarter. In 1999, Tom Bentley, the director of the think-tank, Demos, who had been an adviser to David Blunkett, formerly Secretary of State for Education and Employment, argued that the emphasis on qualifications in schooling must be reduced, and that the skills needed for, what he termed, the 'new knowledge economy' should be integrated into mainstream teaching. He also argued that only those who could apply their knowledge creatively would thrive in a world 'characterised by innovation and flux' (Seltzer & Bentley, 1999). Creativity became the watchword of many in New Labour's 'big tent', the term given to its broad coalition, who were seeking to change direction away from the standards agenda. A publication from the think-tank, Demos, complained that 'the emphasis on raising standards in schools has encouraged a form of "test mania", which means that the development of creative abilities has often been squeezed out' (Jupp *et al.*, 2001). Demos has been identified by Hartley, along with the Department for Trade and Industry and the Department for Media, Culture and Sport, as sites where concerns were expressed in 2000, 'that an overly *dirigiste* approach to the management of teachers and an overly explicit classroom pedagogy would do little to release the creativity and innovation which a knowledge based economy would require' (Hartley, 2003).

Another term associated with the view of the turn required to make schooling conform more to the needs of the so-called knowledge economy is individualised learning. Again, Tom Bentley was at the forefront of the demand for more flexibility in schooling and for a move away from, 'the centrally determined and test-driven approach' in favour of, among other things, 'individualised learning programmes for all pupils' (Bentley, 2002). The Specialist Schools Trust that has its roots in the City Technology Colleges innovation of the 1980s is also a site where calls for creativity and individualised learning linked to Information and Communication Technology often surface. In a recent lecture on pupil centred learning, the then Secretary of State for Education, Charles Clarke, acknowledged the role of the Specialist Schools Trust, in target setting, supporting the use of ICT as a driving force for change in our system and 'recognizing the importance of pupil centred learning and the role of assessment and data within that' (Clarke, 2003).

Much of this emphasis on creativity, individualised learning and ICT is directed at secondary schools, the focus of New Labour's education policies in its second term. Once more (Brehony, 1990) the primary phase is being dragged along in a policy slip-stream which is not principally directed at the phase but at the 14–19 curriculum. Moreover, there is a strong element of post-Fordist ideology (Brehony & Deem, 2005) in this new turn. Post-Fordism, in this normative sense, refers to flexible production, flexible labour and the application of information technologies to the production process and to the administration of organisations. The Schools Stan-dards Minister, David Miliband, in a recent speech entitled 'choice and voice in personalised learning', cited Sabel and Piore (Piore & Sabel, 1984) who are in the institutionalist school of post-Fordist theorists in support of what, following the Prime Minister, Tony Blair, he calls personalised learning. This, he declared, 'is not a return to child-centred theories; it is not about separating pupils to learn on their own; it is not the abandonment of a national curriculum; and it is not a licence to let pupils coast at their own preferred pace of learning'(Miliband, 2004). Ironically, Miliband's rejec-tion of child-centred theories was accompanied by a description of personalised learn-ing that was virtually indistinguishable from definitions of child-centred education used in the past. Some, like Hartley, see in all this a re-articulation of progressivism. 'Now, again', he writes, 'progressivism seems to be waiting in the wings. This time, it would not only be functional for a low-skill service economy; but could also be a preparation for a high-value-added knowledge economy' (Hartley, 2003). Progressiv-ism is a slippery concept (Brehony, 2001) but there is no doubt that its lexicon is being reappropriated by New Labour as is demonstrated further by Charles Clarke's decla-ration that, 'the individual pupil must be at the centre of everything that we do' (Clarke, 2003). This is highly resonant of the Plowden Committees' assertion that, 'at the heart of the educational process lies the child'(Central Advisory Council for Education, 1967).

The new discursive turn traced here was manifest in relation to the primary phase with the publication in 2003 of *Excellence and enjoyment: a strategy for primary schools* (Department for Education and Skills, 2003). Announcing this strategy, Charles Clarke said that the targets for primary would be dropped in 2004 and that he was responding to headteachers' complaints about excessive pressure from top-down targets. The strategy promises more autonomy for teachers and schools. In future, schools would be able to set their own targets (Ward, 2003). Among the key terms used in the document, 'individual' was prominent as in the declaration that, 'learning must be focused on individual pupils' needs and abilities' (Department for Education and Skills, 2003). But as Alexander has noted in a vigorous critique of the strategy, the advocacy of autonomy is contradicted by, 'the continuing pressure of testing, targets and performance tables and the creeping hegemonisation of the curriculum by the Literacy and Numeracy Strategies, with three-part lessons, interactive whole-class teaching and plenaries soon to become a template for the teaching of everything' (Alexander, 2004). The strategy shows few signs of a serious desire to move away from standards in favour of creativity and pupil-centred curricula.

Conclusion

One of the difficulties confronting the analyst of education policy is that of distinguishing symbolic policies (Edelman, 1971) designed primarily to gain electoral advantage, from those that genuinely seek to address problems. Policies, of course, tend in practice to be a combination of both but arguably some, such as class size reduction, were adopted more for their electoral appeal than because they offered genuine solutions to real problems.

One prominent element of New Labour's policies towards primary schools, whether or not they were intended to appeal to the electorate, has been their claim to have policies based on research. Conceived as an antidote to ideology, the mantra 'what works' is itself ideological because it ignores the asymmetries of power and its operation and it rests on the firm conviction that 'what works' can be identified with some degree of precision, whereas most social science research tends to produce not a single answer but several (Lather, 2004). As has been seen, the attitude of New Labour's educational policy formulators to research and evidence in primary education has been one of impatience towards complexity and a demand for unambiguous evidence. At worst, this has led to the selective appropriation of evidence and rejection of that which did not suit New Labour's political purposes, as when the then Secretary of State for Education, David Blunkett, criticised research on homework (Tymms & Coe, 2003).

But over and above crude interventions like this, there is the question of how research evidence can support all of the frequently contradictory ideological elements which make up New Labour (Gewirtz, 2002). Thus while the social democratic strand with its attachment to notions of social justice after a first term of stagnation has produced more money for education and a number of targeted initiatives intended to counteract the effects of poverty and social disadvantage, the New Labourist embrace of standards and testing in the primary school is at variance with it as well as with the perceived need for creativity. Even though it appears that the believers in fostering creativity for the knowledge economy are gaining the upper hand, the top-down habits and the electoral pressures that they serve remain and the contradiction looks irreconcilable. But even if it was, both arguments are framed solely within a discourse of economic utility. The five year strategy in curriculum terms offers the teachers whose task it will be to implement it very little to moderate their hostility to the regime of targets, testing and inspection. They will at best be indifferent to yet another set of contradictory initiatives arriving from outside, and through a combination of coercion and consent will be forced to find new coping strategies and ways of securing their self-identity (Jeffrey, 2002; Woods & Jeffrey, 2002). This situation

might be acceptable if it could be shown that pupils were benefiting from these policies not just in terms of test results but also in respect of fairness and social justice.
There is, unfortunately, little evidence that this is the case.

Note on contributor

Kevin Brehony is Professor of Early Childhood Studies at Roehampton University.
His research interests include educational ideologies, especially child-centred
education, education policy and the origins of education as a subject area. Recent
publications include: 'From the particular to the general, the continuous to the
discontinuous: progressive education revisited', *History of Education*,
30(5),(2001); and 'Researching the grammar of schooling: an historical view',
European Educational Research Journal 1(1), (2002).

References

Alexander, R. (2004) Still no pedagogy? Principle, pragmatism and compliance in primary educa-
tion, *Cambridge Journal of Education* 34(1), 7–34.
Alexander, R., Rose, J. & Woodhead, C. (1992) *Curriculum organisation and classroom practice in
primary schools: a discussion paper* (London, Department of Education and Science).
Anon (1999) Rebel schools flouting law on league tables. *http://news.bbc.co.uk/1/hi/education/
284165.stm* (accessed 9 April 2004).
Ball, S. J. (1999) Labour, learning and the economy: a 'policy sociology' perspective, *Cambridge
Journal of Education*, 29(2), 195–206.
Barber, M. (2002) The next stage for large scale reform in England: from good to great. *http://
www.cybertext.net.au/tct2002/disc_papers/organisation/barber.htm* (accessed 15 June 2004)
Barber, M. & Sebba, J. (1999) Reflections on progress towards a world class education system,
Cambridge Journal of Education, 29(2), 183–194.
Beard, R. (2003) Not the whole story of the national literacy strategy: a response to Dominic
Wyse, *British Educational Research Journal*, 29(6), 917–928.
Bentley, T. (2002) Time to stop 'teaching the test'. *The Observer*. February 10. http://
observer.guardian.co.uk/comment/story/0,6903,648079,00.html
Blair, T. (2004) Universal education and care for under-fives, speech by Prime Minister, Tony
Blair, at the *National Association of Head Teachers conference*, Cardiff. *http://www.labour.org.uk/
tbnaht2004/* (accessed 3 June 2004).
Blatchford, P. (2003) *The class size debate : is small better?* (Buckingham, Open University Press).
Board of Education (1931) *Report of the consultative committee on the primary school* (London,
HMSO).
Brehony, K.J. & Deem, R. (2003) Education policy. in: N. Ellison & C. Pierson (Eds) *Develop-
ments in British social policy 2* (Basingstoke, Palgrave Macmillan), 177–193.
Brehony, K. J. (1990) Neither rhyme nor reason: primary schooling and the National Curriculum.
in: M. Flude & M. Hammer (Eds) *The Education Reform Act 1988: its origins and implications*
(Basingstoke, Falmer), 107–131.
Brehony, K. J. (1998) Even far distant Japan is 'showing an interest': the English Froebel move-
ment's turn to Sloyd, *History of Education*, 27(3), 279–295.
Brehony, K. J. (2001) From the particular to the general, the continuous to the discontinuous:
progressive education revisited, *History of Education*, 30(5), 413–432.
Brehony, K. J. & Deem, R. (2005) Challenging the post-Fordist/flexible organisation thesis. The
case of reformed educational organisations, *British Journal of Sociology of Education*, forthcoming.

Brown, M., Millett, A., Bibby, T. & Johnson, D. C. (2000) Turning our attention from the what to the how: the national numeracy strategy, *British Educational Research Journal*, 26(4), 457–472.

Budge, D. (1999) Strategy research goes to Canada. *Times Educational Supplement*. February 26. http://www.tes.co.uk/search/search_display.asp?section=Archive&sub_section=News+%26+opinion&id=313947&Type=0

Burgess, H. (2000) What future for initial teacher education? New curriculum and new directions, *The Curriculum Journal*, 11(3), 405–417.

Cabinet Office (1999) *Modernising government* (London, Stationery Office).

CCCS (1981) *Unpopular education* (London, Hutchinson).

Central Advisory Council for Education (1967) *Children in Their Primary Schools* (London, HMSO).

CFAS (2003) School Sampling Project Curriculum Survey: Summary of primary school findings 2001-02. *http://www.education.man.ac.uk/cfas/mca/summaries.htm* (accessed 11 June 2004).

Clarke, C. (2003) Pupil centred learning: using data to improve performance. Specialist Schools Trust annual lecture 2003. *http://www.specialistschoolstrust.org.uk/resources/downloads2003.html* (accessed 6 June 2004).

Clinton, W. J. (1999) Transcript: Clinton's State of the Union speech. *http://www.cnn.com/ALLPOLITICS/stories/1999/01/19/sotu.transcript/* (accessed 15 November 2003).

Collins, T. (2004) War on SATs. *Evening Mail*. May 13. http://icbirmingham.icnetwork.co.uk/eveningmail/news/tm_objectid=14236934&method=full&siteid=50002&headline=war-on-sats-name_page.html.

Cunningham, P. (1988) *Curriculum change in the primary school since 1945 dissemination of the progressive ideal* (Lewes, Falmer Press).

Curtis, P. (2003) Funding crisis 'has cost 20,000 jobs', *The Guardian*, 14 October. http://education.guardian.co.uk/schools/story/0,5500,1062729,00.html.

Cutler, T. (2001) Learning from America: policy transfer and the development of the British workfare state, *Social Policy & Administration*, 35(1), 121–122.

Department for Culture, Media and Sport (1999) *All our futures: creativity, culture and education* (Sudbury, Department for Education and Employment).

Department for Education and Employment (1997) Blunkett sets tough new national targets to boost three Rs. *http://www.newsrelease-archive.net/coi/depts/GDE/coi8746c.ok* (accessed 5 March 2004).

Department for Education and Employment (1997) *Excellence in schools* (London, Stationery Office).

Department for Education and Employment and Unit, S. a. E. (1998) *The National Literacy Strategy: framework for teaching* (London, DfES).

Department for Education and Skills (2003) *Excellence and enjoyment : a strategy for primary schools.* (London, DfES).

Department of Trade Industry and Department for Education Employment (2001) *Opportunity for all in a world of change: [a White Paper on enterprise, skills and innovation]* (London, Stationery Office).

Dolowitz, D., P. (2000) *Policy transfer and British social policy : learning from the USA?* (Buckingham, Open University Press 2000).

Dolowitz, D. P. (2004) Prosperity and fairness? Can New Labour bring fairness to the 21st century by following the dictates of endogenous growth? *British Journal of Politics and International Relations*, 6(2), 213–230.

Dolowitz, D. P. & Marsh, D. (2000) Learning from abroad: The role of policy transfer in contemporary policy-making, *Governance – an International Journal of Policy and Administration*, 13(1), 5–24 ⟨Go to ISI⟩://000085236800002.

Earl, L. M., Fullan, M., Leithwood, K. & Watson, N. (2000) *Watching & learning: OISE/UT evaluation of the implementation of the national literacy and numeracy strategies* (Nottingham, DfEE Publications).

Earl, L. M., Levin, B., Leithwood, K., Fullan, M. & Watson, N. (2001) *Watching & learning 2: OISE/UT evaluation of the implementation of the national literacy and numeracy strategies* ([S.l.], DfES Publications).

Earl, L. M., Watson, N., Levin, B., Leithwood, K., Fullan, M. & Torrance, N. (2003) *Watching & learning 3: final report of the external evaluation of England's national literacy and numeracy strategies* (Nottingham, DfES Publications).

Edelman, M. (1971) *Politics as symbolic action* (Chicago, Markham).

Ehrenberg, R. G., Brewer, D. J., Gamoran, A. and Willms, J. D. (2001) Class size and student achievement, *Psychological Science in the Public Interest*, 2(1), 1–30.

Ehrenberg, R. G., Brewer, D. J., Gamoran, A. & Willms, J. D. (2001) Does class size matter? *Scientific American*, 285(5), 78–85.

Emery, H. (1998) A National Curriculum for the education and training of teachers: an English perspective, *Journal of In-service Education*, 24(2), 283–291.

Galton, M. & MacBeath, J. (2002) *A life in teaching? the impact of change on primary teachers' working lives* (London, National Union of Teachers).

Garner, R. (2002) Labour was wrong to cut class sizes, says Blair adviser, *The Independent*, 2 May.

Gewirtz, S. (2002) *The managerial school: post-welfarism and social justice in education* (London, Routledge).

Giddens, A. (1998) *The third way: the renewal of social democracy* (Cambridge, Polity Press).

Giddens, A. (2000) *The third way and its critics* (Cambridge, Polity Press).

Gould, P. (1998) *The unfinished revolution: how the modernisers saved the Labour Party* (London, Little Brown).

Graham, J. (1998) From New Right to New Deal: nationalism, globalisation and the regulation of teacher professionalism, *Journal of In-service Education*, 24(1), 9–23.

Hall, K., Collins, J., Benjamin, S., Nind, M. & Sheehy, K. (2004) SATurated models of pupildom: assessment and inclusion/exclusion, *British Education Research Journal*, 30(6), 801–17.

Hall, S. (2003) New Labour's double-shuffle, *Soundings*,(24), 10–24.

Hallam, S., Ireson, J. & Davies, J. (2004) Grouping practices in the primary school: what influences change? *British Educational Research Journal*, 30(1), 117–140.

Hallam, S., Ireson, J., Lister, V. & Chaudhury, I. A. (2003) Ability grouping practices in the primary school: a survey, *Educational Studies*, 29(1), 69–84.

Harris, S., Keys, W. & Fernandes, C. (1997) *Third International Mathematics and Science Study: second national report part 1; achievement in mathematics and science at age 9 in England* (Slough, NFER).

Hartley, D. (2003) New economy, new pedagogy? *Oxford Review of Education*, 29(1), 81–94.

Jeffrey, B. (2002) Performativity and primary teacher relations, *Journal of Education Policy*, 17(5), 531–546.

Jupp, R., Fairly, C., Bentley, T., Demos & Design, C. (2001) *What learning needs: the challenge for a creative nation* (London, Demos/Design Council).

Lather, P. (2004) Scientific research in education: a critical perspective, *British Education Research Journal*, 30(6), 759–72.

MacLeod, D. (2004) Clarke reports rise in teaching numbers, *The Guardian*, 29 April. http://education.guardian.co.uk/schools/story/0,5500,1206181,00.html.

Miliband, D. (2004) Choice and voice in personalised learning. *http://www.dfes.gov.uk/speeches/search_detail.cfm?ID=118* (accessed 2 June).

Mintzberg, H. (1983) *Structure in fives: designing effective organizations* (Englewood Cliffs NJ, Prentice-Hall).

National Audit Office (2003) *Getting the evidence: using research in policy making: report by the Comptroller and Auditor General* (London, Stationery Office).

Office for Standards in Education (1999) *Primary education: a review of primary schools in England, 1994–1998* (London, Stationery Office).

Office for Standards in Education (2002) *The curriculum in successful primary schools* (London, Office for Standards in Education).

Office for Standards in Education (2002) *The national literacy strategy: the first four years 1998–2002* (London, Ofsted).

Office for Standards in Education (2002) *The national numeracy strategy: the first three years 1999–2002* (London, Ofsted).

OFSTED (2000) Inspection report: Kings Rise Community Primary School. *http://www.ofsted.gov.uk/reports/index.cfm?fuseaction=summary&id=103242* (accessed 18 February 2004).

OFSTED (2003) Inspection report: Rosslyn Junior school. *http://www.ofsted.gov.uk/reports/index.cfm?fuseaction=summary&id=122459* (accessed 18 February 2004).

Paterson, L. (2003) The three educational ideologies of the British Labour Party, 1997–2001, *Oxford Review of Education*, 29(2), 165–186.

Phillips, D. & Ochs, K. (2003) Processes of policy borrowing in education: some explanatory and analytical devices, *Comparative Education*, 39(4), 451–462.

Piore, M. J. & Sabel, C. F. (1984) *The second industrial divide: possibilities for prosperity* (New York, Basic Books).

QCA (1997) Notes on the nature and scope of the review of the National Curriculum. *http://www.qca.org.uk/news/2586_2086.html* (accessed 12 March 2004).

Rabinovitch, D. (2002) Off on the right foot, *The Guardian*, 9 July. http://education.guardian.co.uk/schools/story/0,5500,751463,00.html.

Reynolds, D. & Farrell, S. (1996) *Worlds apart? A review of international surveys of educational achievement involving England* (London, HMSO).

Ritter, G. W. & Boruch, R. F. (1999) The political and institutional origins of a randomized controlled trial on elementary school class size: Tennessee's project STAR, *Educational Evaluation and Policy Analysis*, 21(2), 111–26.

Selleck, R. J. W. (1972) *English primary education and the progressives 1914–39* (London, Routledge and Kegan Paul).

Seltzer, K. & Bentley, T. (1999) *The creative age: knowledge and skills for the new economy* (London, Demos).

Selwyn, N. & Fitz, J. (2001) The national grid for learning: a case study of new labour education policy-making, *Journal of Education Policy*, 16(2), 127–148.

Smithers, R. (2003) Education alliance urges test shakeup, *The Guardian*, 3 December. http://education.guardian.co.uk/primaryeducation/story/0,11146,1098917,00.html.

Smithers, R. (2003) Low NUT ballot lifts threat of tests boycott, *The Guardian*, 17 December. http://education.guardian.co.uk/primaryeducation/story/0,11146,1098917,00.html

Szreter, S. (1997) A deep and disastrous legacy that undermines national learning – the need for more teachers, *New Statesman* http://articles.findarticles.com/p/articles/mi_m0FQP/is_n4354_v126/ai_20052437.

Teacher Training Agency (1997) *Training curriculum and standards for new teachers* (London, TTA).

Tomlinson, S. (2001) Education Policy, 1997–2000: the effects on top, bottom and middle England, *International Studies in Sociology of Education*, 11(3), 261–278.

Tymms, P. & Coe, R. (2003) Celebration of the success of distributed research with schools: the CEM Centre, Durham, *British Educational Research Journal*, 29(5), 639–654.

Ward, H. (2002) Primary review to ease 3Rs pressures, *Times Educational Supplement*, 28 June.

Ward, H. (2003) Thank you Charles … but it's not enough, *Times Educational Supplement*, 23 May.

Whitty, G. (2001) Education, social class and social exclusion, *Journal of Education Policy*, 16(4), 287–295.

Wilby, P. (1997) Adding and taking away in class – why reducing class size is bad policy, *New Statesman*, 3 October. http://articles.findarticles.com/p/articles/mi_m0FQP/is_n4354_v126/ai_20052436.

Woodhead, C. (2002) *Class war* (London, Little Brown).

Woods, P. & Jeffrey, B. (2002) The reconstruction of primary teachers' identities, *British Journal of Sociology of Education*, 23(1), 89–106.

Woodward, W. (2003) Ex-head jailed for exam forgery, *The Guardian*, 8 March. http://www.guardian.co.uk/uk_news/story/0,3604,909874,00.html.

Wyse, D. (2003) The National Literacy Strategy: a critical review of empirical evidence, *British Educational Research Journal*, 29(6), 903–916.

Diversity, specialisation and equity in education

Chris Taylor, John Fitz and Stephen Gorard

[handwritten annotation:]
Data on growth of specialised schools,
Sponsored academies
Expansion of faith based schools

1. Introduction

Recent announcements that the Labour government intends to increase the number of privately sponsored city academies from the existing 44 to a target figure of 200 by 2010 (BBC News, 2004) further emphasises the extent to which it is committed to diversification of state education. It sees this as a means to enhance further the standards of education, especially in historically low-attaining schools in inner urban areas. This initiative builds on the government's commitment to diversifying secondary school provision by increasing, for example, the number of specialist schools, from the present number of 1,445 in 2003, to 2,000 by 2006—well above 50% of all state secondary schools in England. The British government has recently lifted the 'cap' on specialist school funding so that all secondary schools in England that meet the requirements could be given specialist school status. Neither Wales nor Scotland however, has adopted specialist secondary schools.

Because the specialist schools programme is the largest of the diversification initiatives much of this paper is devoted to a detailed consideration of its character and its impacts. However, there are other diversification measures in operation, the most prominent of which are the development of 'academies' and support for the expansion of the number of faith-based schools. As these programmes are not as extensive or as well developed, it can be argued that the general insights about the effect of diversification can best and most precisely be drawn from studies of the specialist schools.

The government argues that their diversity agenda represents a modernisation of the comprehensive system that will contribute to its overall programme of raising standards by generating and disseminating good practice in specialist curricular areas and by establishing centres of excellence in educationally challenging areas. Critics are concerned with several aspects of the push for diversity via specialist schools, faith-based schools and academies. All these schools assume control of their own admissions policies, unlike traditional comprehensive schools. The consequence, it is argued, will be to re-introduce 'selective education' by engineering their intakes to choose the most able or motivated recruits (Thornton, 2001; Hattersley, 2002). This provides a market advantage within the competitive UK system of provision as well as achieving better student performance figures at the expense of other schools in the area. Aside from philosophical arguments about state funding for religious schools, faith-based schools in the British context can be seen as contributing to and sustaining 'parallel communities' where ethnic and language communities are educated in different schools (Garner, 2002; Willis, 2002). Furthermore, the resource advantages and clear mission enjoyed by these different types of schools set them apart from adjacent schools and provide a further market advantage. It is for these reasons that critics are concerned about the emergence of a two-tier system which in turn will serve to reproduce, in new and different ways, existing structures of inequality in English schooling.

The first aim of this paper is to outline empirically the scale, character and scope of state-funded school diversity and provision in the UK.[1] We identify four phases in the development of school diversity. The first phase is characterised by plurality in school provision, encompassing the era of the rise of mass secondary education from 1944 to the 1960s. The second phase of school diversity reforms represents a major shift away from plurality and towards the homogeneous notion of comprehensive schools from the late 1960s until the early 1980s. The neo-conservative attempt to address the apparent 'failure' of the comprehensive era led to the third phase of formal school diversity directed by central government and introduced alongside the increased marketisation of schooling in England and Wales. The fourth and most recent phase of school diversity is defined by the incumbent New Labour government in 1997. It is these attempts to diversify school provision since 1997 that provide the main focus of this paper and it is in this context we examine the empirical evidence of the relations between diversity and school segregation.

The second main aim of the paper is to examine and, where appropriate, analyse the relationship between recent programmes of education diversity and equity.

Drawing upon extensive work measuring the social composition of schools over time it is possible to consider the role that diversity and specialisation have had on equality in education (see Gorard *et al.* 2003 for more about this research). In particular, we go on to discuss the extent to which critics' fears about the emergence of a two-tier system are justified.

Before proceeding with the main discussion three qualifications need to be made. The first is that this paper is primarily concerned with diversity in secondary school provision. This sector is where most new diversity initiatives have taken place and had greatest impact. This is not intended to mean that diversity among state-funded primary schools does not exist. For example, the Beacon School programme included primary and secondary schools. Concerns about the extent to which diversity leads to divisions and segregation, however, have been expressed mainly in relation to secondary schooling.

The second qualification that needs to be made is that the reforms have had very different impacts across the 'home nations'. In Scotland and Wales relatively little diversification between schools exists. Indeed, most of the programmes to extend school diversity by the present Labour Government have been solely for England. Although this paper, therefore, addresses primarily 'English' reforms the findings and argument presented are still relevant to Wales and Scotland. For example, some school diversity —such as faith-based schools and Welsh-medium schools— does exist in these two countries. Furthermore, it is often reported that Welsh and Scottish local authorities, particularly in urban areas, do consider features of the English school diversity reforms when addressing their particular educational issues. Although in Wales and Scotland there are few national policies towards school diversity the response of schools and local authorities to what is going on in England cannot be ignored.

The final qualification is that this paper is primarily interested in the organisation of school provision and not in the curricular and pedagogic practices taking place within schools. It is important to note that the cycle of policy developments in terms of within-school diversity is not in tune with developments of between-school diversity. For example, although the more homogeneous provision of comprehensive schools occurred in the 1960s/1970s, it was not really until the introduction of the National Curriculum and standardised testing in the 1980s that homogeneous provision within schools was established.

2. From plurality to diversity

It is important to emphasise that school diversity in the UK is not new. The 1944 Education Act, as well as introducing compulsory secondary education, effectively consolidated pre-war arrangements—the most important element of which was to enable church schools to receive state funding and become 'voluntary' schools within the state system. The faith schools, most of which were Church of England or Roman Catholic in affiliation, received state funding in exchange for LEA participation on their governing bodies. The ensuing British education system can be characterised as plurality in provision. Parents could express a preference for a particular kind of state school although there was no guarantee that preferences would be realised. For parents, choice could be made between state and private education, between LEA and church schools, between single sex and co-educational schools and, in some areas, between selective and non-selective schools, though not all parents have had the same degree of choice. Parents in Wales were also able to choose between Welsh medium schools, where Welsh is the language of instruction, and English medium schools. At the LEA level, the administrative response to the challenge of secondary education for all, under strong guidance from central government, was secondary school provision in the form of an academically selective tripartite system composed of grammar schools, technical schools and modern schools. Although these different types of schools were meant to cross social class boundaries children from middle-class families were typically over-represented in selective grammar schools (Floud & Halsey, 1961; Silver, 1973; Halsey *et al.*, 1980; Ball, 1986), a phenomenon that, as we will see later, continues to the present.

A second phase of reforms relating to school diversity commenced in the early 1960s. This was characterised by the introduction and expansion of comprehensive schools, including a significant programme of new schools alongside the expansion of social housing. One aim of the comprehensive movement, which in the early years was located in LEAs and teacher organisations, was to remove diversity of school types and provide greater equality of opportunity (Benn & Chitty, 1996; Kerckhoff *et al.*, 1996). However, by 1965 the national government began to request plans for comprehensive school reorganisation from local educational authorities. Eventually comprehensive schools were formally recognised in the 1976 Education Act.

Although this period appears to have the least degree of formal diversification, considerable diversity was still evident. Not only did some grammar schools remain but many ex-grammar schools retained their ethos and, most importantly, their reputation among local communities (Kerckhoff *et al.*, 1996). Comprehensive schools were also quite diverse for a number of reasons: the commitment of local education authorities to the comprehensive movement; the association between new residential development, urbanisation and new comprehensive schools (Taylor & Gorard, 2001); and the way in which comprehensive schools were accommodated in the existing education landscape of, say, religious schools (Roman Catholic and Church of England), modern schools, technical schools, grammar schools and ex-grammar schools (Benn & Chitty, 1996). By the mid 1990s, about 92% of all state secondary students in England and approximately 99% in Scotland and Wales attended comprehensive schools (Benn & Chitty, 1996). Student admission polices were predominantly area based, via the use of catchment areas, operated by LEAs to encourage families to use their nearest schools. Nevertheless, parents, particularly in urban areas, prior to 1988, enjoyed a considerable measure of choice between different types of state school, even in left-leaning LEAs such as the Inner London Education Authority (Hargreaves, 1996).

The neo-liberal policy framework of the 1980 Education Act, the 1988 Education Reform Act and subsequent Conservative government legislation introduced a third policy phase. Diversity in this sense was seen as a key element in the construction of quasi-markets in education. Here the quest was to create state schools outside the control of LEAs and thus give parents a choice between LEA and self-governing schools. The City Technology Colleges (CTCs) programme, which commenced in 1986, represents the first move in this direction and established a pattern for the creation of different kinds of state schools, much of which is evident in today's specialist schools. CTCs were distinctive in that they had a specific technology-focused curriculum, they were intended to be state-private partnerships involving sponsors who would provide site and building, and they were outside the control of LEAs and would receive government grants to support recurrent costs, with additional support from industry to contribute to the technological aspects of the curriculum. As the policy unfolded it became increasingly clear that its intentions were not being fully met, and indeed the involvement of private sector sponsors fell well short of expectations (Whitty *et al.*, 1993).

Diversity was taken further forward in the 1988 Education Reform Act, a central feature of which was the grant-maintained (GM) schools initiative that enabled schools, after a ballot of parents, to opt out of LEA control, achieve a greater measure of autonomy and receive funding directly from central government (Fitz *et al.*, 1993). In the CTC and GM school initiatives LEAs were clearly seen as barriers to change and raising standards, and so diversity denotes creating schools outside LEA control while keeping them in the state system. A subsequent consultative Green Paper in 1992, entitled *Choice and diversity in education* (DFE, 1992) followed by new legislation, became a platform on which to extend diversity via the Technology Schools Initiative. GM and voluntary schools could apply for technology school status, initially in the areas of science/technology, language and sports and receive substantial grants to develop their curriculum specialism. More importantly they were allowed to select up to 10% of their intake by aptitude or ability in that specialism. In 1996, the principle of selection was extended by enabling GM schools to apply to change their admissions policies and select up to 20% of their intake. The conservative government was voted out of office before these measures came into effect.

The perils of devolving admissions policies to GM schools became apparent in the mid-1990s especially in the Greater London area and south east England where it became increasingly difficult for parents in some LEAs to obtain places in nearby high performing secondary schools (Fitz *et al.*, 2002). These difficulties were most intense in areas with high concentrations of GM schools (Taylor *et al.*, 2002).

The diversity programme during this third phase of development, then, was characterised by building a state school sector outside the control of, and therefore undermining, LEAs, funding advantages for self-governing schools, giving some schools control over their own admissions policies and the extension of the principle of selection. Clearly these features of school diversity distinguish this period from the earlier period of school plurality where school type was the key feature in promoting diversity. A useful framework for considering these other features of school diversity together is provided by Bradford's (1995) private-state continuum in educational provision. This conceives school diversity as the blurring of private and public functions of education provision. Taylor (2001a) takes this further by considering the geographical variation in school diversity during this third period of reforms, and argues that different levels of school diversity are achieved in different areas that 'reflect how recent education legislation has impacted differentially across England, creating a mosaic of education markets, each one offering different choice and constraints for parents in the market place' (p. 380).

3. New Labour and school diversity

There are strong continuities between Conservative and New Labour's social welfare and education policy frameworks. The combination of choice and competition policies in public service provision with so-called new public management accountability processes and practices where the emphasis has been on strong leadership and effi-ciency has been evident across administrations. The challenge has been to identify what has been distinctive about New Labour's social welfare and education programmes.

One approach has been to explore the extent to which Labour's policies exhibit features of Anthony Giddens' 'third way' framework (Power & Whitty, 1999). In other words, whether policies combine, and if so to what extent, elements of 'old Labour' where state power and state agencies are employed to assist the poor and the disadvantaged with elements of neo-liberalism. Paterson (2003) has argued, however, that these analyses of the reforms introduced by the new Labour government have been inadequate. Instead, Paterson's more nuanced analysis proposes that there are three educational ideologies underpinning Labour's reforms: (1) the notion of 'New Labourism'—that include themes from the New Right of the 1980s combined with a reinterpretation of 19th Century liberalism; (2) 'developmentalism'—state policies designed to promote the competitiveness of the UK in the global market economy; and (3) 'New Social Democracy'—encompassing the benefits of the free market, governmental intervention to limit the social consequences of the market, the impor-tance of redistributing power, wealth and opportunity, and promoting citizenship and social responsibility.

On this interpretation there would appear to be no single ideology or simple approach underpinning recent reforms but there are distinctive emphases. The first is a willingness to intervene (Paterson, 2003) in the pursuit of higher standards. The National Literacy and Numeracy Strategies, Education Action Zones, the expansion of specialist schools and support for city academies are all examples of this. The second is a willingness to use some of these programmes to provide greater resources for disadvantaged communities. These in turn are the sources for Labour's determi-nation to develop programmes to foster school diversity and as such, we believe, represent a fourth phase.

The early years

Education was a key issue for the Labour opposition in the run up to the 1997 general election. Among traditional Labour supporters the end of academic selection was seen by many as the priority for reforms. However, as Webster and Parsons (1999) have argued, the ruling members of the Labour Party were not consistent on this matter.

Indeed, they focused, rather, on the Conservative government's 'obsession with school structures' and heralded 'standards, more than structures, are the key to success. Labour will never put dogma before children's education' (The Labour Party, 1997). The 'standards not structures' agenda attempted to focus upon non-ideological pragmatism rather than the perceived 'old-fashioned' arguments about selection. Unsurprisingly, when elected in to office in May 1997, the attempts by the New Labour government to end academic selection were more rhetorical than real. The fate of the remaining 160 or so grammar schools, for example, was to be determined by parental ballot rather than by any concerted central government effort to close them.

However, other early reforms did appear to represent a shift away from educational diversity towards greater homogeneity. For example, the Assisted Places Scheme, that enabled supposedly academically able children from disadvantaged backgrounds to attend fee-paying private schools, was phased out. The funds saved from this scheme were used to try to reduce class sizes in Primary Schools.

The new Labour government also announced in its 1997 White Paper the abolition of GM schools. But rather than take that opportunity to reflect a move away from the previous phase of school diversity it actually heralded a fourth suite of reforms promoting and encouraging school diversity. Instead the legislation revised the way in which schools were to be governed and grouped: 'community schools' (schools under LEA control), voluntary-aided schools (VA) (in the main, faith-based schools) and 'foundation schools' (the great majority being former GM schools) (White *et al.*, 2001). Not only did this formally acknowledge plurality within the state education system it maintained the autonomy that VA and former GM schools had in controlling their own admissions policies.

In pursuit of standards driven reforms, the Labour Government White Paper also announced its intention to embrace 'partnerships' with private and non-governmental organisations whenever these would prove to be beneficial. It therefore accepted the continued existence of City Technology Colleges as independent state-funded education institutions for example. However the blurring of the public–private divide, as represented by the CTCs, in fact became the model that was to inform the creation of initiatives such as education action zones and later city academies. Moreover its declared policy of zero tolerance for underachieving schools has given rise to an unprecedented willingness, via the mechanism of school inspections, to pass control of 'failing' schools and LEAs to commercial and not-for-profit agencies, which in turn has the potential to extend the process of privatisation (Fitz & Beers, 2002).

Alongside the continuance of neo-liberal elements of educational policy, however, there has a been a distinctive shift towards the reform of urban schools and to direct more resources—some derived from the private sector—to schools and groups of schools serving disadvantaged communities. This provided a broad framework within which diverse kinds of secondary schools were able to emerge within programmes such as Education Action Zones and Excellence in Cities.

The 1998 School Standards and Framework Act continued to extol the virtues of 'standards not structures' and attempted to harmonise the increasingly frustrating admission processes that emerged from previous policies to accommodate open enrolment (Fitz *et al.*, 2002; Taylor *et al.*, 2002). It also initiated this government's programme of school diversity with the continued expansion of specialist schools and the establishment of Beacon Schools. But it was the 2001 White Paper *Schools achieving success* and the more recent 2003 strategy document *A new specialist system: transforming secondary education* where the promotion of greater school diversity was made more explicit. Indeed, there is now a School Diversity unit within the Department for Education and Skills (DfES) whose primary responsibility is to encourage and investigate greater school diversity. As a result of government action within the state sector, alongside LEA controlled comprehensive schools, foundation and VA school (which have been encouraged to expand in number), there are Beacon Schools, Training Schools, Federations, Leading Edge Partnership schools, specialist schools and most recently, city academies. We will discuss the last two initiatives in more detail later in the paper. The thrust of all these initiatives is to enable schools to differentiate themselves according to their individual ethos, special character and areas of specialist expertise. Furthermore, they draw upon the historical nature of school diversity in Britain as a justification for this continued approach. The flagship for school diversity since 1997 has been the specialist schools programme and we now turn to discuss this policy in more detail.

Specialist schools

Specialist schools were first established in 1994 by the previous Conservative government. However, the scope and nature of these schools has changed dramatically since 1997. Figure 1 illustrates the year-on-year rise in the number of specialist schools, including their rapid expansion from 1999. There are currently 1,686 specialist schools, which account for 54% of all state-funded secondary schools. It is intended to have 2,000 specialist schools by 2006.

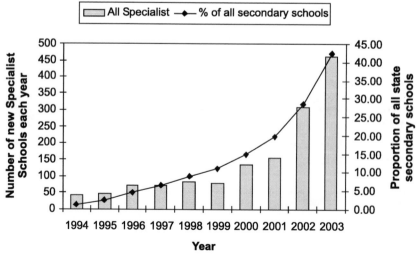

Figure 1.   The rise of specialist schools, by year: England 1994–2003
NB. Figures are given for September of each year.

Specialist schools continue to deliver the National Curriculum but are meant to provide a special focus on their chosen subject area. Initially specialist school status was only given to GM schools that had a particular strength in technology. But just as the number of specialisms was expanded, so were the types of schools that could apply for this status. For many years there were only four specialisms: technology, arts, sports and language. But since 1997 the number of specialisms has risen to ten to also include: science, business and enterprise, maths and computing, engineering, humanities and music. Schools may now combine these specialisms; in addition they may apply for specialist status by proposing a curriculum with a strong 'rural dimension'.

To obtain specialist school status schools must apply for this recognition. Originally this was on a competitive basis but since the cap on funding specialist schools was removed in 2002 it is now largely based upon meeting certain requirements. Schools of all types are also now allowed to apply for specialist schools status. However, the legacy of the 'exclusive' nature of this scheme continues to mean that some schools are under- and over-represented in the programme, although this is declining (Gorard & Taylor, 2001). But one key barrier to entry remains—that is, schools in Special Measures or with serious weaknesses will not be given specialist school status. Furthermore, schools must show they have high examination performance or be on an upward trajectory for school improvement for them to be considered.

When applying, schools must also raise £50,000 in unconditional sponsorship towards a capital project. If successful, specialist schools can currently expect to receive from the government an additional £100,000 towards the capital project and £126 per pupil per year for four years in addition to their standard recurrent funding. Specialist schools are expected to spend a third of their additional recurrent funding on sharing their expertise with other schools. This can include opening their premises for use by adjacent schools, sharing technology with them or enable staff to lead staff development and share expertise with teachers in other schools. But in light of the competitive environment secondary schools are now in research suggests that collaboration tends to be with primary schools or other non-school agencies rather than other secondaries (Davies *et al.*, 2002; Bell & West, 2003; Penney, 2004).

Academies

The Secretary of State described academies as 'state-funded independent schools that will work with other schools to provide a first rate, free education for pupils of all abilities' (Clarke, 2003). As with specialist schools, it is envisaged that these schools will involve a partnership between sponsors—'individual benefactors ... business, faith or voluntary groups'—who are expected to provide up to 20% or £2 million of the capital costs, and the government, which will be responsible for recurrent costs (Clarke, 2003). Furthermore, the sponsor or their representative is expected to join the governing body of the school but, unlike its predecessor, City Technology Colleges, local education authorities are seen as a key partner in their establishment and development. The first three Academies were opened in September 2002, followed by a further nine in 2003. Currently there are 44 Academies already open or in development, and after its most recent announcement the government is aiming to have at least 200 by 2010, with at least 30 of these located in London. In terms of school numbers the Academy programme has been significantly more successful than the previous Conservative governments' attempts to establish City Technology Colleges.

The rhetoric in establishing Academies has been in terms of addressing under-attainment and raising standards. It is the intention, therefore, that Academies are located in educationally challenging areas, and the Government stresses they are all-ability schools. Initially they were to be limited to inner city areas but since the 2002 Education Act they can be established in challenging suburban and rural areas also.

Beacon schools and the leading edge partnerships

Another key part of New Labour's school diversity programme is the Beacon Schools initiative. These are schools identified as high performing that are funded to be centres of excellence, sharing effective practice and offering advice to other schools. These were established in 1998 and at time of writing there are 1,052 Beacon Schools—including 254 secondary schools, 42 nursery schools, 678 primary schools, 6 middle schools and 71 special schools. Such schools receive on average an additional £38,000 per year to work with other schools and teachers. Research on these schools is limited, although there has been a government-funded review of Beacon Schools by the NFER (Rudd *et al.*, 2002).

Although only operational for six years this scheme is being gradually phased out. Since 2002, secondary Beacon Schools have been replaced by the Leading Edge Partnership programme. This new programme adopts a slightly different focus since it tries to identify schools that are already innovative. Furthermore, identification is made of schools already working in collaboration; there is a lead school but it is the partnership of schools that receives the additional £60,000 per year for three years. It is also notable that there is no formal 'badging' of this more recent scheme as opposed to the Beacon School programme. The government argues that there is a negative impact of such labelling or identification, probably acknowledging the difficulty of getting schools to collaborate when they are given an apparent advantage in the market place.

Federations and diversity pathfinders

These two diversity programmes build upon the collaborative features of the New Labour government's educational agenda. To date 18 'federations' have been approved, and the term 'federation' is used to encompass different types of collabo-rative groups and/or partnerships. The innovative use of 'federations', which have been heavily promoted by the Institute of Public Policy Research (IPPR)—reportedly this government's most favoured think-tank—means that their definition and objec-tives are still rather vague. However, they do rely upon some formal acknowledgement of collaboration between institutions. For example, the 2002 Education Act allows for federations to have a single or joint governing body across two or more schools.

Diversity pathfinders are another form of collaborative enterprise, although in this case it is local education authorities (LEAs) who lead their development. They are also more about the organisation of school diversity as opposed to the pedagogic values of collaboration and sharing expertise. The scheme was established in 2001 to demonstrate the 'benefits' of school diversity within particular LEAs. There are currently six local authorities in the scheme from urban and rural areas of England: Cornwall, Portsmouth, Newham, Hertfordshire, Birmingham and North Tyneside.[2] Each authority is taking a different approach to 'managing' school diversity. For example, in Cornwall the authority is encouraging all maintained secondary schools to obtain Specialist school status 'coherently'. In Birmingham, by contrast, six schools are working closely together within a formal management structure, focussing upon staff development, an intranet and building a corporate identity.

Faith-based schools

Although not seen as a formal part of the Labour Government's school diversity programme, faith-based schools clearly make a major contribution to offering a greater choice of schools and encouraging schools to have distinct identities and ethos. Indeed New Labour has encouraged the expansion of faith-based schools through its support of the Dearing report *The way ahead: Church of England schools in the new millennium* (2001) and in its own 2001 White Paper *Schools achieving success*. The Dearing Report proposed a need for 100 new Church of England secondary schools before 2008. This was based upon three key arguments; that overall demand for places in Church of England schools exceeds provision, that there is obvious under-provision in some areas of England, and that faith-based education should remain central to the mission and work of the Church of England. The Government's White Paper adds two further arguments for the general expansion of faith-based schools. First, they argue that it is only 'fair' that the diversity of faith-based provision should extend beyond the dominance of Church of England and Roman Catholic schools. Such expansion of faith-based education should, therefore, meet the needs of other minority faiths by increasing, for example, the number of state-funded Muslim schools and Jewish schools. The second strand to their argument in encouraging faith-based education is that they take the view that such schools generally achieve higher standards and are consequently very popular. However, this justification does not seem to problematise the relationship between educational attainment and the nature of faith-based school intakes; this is returned to later in the paper.

The modernisation of comprehensive schools

Another key feature of the New Labour government's approach to school provision has been the modernisation of comprehensive schools. Clearly, their programme of school diversity can be seen as part of that process to change the comprehensive school system to meet the needs of a changing society and economy. The former Education Minister, Estelle Morris, has indeed argued 'specialist schools have had a lot of nonsense written about them. In fact they are modern comprehensives which gain better results when compared with similar schools, which set more challenging goals and which are supported financially to do so' (2001, p. 4). This is a view shared by the Government's senior advisor on specialist schools, Sir Cyril Taylor, 'specialist schools are intended to strengthen the comprehensive school system, not to threaten it' (2001b, p. 15). Features of the comprehensive ideal also appear in the school diversity programme, such as the move towards all-ability Academies and removing the opportunity for new specialist schools to select a proportion of their intakes.

The Government's attempts to increase the transparency and fairness of admission processes can also be seen as reflecting the principles of comprehensive schooling. While the third period of school diversity under the Conservative government encouraged the decentralisation of admissions procedures and policies to schools the fourth era of school diversity under New Labour has attempted to regain some centralised management and control of school admissions. However, this has not been successful in returning the control over admissions to a level seen during the comprehensive era. Although LEAs have been given increased responsibility, and some coordination of the procedures now exists between schools, most of the changes have been in the form of guidance notes and heavily influenced by particular tensions that, it can be argued, are unique to London.

These efforts are characteristic of what Paterson (2003) refers to as the New Social Democracy—a concern that government should attempt to limit or reconcile the social injustices of the market—that has been a key thread to New Labour's approach to education reforms. We next consider two key features of all these programmes of school diversity, funding and admissions and the issue of equity.

4. Funding and admissions

There are two important characteristics that are common to all these programmes of school diversity, including those of the Conservative governments since 1979. The first of these relates to the funding of schools that represent the diversity agenda. The funding of these schools differs somewhat to the funding of traditional LEA-maintained schools. The government provides their funding direct to schools and colleges. Not only has this reduced the responsibility of LEAs, however, it has also severely limited their ability to provide services and functions to schools, particularly the traditional LEA-maintained schools. Furthermore, nearly all the schools that are part of the diversity reforms enjoy the benefits of additional funding, both in terms of capital costs and in recurrent funding. Not only do they receive these additional funds but since many of them have private sponsors, of one kind or another, they have more than one potential source of income if extra resources are required for refurbishment, for example.

The second common feature of schools in these programmes of diversity relates to admissions. Although open enrolment is universal the procedures for applying for school places and for allocating oversubscribed school places varies enormously. In particular, schools that join these programmes of diversity are given some degree of autonomy in organising their admissions. In some cases, such as the original City Technology Colleges and early specialist schools, schools could select between 10% and 20% of their intakes on the basis of aptitude or ability in their chosen specialism. Even where schools do not introduce selection by aptitude or ability the way they organise and run their admissions can lead to covert and overt selection (West & Hind, 2003).

5. School diversity and social equity

There are two main equity issues that are of importance in terms of school diversity. The first is whether the school reforms, whatever form they take, have an equitable impact on the education standards of all pupils and groups. A second related but also separate issue is whether changes in school provision, and the increased diversity of schools, is leading to greater or lesser segregation of pupils on the basis of their social (and ethnic) characteristics. Not only does the increasing or decreasing segregation of children from different social backgrounds have a direct influence upon the relative performance of schools as measured by public examination results, it also has important impacts on social mobility, citizenship and social exclusion/inclusion. It is this latter equity issue that is the focus here since it is necessary to consider this first before fully addressing the issue of standards and equity.

While it is perhaps still too soon to identify the overall impact of New Labour's school diversity programme on social equity, some initial observations can be made. For example, it is possible to examine the long-term impact of school diversity, particularly of programmes that pre-date 1997, and recent trends in the socio-economic composition of school intakes. These findings can begin to give some indication of what the consequences of the fourth phase of school diversity reforms will be on social equity.

In our research we have examined the impact of increased marketisation on socio-economic (and ethnic) segregation over the last few years (see Gorard *et al.*, 2003). This has investigated the change in the composition of all secondary school intakes in England and Wales, year-on-year, since 1989. It has also examined the geography of segregation between schools, via the identification of patterns of spatial variation of trends in segregation between schools. Socio-economic segregation of student compositions, as assessed by the proportion of pupils with a specific characteristic who would have to exchange schools for this characteristic to be spread evenly, declined between 1988–1997. This decline in segregation has been measured in terms of poverty, special needs, first language and ethnicity. The period involved increasing parental choice, a growth in out-of-catchment placements, and a large growth in appeals (Taylor, 2001a; Taylor *et al.*, 2002).

Our analysis of these trends and the geography of school segregation have highlighted a number of key factors that may explain these changes. These include: the geography of local education markets, including residential segregation; local school reorganisation, and particularly the impact of local education authorities in closing or amalgamating schools; and the impact of the admission procedures. We have already

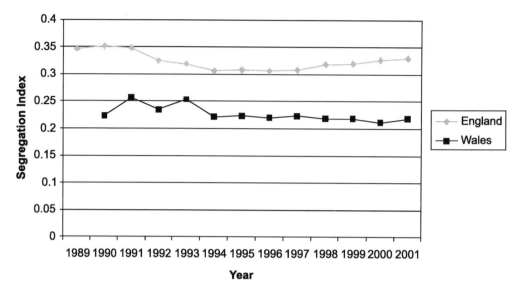

Figure 2.   Segregation of free school meal pupils between secondary schools

discussed the proliferation of admission processes and practices to emerge from the increased marketisation of schooling throughout the 1980s and 1990s. But many changes to school admissions have primarily been a direct consequence of increasing school diversity.

It is notable, then, that since 1997 socio-economic segregation in England has begun to rise slightly (Figure 2). Although there are potentially many explanations for these rises, particularly at the local level, it does coincide with the arrival of the New Labour government and, in particular, the encouragement of greater school diversity. Indeed, an increase in school diversity will have only added to the greater complexities of the school admissions process, alongside an increasing number of schools with autonomous power in deciding how to admit pupils.

Figure 2 employs a segregation index to show the spread of children who receive free school meals (FSM) between schools. We discuss the segregation index in detail elsewhere (Gorard *et al.*, 2003) but it shows the proportion of FSM children who would have to move school for each school to take its fair share. This table shows about a third of FSM children would have to change school in order to achieve an even spread. Thus, were the segregation index to show 0, then all schools would have their fair share of FSM children and could therefore be deemed socio-economically 'mixed'. The higher the index the more schools are segregated or different in terms of their intakes. A very high segregation index figure would denote a system clearly divided, say, into so-called 'privileged' and 'sink' schools. If the index rises or falls over time then the schools have become more or less segregated.

This figure illustrates that Wales, where secondary education is very largely provided by LEA comprehensive schools and where there are few grant-maintained, low numbers of fee-paying, selective, and specialist schools, has markedly lower levels of segregation than the English average. One possible conclusion is that choice without diversity tends to lead to lower levels of segregation than simple allocation of school places by area of residence (Taylor & Gorard, 2001).

Although levels of segregation in England in 2001 still remained lower than they were in 1989 when open enrolment was first introduced, there is great variation in the levels of segregation in different regions and locales. In general, LEAs with higher proportions of foundation, selective or specialist schools have higher levels of socio-economic stratification between schools (Gorard & Fitz, 2000). Within LEAs the relationship between school types and segregation is an ogival one. Areas with high levels of selective, voluntary-aided, grant-maintained or fee-paying schools have higher levels of segregation than their neighbours, and show no change in segregation over time (e.g. Bromley, Buckinghamshire, and Haringey). Areas with large changes in segregation over time or lower initial levels of segregation contain only LEA-controlled comprehensive schools. Diversity with choice therefore appears to tend towards segregation/selection. This remains the case in the analysis of our national dataset whatever the publicised criteria of allocation to schools are (and the considerable range of these criteria can be seen in White *et al.*, 2001). These general findings spell out a possible warning for a policy, such as the current one, that combines parental choice, school diversity and autonomy in allocating school places.

We have also undertaken detailed analysis of the relationship between socio-economic segregation and a particular form of school diversity, that of specialist schools (Gorard & Taylor, 2001). This analysis incorporated our examination of the changing nature of school intakes alongside interviews with local authority admissions officers and senior staff from specialist and non-specialist schools. We concluded that it would appear that the specialist school programme *per se* does not lead to, as critics have feared, a two-tier system of admissions. The evidence from this study, however, does show that specialist schools that retain some autonomy over their admissions arrangements are less likely to admit pupils living in poverty. Combining the 'specialist school' form of diversification with the 'school autonomy' form of diversification, as represented by voluntary aided and foundation schools, is leading to a two-tier education system. This process arises in two stages. First, since specialist school status increases the popularity of a school (West *et al.*, 2000) these schools are more likely to apply criteria in allocating places when they are oversubscribed than other schools. And second, their over-subscription criteria can be applied to ensure they get the most able and consequently the most socially 'advantaged' children.

To illustrate this, Table 1 outlines the proportion of schools whose intakes have become more 'privileged' between 1994/95 and 1999/00. We consider here that schools with more 'privileged' intakes already had less than their 'fair share' of children from families in poverty, as measured by their entitlement to free school meals, and that this proportion over those five years declined further. We also assume that their 'fair share' is the equivalent to the proportion of such pupils across all schools in their respective local authority. Some commentators have questioned the basis of what should be considered the 'fair share' or basis for such measurements. However, our own analysis of this important factor directs us to use local authorities, since it is convenient and more importantly, in terms of trends, very similar to findings using other

Table 1.   Schools with increasingly more 'privileged' intakes, 1994/95–1999/00

School Type	% schools more 'privileged'
All schools	29%
Grammar schools	75%
Community Schools (no element of diversity)	23%
Foundation schools (no grammar)	31%
Voluntary-Aided schools (no grammar)	45%
Comprehensive (14–18)	69%
Secondary Modern	17%
Specialist schools (all)	37%
Of which Language colleges	*43%*
Of which Foundation schools	*43%*
Of which Voluntary Aided schools	*57%*

methods (Taylor *et al.*, 2003). It is also important to note that in this analysis we merely distinguish between schools that have become more 'privileged' and those that have not. We do not, for example, consider here to what extent they have become more 'privileged'. This level of analysis we discuss elsewhere (Fitz *et al.*, 2003), but to provide an analysis of equity and general school diversity we focus solely on this binary definition.

Table 1 shows that 29% of all secondary schools, or 23% of Community schools without any form of diversity, had increasingly more 'privileged' intakes over that period. In other words these schools were allocating relatively fewer places to pupils eligible for free school meals than other schools in their local authority, and that over time they admitted even fewer pupils from socio-economically disadvantaged areas. It is these schools, in effect, that have been driving the levels of segregation between schools upwards since 1996/7 (see Figure 2). Table 1 also illustrates that 37% of specialist schools, at that time, had more 'privileged' intakes. This suggests that specialist schools are more likely to have privileged intakes than other non-specialist schools.

It is important to note, however, that 63% of specialist schools did not become more 'privileged'. They may have admitted fewer pupils eligible for free school meals, but if they had then they were already taking more than their 'fair share'.

Nevertheless, once we begin to examine in detail different types of specialist schools it becomes clear that particular specialist schools were more likely to become 'privileged' than others. For example, specialist schools that chose to specialise in, say, languages were more likely to become 'privileged'. These contrast, for example, with schools that chose to specialise in sports, which were less likely to become more 'privileged'. Furthermore, as proposed above, a higher proportion of schools with more privileged intakes occurred where schools combined their specialist status with further autonomy and diversity. For example, 43% of Specialist Foundation schools and 57% of Specialist faith-based, or voluntary-aided, schools increased their 'privileged' intakes over that period.

Table 1 extends this analysis to include other forms of school diversity, such as grammar schools (i.e. selective), foundation schools (typically former GM schools) and faith-based schools. Grammar schools have, for many decades, admitted socio-economically privileged intakes because they select their intakes on the basis of academic ability. So prior to open enrolment and prior to greater school diversity these schools already served privileged intakes. Although few in number, it is perhaps surprising, then, that three-quarters of grammar schools have become *more* 'privileged' between 1995 and 2000. Of course all of these schools already admitted relatively far fewer pupils eligible for free school meals than the average for their area. It is therefore the case that they were more likely to meet the first criteria we are adopting here, i.e. that they were already admitting below their 'fair share' of pupils eligible for free school meals. But it is also possible that the fight for places at such schools has increased since open enrolment was introduced and parents have been encouraged to choose a school for their children. With greater competition for places at grammar schools the benchmark in 11+ tests will have risen. This in turn may have reduced the opportunity for children from relatively poor backgrounds to be allocated a place.

The past historical favourability and élite status of grammar schools over other schools continues today in ex-grammar schools. For example, only 17% of secondary modern schools admitted more 'privileged' intakes during this period. In contrast, 69% of comprehensive 14–18 schools, many of which were formerly grammar schools in the 1970s (Kerkchoff *et al.*, 1996), became more 'privileged'.

Table 1 also illustrates the élite status of two other types of schools. Foundation schools (typically former Grant Maintained schools) were more likely to have admitted more 'privileged' intakes than non-diverse types of schools (31%). Although these schools benefited, in the past, from additional resources, and continue to have some autonomy in their admissions policies, they have not all been able to use this to gain élite status or privileged intakes. The mix of schools that originally became Grant Maintained (Fitz *et al.*, 1993) has meant that such schools did not become as popular as other types of schools. We have shown elsewhere that GM status helped to differentiate some of these schools in the market place from other LEA-maintained schools. However, their overall impact on the education market has perhaps been rather limited (Taylor, 2001c).

Faith-based schools, or voluntary-aided schools, on the other hand, occupy a unique position in the education market (Ball *et al.*, 1995; Taylor, 2001c). As a consequence they have maintained 'privileged' intakes and, between 1994/95 and 1999/00 just under half of such schools admitted even more 'privileged' intakes. Faith-based schools retained the right to control their admissions policies in order to provide places for families who were committed to a religious education and in order to sustain the ethos of the schools. Faith-based schools have historically been associated with selection, by interviewing able, well-motivated children, often acting as havens for disaffected parents seeking an alternative to the neighbourhood comprehensives. But critics have argued, with some justification, that interviews conducted with applicant families can become a convenient form of selection by proxy, a process which screens out less desirable students and families (Toynbee, 2001). Recent studies report that faith-based and voluntary schools were more likely to use interviews and to employ admissions criteria to 'select out' students than LEA community schools (Couldron, 2003; West & Hind, 2003).

6. Conclusions

We have shown that policies aimed at diversifying secondary education, first introduced during the 1980s and early 1990s by previous Conservative administrations, continue today under the control of a New Labour government. However, the diversity agenda of the current government departs in a number of ways that also reflects their approach to education policy more broadly. On the one hand it has continued to follow the neo-liberal programme by expanding school diversity, well beyond the scope and extent achieved by the previous Conservative administrations. This is best illustrated in the specialist schools programme, which now includes more than half of all state-funded secondary schools, and Academies, that now exceed the number of City Technology Colleges introduced by the Conservatives. Although this does not constitute a departure from the approach taken during the 1980s and early 1990s it does represent a significant advancement in fostering school diversity.

Also distinctive is Labour's focus on urban reform and its greater support for schools in disadvantaged communities. The policies intended to achieve this were not without controversy because they were based on partnerships with private and not-for-profit organisations. Nevertheless these programmes represent, in Paterson's terms, attempts to mute the impact of the market on schools vulnerable within in it.

The approach of New Labour towards the promotion of school diversity does also differ in other ways from that of the previous Conservative governments. While it has not been resolute in its determination to close grammar schools it has entertained the idea by giving parents the right to ballot for their closure, albeit employing guidelines that make closure very difficult to achieve. Furthermore, they have given local authorities and Admission Adjudicators some power, through admission forums, to reduce the level of academic selection among other schools. Again, their actions could have been more substantial, but authorities, such as Hertfordshire, have used these mechanisms to considerably reduce the level of selection among their schools. Selection, however, remains an issue with Labour's policies more generally and one which has caused discomfort within the ranks of the government's supporters.

They will have been relieved that very few specialist schools have chosen to use their right to select a proportion of their intakes on aptitude. What was initially an uncomfortable period, when successive ministers for education were made to justify the use of selection in one of their flagship initiatives, has now been modified, preventing future specialist schools from academically select their intakes. This also applies to Academies.

Another key feature of New Labour's approach to school diversity has been the importance of collaboration between schools. Specialist schools, even prior to 1997, were meant to use some of their additional resources to share expertise with neighbouring schools. However, it soon became clear that their support for neighbouring schools has been limited (Yeomans *et al.*, 2000; OFSTED, 2001). One of the main failings, it could be said, is that such schools wish to retain their relative advantage in the education market place. Collaborating, cooperating and/or sharing their expertise and additional resources does run counter to the competitive nature of a well established education market. It is perhaps not surprising, therefore, that collaborative links have tended to emerge predominantly with feeder primary schools and not with other non-specialist secondary schools.

It is possible to argue that one attempt by the Labour government to address this issue has been the establishment of the Diversity Pathfinders strategy—helping local authorities, such as Cornwall, in encouraging schools to obtain specialist school status in a complementary, rather than competitive, way.

Another strategy, Beacon Schools, was also introduced to enable collaboration and sharing of expertise and good practice. However, by further differentiating between schools, the education market place has the potential to severely constrain greater collaboration between schools and prevent the spread of bottom-up innovations in teaching and learning that was envisaged. However, by replacing the Beacon school scheme in the secondary sector with Leading Edge Partnerships, the New Labour government continues to try and find a way of achieving this more social democratic objective within its diversity agenda. Instead of identifying schools of excellence and then encouraging them to share their expertise Leading Edge Partnerships are chosen because they already work effectively in partnership. Similarly, there is no formal badging of this scheme and the resources are managed by the partnerships, not individual schools.

Clearly New Labour's investment in encouraging greater collaboration between schools could be characteristic of one of the overarching educational ideologies identified by Paterson (2003) as New Social Democracy. It could be argued, therefore, that this helps distinguish the New Labour approach to school diversity from previous approaches. The New Labour government would appear to argue that this represents the modernisation of comprehensive schooling.

If Ministers and policy advisors are alluding to a return to the pursuit of social equity, another supposed characteristic of comprehensive schooling, then they may also be mistaken. We have provided clear evidence that since 1997 socio-economic segregation between all secondary schools in England has risen. Whatever the causes of this have been this has may well have been an unintended consequence of New Labour's education agenda. We have also demonstrated that, for example, in Wales, where school diversity is limited, socio-economic segregation between secondary schools is significantly lower than in England and has continued to decline when segregation in England began to rise. In this paper we have also discussed the greater propensity of some schools that control their own admissions policies to admit increasingly 'privileged' intakes from 1994/95 to 1999/00. If we consider this alongside other evidence that the admissions process can favour such schools then it would seem that pursuing a programme of school diversity leads to greater social inequity. A combination of additional resources, growing popularity and autonomy for admissions allows some schools, whether consciously or not, to recruit children from advantageous socio-economic backgrounds. The proposed expansion in the number of city academies needs to be viewed in this light.

Since such schools are, in effect, attracting more able pupils, this is likely to result in an improvement of their overall examination performance. This raises another important concern about the New Labour school diversity programme. Supposed evidence of increasing education standards is used by the current government to further encourage school diversity. However, as we have seen, improvement may in reality arise because such schools are able to maintain a privileged position within the education market, and by increasingly attracting particular children from particular backgrounds. It is also the case that for schools to obtain specialist school status their pupils must already be achieving high examination standards or that over time they are already improving. It is unsurprising, therefore, that with additional resources and growing popularity, the specialist schools programme may appear successful to the government. Similar concerns exist about the evidence base underpinning the policy aimed at the further expansion of faith-based schooling.

To conclude, there are several policy objectives that inform New Labour's version of school diversity. The previous Conservative governments primarily saw diversity of schooling as a way of extending choice within the education market place, and in bypassing what they believed were largely bureaucratic local authorities. New Labour, however, have used the school diversity agenda primarily as a vehicle for raising standards in schools. For example, schools are typically offered additional resources in return for reforming their teaching and learning, organisation and/or governance in the 'desired' way. The problem with this is that the 'other' schools, schools that remain as LEA-maintained Community schools with no formal special 'status', are not offered additional resources for remaining so. Inevitably, this leads to a growing disparity between the 'winners' and the 'losers' of the New Labour education agenda.

It is also difficult to see how the New Labour approach to school diversity, that encourages greater collaboration between schools, can overcome the disparity between the haves and the have-nots. Although fostering greater cooperation and networking between schools may be a useful strategy to raise standards across all schools, this perhaps naively ignores the presence of school choice and competition that is now firmly established in the education system. If the government wishes to modernise comprehensive schooling for a changing society it must first recognise that the education system and the consumption of education has changed considerably since the 1970s.

Notes

1. Although the paper is primarily concerned with school diversity in England.
2. There are two additional associate pathfinders to these: Warwickshire and Middlesbrough.

Notes on contributors

Chris Taylor is a lecturer in the Cardiff School of Social Sciences, Cardiff University. His interests are in the marketisation and geography of education provision. He has also recently been involved in the development and enhancement of research capacity among education researchers in the UK as manager of the TLRP Research Capacity Building Network.

John Fitz works in the Cardiff School of Social Sciences, Cardiff University. He is a professor of education policy, and has spent many years examining changes to UK school provision. He is also interested in the politics of policy making and policy implementation.

Stephen Gorard is professor of education in the Departmental of Educational Studies, University of York. His main interests are in differential attainment, school compositions and patterns of participation. He writes extensively on the nature, quality and methods of education research.

References

Ball, S. (1986) *Education* (London, Longman).

Ball, S., Bowe, R. & Gewirtz, S. (1995) Circuits of schooling: a sociological explanation of parental choice in social class contexts, *Sociological Review*, 43(1), 52–87.

BBC News (2004) 200 City Academies promised, downloaded from http://news.bbc.co.uk.

Bell, J. & West, A. (2003) Specialist schools: an exploration of competition and co-operation, *Educational Studies*, 29(2/3), 273–289.

Benn, C. & Chitty, C. (1996) *Thirty years on: is comprehensive schooling alive and well or struggling to survive?* (London, David Fulton).

Bradford, M. (1995) Diversification and division in the English education system: towards a post-Fordist model? *Environment and Planning A*, 27, 1595–1612.

Brighouse, T. (2002) Comprehensive schools then, now and in the future—is it time to draw a line on the sand and create a new ideal? *The Caroline Benn, Brian Simon Memorial Lecture*, September 2002.

Clarke, C. (2003) *A new specialist system: transforming secondary education* (London, DfES).

Couldron, J. (2003) Memorandum of Evidence presented to the House of Commons Education and Skills Select Committee.

Davies, P., Adnett, N. & Mangan, J. (2002) The diversity and dynamics of competition: evidence from two local schooling markets, *Oxford Review of Education*, 28(1), 91–107.

DFE (1992) *Choice and diversity: a new framework for schools* (London, HMSO).

Dore, C. & Flowerdew, R. (1981) Allocation procedures and the social composition of comprehensive schools, *Manchester Geographer*, 2(1), 47–55.

Fitz, J. & Beers, B. (2002) Educational management organisations and the privatisation of education in the US and the UK, *Comparative Education*, 38(2), 137–154.

Fitz, J., Halpin D. & Power, S. (1993) *Education in the market place* (London, Kogan Page).

Fitz, J., Taylor, C., Gorard, S. & White, P. (2002) Local Education Authorities and the regulation of educational markets: four case studies, *Research Papers in Education*, 17(2), 125–146.

Fitz, J., Gorard, S. & Taylor, C. (2002) School admissions after the School Standards and Framework Act: bringing the LEAs back in? *Oxford Review of Education*, 28(2), 373–393.

Floud, J. & Halsey, A.H. (1961) Social class, intelligence tests and selection for secondary schools, in: A.H. Halsey, J. Floud & C. Arnold Anderson (Eds) *Education, economy and society: a reader in the sociology of education* (New York, the Free Press and London, Collier-Macmillan), 209–215.

Garner, R. (2002) Inquiry urged into faith schools plan, *Independent*, 6 November, downloaded from www.independent.co.uk.

Gorard, S. & Fitz, J. (2000) Investigating the determinants of segregation between schools, *Research Papers in Education*, 15(2), 115–132.

Gorard, S. & Taylor, C. (2001) The composition of specialist schools in England: track record and future prospect, *School Leadership and Management*, 21(4), 365–381.

Gorard, S., Taylor, C. & Fitz, J. (2003) *Schools, markets and choice policies* (London, Routledge-Falmer).

Halsey, A.H., Heath, A. & Ridge, J. (1980) *Origins and destinations: family, class and education in modern Britain* (Oxford, Clarendon Press).

Hargreaves, D. (1996) Diversity and choice in school education: a modified libertarian approach, *Oxford Review of Education*, 22(2), 131–141.

Hattersley, R. (2002) Selection returns by stealth, *Guardian*, 25 February, p. 16.

Kerckhoff, A.C., Fogelman, K., Crook, D. & Reeder, D. (1996) *Going comprehensive in England and Wales; a study of uneven change* (London, The Woburn press).

Morris, E. (2001) We need your help to make a difference, *Education Review*, 15(1), 2–7.

OFSTED (2001) *Specialist schools: an evaluation of progress* (London, OFSTED).

Paterson, L. (2003) The three educational ideologies of the British Labour Party, 1997–2001, *Oxford Review of Education*, 29(2), 165–186.

Penney, D. (2004) Policy tensions being played out in practice. The specialist schools initiative in England, *Journal for Critical Education Policy Studies*, 2, 1 http://www.jceps.com.

Rudd, P., Rickinson, M., Blenkinsop, S., McMeeking, S., Taylor, M. & Phillips, N. (2002) *Long-term external evaluation of the Beacon Schools initiative 2001–2002* (Slough, National Foundation for Educational Research (NFER)).

Power, S. & Whitty, G. (1999) New Labour's education policy: first, second or third way? *Journal of Education Policy*, 14(5), 535–546.

Silver, H. (Ed.) (1973) *Equal opportunity in education* (London, Methuen).

Taylor, C. (2001a) The geography of choice and diversity in the 'new' secondary education market of England, *Area*, 33(4), 368–381.

Taylor, C. (2001b) Why one size does not fit all pupils, *Education Review*, 15(1), 15–20.

Taylor, C. (2001c) Hierarchies and 'local' markets: the geography of the 'lived' market place in secondary education provision, *Journal of Education Policy*, 16(3), 197–214.

Taylor, C. (2002) *Geography of the 'new' education market* (Aldershot, Ashgate).

Taylor, C. & Gorard, S. (2001) The role of residence in segregation: placing the impact of parental choice in perspective, *Environment and Planning A*, 33(10), 1829–1852.

Taylor, C., Gorard, S. & Fitz, J. (2002) Market frustration; admission appeals in the UK education market, *Educational Management and Administration*, 30(3), 243–260.

Taylor, C., Gorard, S. & Fitz, J. (2003) The modifiable areal unit problem: Segregation between schools and levels of analysis, *International Journal of Social Research Methodology*, 16(1), 41–60.

The Labour Party (1997) *New Labour: because Britain deserves better*. 1997 Election Manifesto.

Thornton, K. (2001) Specialists spark 'two-tier' fears, *Times Educational Supplement*, 8 June, p.34.

Toynbee, P. (2001) Keep God out of class, *The Guardian*, 9 November, downloaded from www. http//education.guardian.co.uk 20 March 2002.

Webster, D. & Parsons, K. (1999) Labour Party policy on educational selection 1996-98: a sociological analysis, *Journal of Education Policy*, 14(5), 547–559.

West, A., Noden, P., Pennel, H. & Travers, T. (2000) *Examining the impact of the specialist schools programme*, Research Report RR196 (London, DfEE).

West, A. & Hind, A. (2003) *Secondary school admissions in England: exploring the extent of overt and covert selection* (London, Research and Information on State Education Trust).

White, P., Gorard, S., Fitz, J. & Taylor, C. (2001) Regional and local differences in admission arrangements for schools, *Oxford Review of Education,* 27(3), 317–337.

Whitty, G., Edwards, T. & Gewirtz, S. (1993) *Specialisation and choice in urban education: the City Technology Colleges experiment* (London, Routledge).

Willis, P. (2002) Increased tension, *The Guardian,* 4 February, downloaded from http://education.guardian.co.uk

Yeomans, D., Higham, J. & Sharp, P. (2000) *The impact of the specialist schools programme: case studies,* Research Report RR197 (London, DfEE).

Labour government policy 14–19

Richard Pring

14–19[1]

Any division of education into phases must have a certain degree of arbitrariness about it. Young people develop at different rates; they have different aptitudes and aspirations. But divisions there have to be, howsoever rough and ready. It was once believed that 'a tide begins to rise in the veins of youth at the age of 1— they call it adolescence' (Norwood Report, 1943). And so, for most parts of the United Kingdom, the age of 11 was when primary schooling ended and secondary schooling began.

There is no such psychological backing (valid or invalid) for a change at 14. But, almost by stealth, various changes are taking place at that age which marks it off as a time for rethinking both the curriculum and the institutional provision and support. It is the end of Key Stage 3, when all young learners will have been tested and graded. Choices are made for the first time in their educational career about the subjects to be studied—in preparation for GCSE. Parts of what, in 1988, was a National Curriculum for all can at 14 be disapplied (history, geography, modern languages, the arts), a measure which was particularly directed to students who were less academically able or disengaged. Students are obliged between the ages of 14 and 16 to have work experience. They have the opportunity to study full or part-time in colleges of further education—and over 100,000 do so. Careers guidance is offered, and in many schools becomes part of the timetable. And what are referred to as 'vocational options' are introduced.

Furthermore, as an increasing number of young people remain in education and training beyond the compulsory school age of 16, so does the 'break' at 16 seem incongruous. Greater continuity is sought across the 16 age divide.

It is as though the educational programme has to change direction somewhat—to shift from a programme before the age of 14 of learning 'for its own sake', and for the acquisition of 'basic skills' in literacy and numeracy, to a programme after 14 which is 'more relevant' to the world after school—the world of work or of further training or of higher education. Choices have to be made which affect one's life—choices concerning further studies, further training, employment and career. And so schooling has to be 'more relevant'. And 'lack of relevance' is often seen by both learners and employers to be a matter for criticism. Students become disengaged from learning because they do not see the point. Employers say that the educational system is not providing the future employees with the knowledge, skills and attitudes necessary for successful economic performance.

There are several assumptions in what has been said which need to be questioned, and indeed they are questioned in the penultimate section of this paper. However, such assumptions do seem to lie beneath many of the changes which are currently taking place—and which seem to have been endorsed by the Labour government since its election in 1997.

Labour policy 14–19

Assessing the achievements of the Labour Government's policy 14–19 is complicated for the following reasons. The aim of that policy (reflected in the series of policy papers summarised below) would seem to be threefold: social inclusion, higher standards and greater relevance to economic performance. But each of these terms (and thus the policies they describe) is open to different and contested interpretations. What count as appropriate standards, the most appropriate ways of including all young people, and the relation of different kinds of learning to economic success are not universally agreed. Indeed, they are extremely controversial, in particular since they embody wider moral debates, seldom acknowledged, concerning the aims of education and the values which the system ought to be both embodying and promoting.

Social inclusion

As soon as Labour was elected, it produced a Green Paper *Excellence for all children: meeting special educational needs* (1997),[2] which declared the commitment to inclusion in mainstream schools of 'all children who will benefit from it'. Subsequent Green and White Papers extended the idea of greater social inclusion. *The learning age* (1997) sought to remove barriers to participation through Individual Learning Accounts and through improved guidance and information (for example, the 'learning direct' telephone helpline). *Learning to succeed: a new framework for post-16 learning* (1999) focused careers service provision on 'those in greatest need'—which led eventually to the establishment of ConneXions. A major aim of policy has been to increase participation and retention, especially of the rather long tail of young people who leave education and training opportunities as soon as possible. Many join the ranks of the NEETs (Not in Education, Employment or Training). This is seen partly as a curriculum matter – to be solved by increased choice and the availability of more vocational and work related courses. But it is seen also as partly a financial matter— hence, according to the 2004 document *Opportunities and Excellence Progress Report,* Educational Maintenance Grants will be available nationally for 16 to 18 year olds from 2004 onwards.

Therefore, any assessment of policy must look carefully at participation and retention of young people across the social spectrum, not only in numbers and proportions, but also, more subtly, in terms of distribution across courses and institutions.

Higher standards

Following the 1997 White Paper, *Excellence in schools,* a Standards Task Force was established as well as a Standards and Effectiveness Unit at the DfEE. Education Action Zones were created which targeted support and resources where it was most needed, especially in the inner cities. To raise standards, so it was understood, required, first, a clearer definition of what those standards are, and, second, a set of targets for the proportion of young people who should reach those standards. The first is a notoriously difficult task. Standards logically relate to the aims which one is seeking to pursue. Change the aims and you change the relevant standards. As the policy of greater social inclusion is pursued (and thus encouragement to remain in full-time education), so aims of a more vocational nature are recognised, requiring different definitions of standards. Therefore, there has been a lot of work undertaken by the Quality Assurance Agency (QCA), and, within the QCA's framework, by the examination boards, to create vocational qualifications with their own distinctive standards. There has been the further task of establishing 'equivalence' between these different qualifications— to locate the differences within the same overarching framework of 'levels'.

Of primary concern has been the emphasis upon basic standards of literacy and numeracy at Key Stages 3 and 4. The Moser Report (1999) showed the very high proportion of adults with low standards of literacy, despite their '15,000' hours of schooling. And poor literacy would have profound effect upon the personal and social lives of young people as well as upon the economic well being of the community. The Smith Report (2004), *Mathematics counts,* reported that the overwhelming number of teachers, university academics and employers thought that the curriculum and assessment in mathematics was quite inadequate, that the present mathematics curricula were demotivating for the less able and that the subject was in crisis.

Economic relevance

There has been a prolific output of policy documents concerning the 'skills revolution', in particular, the need to provide a more skilled workforce through a transformed educational and training system. The most significant was the 2003 White Paper issuing jointly from the DfES, the Treasury, the Department of Trade and Industry and the Department for Work and Pensions, entitled *21st century skills: realising our potential.* It is difficult to summarise in a few words the grandiose vision captured within this paper (see Pring 2004 for a detailed account and critique). Its aim is to provide the framework in which Britain might prosper economically in a highly competitive world. The essential ingredient is a skills revolution—ensuring that many more people acquire relevant skills. Educational providers play a crucial role in this, but that role must be seen within the wider context of a partnership with employers, the Regional Development Agencies, the (occupational) Sector Skills Councils and the local Learning and Skills Councils. The precise way in which all these interrelate is not clear, but it is assumed that it is possible: first, to identify in some detail the skills required at different levels, in different occupations and in different regions; second, to match these *demands* for different levels and kinds of skill with educational and training *supply*; third, to create the partnerships between schools, colleges, universities, employers, private learning providers and funding agencies for the most efficient delivery of the required skills.

These different but interconnected aims could, of course, be pursued without any reference to a distinctive 14–19 phase. But they were seen to have a distinctive 14–19 flavour. The Green Paper *14–19: Extending opportunities, raising standards* (2002) addressed particularly social inclusion and the raising of standards. It anticipated a new framework of qualifications which would include—and give greater value and status to—vocational qualifications (including work based learning) from the age of 14 upwards. By proposing an overarching diploma at different levels, the document indicated that almost all learners would receive a qualification which reflected both the content of what had been learnt and the level at which that learning had been completed. Though there would be different pathways, there would be a common strand of literacy, numeracy and ICT. To achieve the more flexible, multi-pathway through the system from 14 to 19, elements of the National Curriculum, previously compulsory, could be 'disapplied'. Participation would be improved, so it was believed, if there were greater choice of learning pathways and if those choices included more vocational and work based (or work related) courses, leading to vocational GCSEs and eventually advanced vocational qualifications at 18 or 19.

After a period of consultation, most of the Green Paper proposals became firm policy in the (2003) White paper *Opportunity and excellence.* Furthermore, the 2004 document *Opportunities and excellence progress report* budgeted for £60 million for 'Enterprise Education Entitlement' from 2005/6 to provide all 15/16 year olds with the equivalence of five days enterprise activity, including the employment of 250 enterprise advisers. Enterprise is a further skill required in the 'skills revolution' and the fight for economic prosperity. As a prime aim of education is increasingly seen to be about economic achievement both for the individual and for the wider community, so 'enterprise' becomes the new educational virtue. But it would be a mistake to understand all these developments simply in terms of economic success. Following the Crick Report (1998), education for citizenship has also been seen as an important educational aim. Not only is a skilled workforce required. That workforce must also be equipped with the understanding and attitudes and dispositions to be responsible citizens. Citizenship is now a compulsory part of the curriculum post-14.

Subsequently, the Tomlinson Working Group was established to review and make proposals for the framework of qualifications which would encourage greater participation and retention and would define standards at different levels of achievement. It reported in October, 2004. It was important to provide a framework which would give greater flexibility of choice, which would encourage a greater number of young people to remain in education and training and which would provide clear and guided lines of progression.

In sum, the Labour government, concerned about the underachievement of a large minority of young people and about the comparatively low participation rate post-16, has put forward measures to increase the interest of young people in remaining in some form of education and training and to make that financially possible for them. It has broadened the understanding of what would count as appropriate standards of achievement by opening up more vocational routes and by seeing the value in work related and work based learning. It has seen, too, the importance of guidance and counselling, giving careers guidance a higher profile and creating a ConneXions Service which addresses particularly the needs of the most vulnerable and disengaged. It has emphasised the importance of the key skills of literacy and numeracy as necessary conditions for progress in any other aspect of education or training. Finally, it has insisted upon the need for the educational system to produce the kind of skills, knowledge and qualities which will serve the economy in a very competitive global market. 'Inclusion', 'relevance' and 'standards' have been the watchwords, and policies and funding have been applied to ensure that these aims are achieved.

Assessment of the policy

These aims (namely, social inclusion, higher standards and economic relevance), howsoever operationalised, must in many ways be seen as long term. It may be the case that 'reforms' put in place might not bear fruit within a few years, or be reflected in short term targets. They are laying the foundations for improvement. There is, for example, as much faith as there is science in the reform of qualifications or in the creation of foundation degrees.

None the less, evidence there is as to whether these aims are being achieved, if only slowly and stealthily. In examining this evidence, I shall focus upon five aspects of government policy, namely:

- Reform of qualifications
- Participation and retention
- Work-based learning
- Institutional provision
- Equality of esteem

Reform of qualifications

One way of meeting the aims would be to reform the examination system to make sure that a wide range of achievement (both academic and vocational) is acknowledged and that there might be progression through the various levels and varieties of study. Following the Dearing Report (1996), the government introduced *Curriculum 2000*. According to Hodgson and Spours (2003), the

> primary aim [was] of making all advanced level qualifications more accessible and more equally valued, thus providing learners with greater flexibility to move between the qualifications tracks and to build programmes of study based on different types of qualifications.

To achieve this, students would be encouraged to take a wider range of subject post-16. These subjects would be selected from both academic and vocational pathways or indeed from a mixture of both. Modular, rather than linear, courses would be the norm, with assessment at the end of the first year of advanced level study.

The subsequent National Qualifications Framework had three broad categories: (a) the general (or academic), namely, a two-part General Certificate of Education (GCE) A Level, with Part I being taken at the end of Year I; (b) the 'vocationally related' school or college based course, formerly the Advanced General National Vocational Qualification (GNVQ); and (c) the occupationally specific National Vocational Qualification (NVQ). There was also the attempt to introduce the Advanced Extension Award, so that greater discrimination might be made between the increasing numbers who were obtaining top grades at A Level.

There were some well known difficulties in the introduction of Curriculum 2000. Originally the A Level Subsidiary subjects (Part I) were to be five (preferably contrasting) with a view to broadening the post-16 experience which, for a long time had been criticised as too narrow. However, in fact, few schools, logistically, were able to teach five subjects at that level, and the norm reduced to four. Furthermore, in a disproportionate number of cases the fourth subject was complimentary rather than contrasting, thereby not providing the greater breadth of learning which originally had been envisaged. Finally, many students used the results at Part I to decide upon the subjects to be taken at Part II. One major victim was mathematics. According to the Smith Report (2004), already referred to, Curriculum 2000 'reform' led to a 15% fall in entry to Part II—with consequent follow-on problems for matriculation to mathematics based courses in universities. One important lesson from these curriculum reforms is that, such is the interrelationship of different parts of the system, that changes in one part have unforeseen consequences in other parts.

There is a wider concern, not the result of government reforms, but seemingly not helped by them, over the decline in certain key subjects taken at A Level. The number of sixth formers studying French and German has halved since 1992. Those taking physics fell from 46,000 in 1985 to 31,000 in 2002. The Smith Report (2004) pointed to the decline in the numbers taking mathematics.

However, it would be wrong to dwell solely upon these failures. Curriculum 2000 was a serious attempt to respond to the changes in schools and colleges, and to reflect the increasing number of young people, of different levels of achievement and of different aspirations, remaining in education and training. By creating the Advanced Certificate of Vocational Education, it went some way towards creating greater equality of status, although the strong tendency has been for students to opt for the more academic route rather than for the vocational A Levels. The Tomlinson proposals have built on the experience of Curriculum 2000.

Participation and retention

Participation is often seen to compare unfavourably with that in other countries of the developed world, and indeed remains below average for OECD countries. In 2001, 75% of the 15 to 19 age group participated in some form of education and training in the UK, compared with approximately 90% in Belgium and Germany. What is clear from the data is that the successfully increased participation achieved between 1986 and 1993 has not been maintained, although there are very significant variations according to locality, gender and occupational sector.[3]

The early success was reflected in the growth of qualifications which related to the more vocationally related courses introduced—including those of the City and Guilds of London Institute (CGLI) and the Business and Technical Education Council (BTEC). On the other hand, there would now seem to be lower retention rates within the full-time vocational pathways. But the significance of this is always difficult to assess. It could be the case that the 'drop outs' are in fact 'dropping in' to employment, made possible by the experience gained on the (unfinished) course.

One might look at the data in a slightly different way, namely, in the proportion of young people gaining different sorts of qualification. Thus, there was an increase of young people in England gaining Level 2 qualifications from 32.8% in 1989 to 51.2% by 2002, but these figures hide the discrepancy in achievement between boys and girls, the girls doing quite a lot better (see Nuffield Review, 2004, Part III).

On the other hand, research also shows that Britain compares well with other countries in raising the proportion of the population obtaining qualifications at Levels 2 and 3 (see Steedman *et al.*, 2004) This success is helped by the inclusion of qualifications of those over the age of 19. None the less, it reflects the success of the effort to improve qualifications, of which the participation of young people is one key aspect.

There has for many years been a sizeable majority of young people who are disengaged from education. Possibly as many as 7% of the 16/17 year olds join the ranks of the NEETs (Not in Education, Employment or Training) when they leave school. An emphasis of recent government policy has been to ensure that this group is included in education and training. To this end, there has been created the Increased Flexibility Programme, which tries to link the learning experience much more closely to their every day lives. There has also been a stress upon work based learning, especially through the renewed apprenticeship system. It is too early yet to evaluate the results of the Flexibility Programme.

But it is important to see the problem of 'disengagement' in perspective. There is little evidence that the UK is different from other countries with large urban areas.

Serious efforts have been made through the Education Action Zones and now Excellence in Cities to break the mould—to re-engage often alienated youth. It is difficult to assess the success of such initiatives. Excellence in Cities is new and replaces but builds upon Education Action Zones. But the problem perhaps needs to be tackled by a more radical appraisal of the curriculum for many young people and of the cultural influences upon the decisions they make (see Ball, 2004).

The Nuffield Review is addressing this problem It has tentatively concluded, in the light of the evidence it has reviewed, that the reasons for either remaining in or dropping out of education and training are much more complex than many policy initiatives would assume—the availability of unskilled employment, financial hardship, peer pressure, sense of failure at school, and so on (see Hodkinson, 2004).

Work based learning

The government believes that the more practical and work based learning experience is, for many young people, especially those disengaged from school or college, a more effective and motivating way of learning. Therefore, work experience (or work related learning) has been made a requirement for all young people aged 14–16. Indeed, parts of the National Curriculum have been 'disapplied' for those for whom work based learning is thought to be more appropriate. Furthermore, work based learning is strongly promoted through what were originally called Modern Apprenticeships.

It is difficult to assess the value of work based learning (see West, 2004). What we do know is that there has been a reduction of about 12% in the uptake of work based learning amongst 16–17 year olds. Not enough is known about the quality of that learning. It is organised mainly by Private Learning Providers, of which there are over 1000. There is no doubt that many provide an excellent service, but the evidence would point to a rather patchy quality across the many kinds and locations of work based learning. In 2002/3, the Adult Learning Inspectorate (ALI) judged 46% of work based learning provision to be inadequate. But that showed considerable improvement on the previous inspection (see ALI, 2003)

Modern Apprenticeships (see West, 2004) were established in 1993. The purpose was to create a work based learning experience which would deliver world class standards in occupational skills at Level 3. These were seen to be an alternative pathway into employment for young people who could reach Level 3—and thus access to higher education. But there did seem to be some confusion in policy. The aim was to recruit up to 28% to such apprenticeships at the same time that the target for entry to university was set at 50%. Was not a target of over 75% for Level 3 rather too ambitious?

By 1997, Modern Apprenticeships were divided into Advanced Modern Apprenticeships (AMA), which were at Level 3, and Foundation Modern Apprenticeships (FMA), which were at Level 2. The 'Modern' was dropped from the title. Even then the achievements were nowhere near the targets set. In 2002/3, only 23% of those leaving the FMA completed the whole framework (which included key skills); only 36% achieved the National Vocational Qualification (NVQ) part of the framework. Only 33% achieved the whole framework of the AMA; only 43% reached NVQ Level 3.

One criterion for assessing the actual as opposed to the claimed importance attached to work based learning is the amount of funding allocated to it. The Association of Learning Providers reported to this year's Spending Review that, out of the Learning and Skills Council's budget of £8.6 billion, only 6% is spent on work based learning (*Times Educational Supplement*, 26 March 2004).

Institutional provision

In pursuit of these policies certain institutional changes were deemed to be necessary.

First, the system needed to be made more accountable in relation to the targets which central government defined (for example, minimum performance levels for GCSE attainment by 2006, according to *Excellence in schools*, 1997). Overall targets were cascaded down to local education authorities (LEAs) which would now be inspected by Ofsted and assessed in relation to those targets. And *Success for all: reforming further education and training* (2001) tied funding of colleges of further education (CFE) to college development plans and improved targets. Target setting was not new, but it has taken on a more vigorous role under Labour, despite the failure in many cases to reach what often appear to be arbitrarily set targets. As Keep (2004) argued, 'target chasing is the dominant focus of management activity as targets for learning achievement are cascaded down from the Treasury to the DfES'. Only one in six of the targets set by the National Advisory Council for Education and Training for 2002/3 were met; only one in four for 2002 was met.

Second, following *Learning to succeed: a new framework for post-16 learning* (1999), the funding of all post-16 education and training was to come from the newly established Learning and Skills Council (LSC)—including that for sixth forms, previously under the control of the LEAs. Subsequently, the LSC, through its 47 local councils, launched Strategic Area Reviews (StARs) to ensure, according to *Success for all: reforming further education and training* (2001) 'the right mix of provision ... to meet learner, employer and community needs' and to further ensure that there would be collaborative networks throughout the country. Again, collaboration between schools, colleges and training providers was emphasised by the 2002 Green Paper *14–19: extending opportunities, raising standards*.

Third, the system of education and training provision which Labour inherited was itself rather complex. On the one hand, schools were responsible to the local education authorities. On the other hand, colleges of further education were 'incorporated' and funded, not by the LEAs, but by the Further Education Funding Council. The colleges, in turn, had a history rooted in vocational preparation, especially for part-time students. But, in recent years, they had increasingly encroached upon the traditional 'academic' areas of study of the sixth forms of schools. Similarly, the schools, in encouraging young people to remain in education, were increasingly offering vocational courses traditionally associated with the colleges, even though they may not be properly equipped for doing so (e.g. in hotel and catering or in business studies). But even that is a simplistic picture. In 'further education', there were colleges which provided a wide range of vocational and non-vocational courses, at different levels, both full-time and part-time. There were also the sixth-form colleges, which generally focused only on A Levels, and Tertiary Colleges, which provided all education and training post 16 for a given area. Schools were similarly heterogeneous (11 to16 and 11 to 18)—mainly comprehensive, but with a substantial number of grammar schools in certain parts of the country, City Technology Colleges and Grant Maintained Schools directly funded by government. How, with such a complex and competitive system (competitive both between schools and between schools and colleges), could Labour create a coherent system 14 to 19 which has flexible routes through the system and where choice of subject or pathway depends, not on the particular institution one happens to be in, but upon ability and aspiration? The promotion of partnership was the answer—especially between schools and colleges and across schools. And there are now many examples of such partnerships. But much militates against them, in particular the ways in which schools and colleges are still funded on a different basis and the way in which each institution, for purposes of accountability, is treated as an autonomous unit.

Fourth, despite the frequent reference to partnership in order to meet the aims of greater social inclusion, higher standards and economic relevance (reflected in the Strategic Area Reviews), there was also a policy of expanding specialist schools to increase diversity within the secondary system (*Schools: building on success,* 2001) and finally to create mainly government funded City Academies within the private sector (*Schools: achieving success,* 2001). A difficulty in understanding Labour policy at the secondary phase lies in reconciling the greater autonomy, competition and fragmentation of the system, on the on hand, with the recognition of the need for cooperation and partnership, on the other.

Fifth, this paper has given passing reference to the changing funding arrangements. Funding according to targets successfully achieved has become one of the 'levers' or 'drivers' of the reformed management of the education system. But, as 14 to 19 comes to be seen as a whole, the differential funding between different institutional providers becomes an anomaly.

Finally, as has already been mentioned, 14–19 education and training has to be seen within a wider framework of the 'skills revolution', in which the DfES is one of several government departments trying to construe and then manage a much bigger cooperative venture. That involves (i) Regional Development Agencies, identifying the training needs of each region; (ii) Sector Development Councils for each major occupational group, identifying the skill needs nationally for that kind of occupation; (iii) the Learning and Skills Council (and its local branches) which funds the education and training post-16 (school and college and work based) and, in doing so, will take into account the regional and sector analyses; (iv) the LEAs, still responsible for funding education up to 16; (v) the incorporated colleges which remain essential for the provision of further education and colleges; (vi) the employers whose cooperation is essential to the provision of work based and work related education and training; (vii) higher education which not only takes on the products of the 14 to 19 system but also is a major economic force in each region, and (viii) the various examination boards which need to respond to all this in creating the assessment system which will be credible in the eyes of the users.

Equality and esteem

'Equality of esteem' between different pathways— the more general or academic, on the one hand, and, on the other, the more vocational—is understandably seen as a major policy aim. There is a deep rooted disdain within the educational system for the more practical and vocational modes of learning. This is long standing and was trenchantly analysed some time ago (see Wiener, 1985, and Barnett, 1986). But as was found in the past (see Olive Banks, 1955, *Parity and prestige in English secondary education*) such esteem cannot be bestowed. The reforms of a qualification system can go some way to redress the balance, and it is a commendable aspect of the reform of qualifications outlined above that the government is seeking to put vocational qualifications within the same diploma framework as the more academic and traditional ones.

However, the attainment of such parity of esteem depends on other factors, some of which are not within the easy grasp of government. Parity of esteem depends largely upon the 'currency' of the qualifications—what they will 'buy' in terms of entry to employment, further training or higher education. But also the complex institutional framework outlined above is unhelpful. Different sorts of institution specialise (even if not by choice) in particular kinds of course. In 2001, sixth form colleges (many of which had formerly been grammar schools) admitted fewer than 7% of those with less than five GCSEs at grade C; 70% of those studying for Level 2 qualifications went to Colleges of FE; only 22% remained in school sixth forms. There are wide differences between institutions, some evidence of selection, and thus a strong chance that many are forced into 'selecting' courses which are less prestigious and not their first preference. This re-enforces the argument, in the previous sub-section, that, to achieve its aims, the government needs to reform the institutional framework so that co-operation rather than competition (on an unequal playing field of funding and prestige) might prevail (see Stanton, 2004).

In conclusion, therefore, the new Labour government in 1997 wanted to address the low participation and retention rate (as that compares with other countries); it wanted to make closer links between the system of education and training and the economic needs of the country and the individuals learners themselves; and it wanted to raise standards generally. In part, this might be seen as essentially a curriculum and teaching matter—to be solved by greater subject choice, the creation of more practical, work-based and vocational courses and the reform of the framework of qualifications.

However, the government saw that this required much more than a reform of learning styles, of curriculum and of qualifications. There needed to be a change of attitude towards more vocational studies. There needed to be a reform of funding and of institutional provision. There needed to be much closer partnership between educational and training provision, on the one hand, and, on the other, the needs of employers within the different occupational sectors and the different regions. Many of the changes which have taken place have tried to address these institutional issues. But at time it seems rather half-hearted and even contradictory, reflected particularly in the encouragement of partnership, on the one hand, and the encouragement of fragmentation of and competition between schools, on the other, through the establishment of City Academies (now, simply 'academies') and the expansion of specialist schools. Funding issues remain to be addressed so that institutions, providing the same service, might be on a level playing field. Much closer links, not just voluntary partnerships, between institutions need to be established if all young people are to receive the same opportunity to pursue the course which they want and which most suits them and if such courses are to be properly resourced and staffed. Above all, there are serious questions to be asked about the capacity of central government or its agencies (LSC, Regional Development Agencies and Sector Skills Councils) to manage such a massive interrelated system on the evidence which is available

Education, education, education: where is it?

There is no doubting the determination of the Labour government since its election in 1997 to transform the educational and training opportunities for all young people. In its view, far too many exited from the system as soon as they could, thereby being excluded from opportunities which education and training afforded them. Furthermore, the country needed what is often referred to as a highly skilled workforce in a very competitive world. The government brought together a moral drive for greater social inclusion and an economic drive for greater prosperity. There was also a deep concern about the lack of basic skills of literacy, revealed in the Moser Report (1999), and numeracy. Add to that the perceived importance of ICT. There was, therefore, a renewed emphasis at the political level, but also at the very practical level of resources and assessment, upon these three 'key skills'.

To achieve these broad aims, quite radical changes were judged to be needed within a much more coherent and integrated progression from the period of compulsory schooling through to further and higher education and training and into employment. What previously had been seen as sharp divisions—between education and work, between pre and post 16, between secondary, further and higher education, between academic and vocational, between those capable of further education and those unable to benefit from further study—were no longer seen to be so. Indeed, the more blurred the division became the more would one be able to provide appropriate opportunities for all—not just for the privileged few.

And yet, in all the documents referred to and in all the practical measures put in place, there is no clear statement of *educational* aim or purpose, hardly any reference (except in the introduction of citizenship) to the kinds of qualities and values which make young people into better human beings, no vision of the kind of society which a more skilled workforce should serve, no idea of the kind of learning which one should expect of an educated person in the present economic, social and environmental context. The policy is trapped in a language which militates against the broader moral dimension of education—the language of skills and targets, of performance indicators and audits, of academic studies and vocational pathways, of economic relevance and social usefulness.

What is worth learning? Certainly, young people need to learn those skills and attitudes which will enable them to earn a living and to contribute to the economic well-being of themselves and of the wider society. But not all learning is judged to be worthwhile in such a limited sense of utility. We have inherited a world of ideas through which we have come to understand the physical and social and moral worlds in a particular way. It is an inheritance, and it is the job of education to enable the next generation to gain access to that inheritance, to grasp and understand those ideas and to gain a deeper understanding of the world in which they live. And there are pressing problems which beset us all and which need to be understood and grappled with—problems of the environment, of social and ethnic relations, of violence and injustice, of the exercise of power, of the prevalence of poverty. And such issues and problems are the very stuff of literature and the arts, of drama and of history, which did have and should retain a central place in the education of all young people.

Furthermore, we do not live by bread alone; there is the need to introduce young persons to ideals which enable them to transcend immediate wants and desires, to be inspired to make the world a better place, to persevere when the going gets tough. The teaching of the arts and the humanities at their best are precisely that—an introduction to that perennial discussion of issues, which affect us deeply, and to different visions of what is good and worth pursuing.

However, in all the documents, the importance of the arts and the humanities, of drama and poetry, or of modern languages, receive no mention—except as subjects, which unlike mathematics and science, can be 'disapplied' at the age of 14. It is believed, without evidence, that the unmotivated will become motivated once that which is to be learnt is seen to be 'vocational'. Those, however, who have seen good drama teaching in schools will know how false that assumption is. Drama and the arts generally have the capacity to engage all young people, precisely because they address those matters which are of deep personal concern, and yet do so through a means which transcends the uniqueness of each person's particular life.

The pity is that we have been here before and yet, having no educational memory, the Labour government seems unable to learn from the past. When the school-leaving age was raised to 16 in the early 1970s, it was felt by many that the resulting disillusion of those forced to stay on would be resolved by a strong dose of practical and vocational studies. It was, however, a tribute to Lawrence Stenhouse (see Stenhouse, 1975) and others that a different philosophy prevailed. The humanities and the arts, far from being downgraded to an option for those who wished to study them, became central to an exploration of what it means for each young person to be human and to how society might itself become more human. The themes of Shakespeare were also the topics which most concerned young people—the use of violence, relations between the sexes, ambition and jealousy, injustice and poverty, racism and tolerance, relations with parents and authority. The job of the teacher was to make the links between the personal concerns of the young people and the literature, poetry, drama, art and narratives of other people and other times. Highly disciplined discussion was at the centre of the learning experience, lacking therefore precise targets to be attained. For who can set precise targets to a well informed and vigorous conversation?

In raising the status of the 'vocational pathways', from the very best of motives, is not the Labour government reinforcing the dubious distinction between the academic and the vocational—a distinction which leaves little space for those areas of learning which fit into neither category and yet are an essential part of an *educational* experience?

Conclusion

The threefold aim of the government policy is higher standards, greater social inclusion and economic relevance.

Many of the reforms which the government has put in place can be assessed only in the long term—for example, the establishment of such agencies as the Leaning and Skills Council and the Sector Skills Councils, or the creation of a more unified framework of qualifications, or the steps taken to increase participation and retention in different forms of education and training, or the creation of a better trained work force.

The evidence so far is mixed. The state of mathematics education and levels of numeracy are a matter of grave concern. There remains a large minority of young people unaffected by the measures taken to engage them in education and training. Work based learning remains patchy in quality, although improving. There are clear tensions in policy between the advocacy of co-operation and partnership, on the one hand, and policies which create fragmentation and competition, on the other. The development of further institutions under different regulations and funding arrangements exacerbates the inequality of status and opportunity. And, finally, there is an absence of debate on the broader aims of education, of an historical grasp of the issues which have been tackled in several initiatives within the last two or three decades, of the links between the provision of education and training, on the one hand, and deliberation over the kind of society and worthwhile form of life we should be introducing young people to. Hence, so many of the government documents and of the connected discussions are trapped into an impoverished language of skills and qualifications without the deeper consideration of the kind of learning which should be promoted.

Notes

1. Many papers referred to for evidence were commissioned by the Nuffield Review of Education and Training 14–19 for England and Wales. These can be found on the website 'www.nuffield14–19review.org.uk'. Thanks are due to all those who have contributed to this large scale, three year review, the first year of which is summarised in the Annual Report (Nuffield Review, 2004).
2. See the detailed list of policy documents in the appendix of the Nuffield Review Annual Report, 2003/4 (Nuffield Review, 2004) upon which these sections draw. It was compiled by Alis Oancea and Susannah Wright, research officers for the Review.
3. See Part III of the Nuffield Review Annual Report, 2003/4, compiled by Geoff Hayward, for a very detailed analysis of the data on participation and retention.

Note on contributor

Richard Pring is Lead Director of the Nuffield Review 14–19 Education and Training England and Wales. He was Director of the Oxford University Department of Educational Studies, 1989 to 2003.

References

ALI (2003) *Chief Inspectors Annual Report, 2002–3* (London, DfES).
Ball, S. (2004) Participation and Progression in Education and Training 14–19: Working Draft of Ideas, Discussion Paper for Nuffield Review Working Day 6.
Banks, O. (1955) *Parity and prestige in English secondary education* (London, Routledge & Kegan Paul).
Barnett, C. (1986) *The audit of war* (London, Macmillan).
Crick Report (1998) *Education for citizenship and the teaching of democracy in schools* (London, DfEE).
Dearing Report (1996) *Review of qualifications for 16 to 19 year olds* (Hayes, Middlesex, SCAA).
Hodgson, A. & Spours, K. (2003) *Beyond A Levels* (London, Kogan Page).
Hodkinson, P. (2004) *Learning careers and career progression*, Nuffield Review Working Paper 12.
Keep (2004) *The multi-dimensions of performance: performance as defined by whom, measured in what ways, to what ends?* Nuffield Review Working Paper 23.
Moser Report (1999) *Improving literacy and numeracy: a fresh start* (London, DfES).
Norwood Report (1943) *Secondary schools curricula and examinations* (London, SSEC).
Nuffield Review (2004) *Annual Review 2003–04* (copies from University of Oxford, Department of Educational Studies).
Pring, R. (2004) The skills revolution, *Oxford Review of Education*, 30(1), 105–116.
Smith Report (2004) *Making mathematics count* (London, The Stationery Office).
Stanton, G. (2004) *The organisation of full-time 14–19 provision in the state sector*, Nuffield Review Working Paper 13.
Steedman, H., McIntosh, S. & Green, A. (2004) *International comparisons of qualifications: skills audit update* (London, DfES).
Stenhouse, L. (1975) *Introduction to curriculum instruction and research* (London, Heinemann).
Tomlinson Report (2004) *14–19 curriculum and qualifications reform*, Final Report of the Working Group on 14–19 Reform (London, DfES).
West, J. (2004) *Work-based education and training for 14–19 year olds*, Nuffield Review Working Paper 14.
Wiener, M. (1985) *English culture and the decline of the industrial spirit, 1850–1980* (Harmondsworth, Penguin).

New Labour and higher education

Alan Ryan

1. Ideological and policy dilemmas of Labour—New and Old

I have often written unkindly about New Labour's policy towards higher education. Here I dispassionately analyse issues that any Labour government will find difficult. The task is the easier inasmuch as I am a beneficiary of the educational ambitions of the Labour politicians who ran the London County Council immediately after World War Two, and I have always shared those ambitions. The dilemmas that afflict Labour policy are those on whose horns I have felt myself impaled in everyday academic life for the past 40 years. To the extent that I suggest that the two Labour administrations of 1997 and 2001 have made avoidable errors, I do not ascribe them to wickedness, but to ministerial inexperience, the exigencies of political competition and the unintended consequences of decisions made many years before.

New Labour came to power determined to do what previous Labour governments had found difficult: to balance the books, and to be *seen* to be balancing the books. Public service workers were not to have a field day, the welfare state was not to be vastly expanded; 'giveaways' were anathema to the new Chancellor; 'something for something' was the motto. Kenneth Clarke, the very successful Chancellor in the outgoing Conservative government, was astonished to discover that the new government meant to adhere for two years to spending targets that he had had no intention of sticking to if he had been returned to office. Because Clarke bequeathed the 1997 Labour government an economy that had grown robustly for four years and had a lot of steam left in it, tax receipts rose rapidly, unemployment continued to drop and a substantial surplus was piled up. Little was destined for higher education; and this was in line with traditional Labour thinking and New Labour plans. HE mattered, but other things had more claim on public spending.

If the notion of the state as Mother Bountiful was a casualty of New Labour's new relationship with Prudence, traditional dilemmas remained sharp. On any reckoning, the stage of a child's life where the greatest damage is done by deprivation—familial, social, nutritional, medical, and educational—is the earliest. It is not only a matter of highly educated middle-class parents reading bed-time stories to their children where their poorer and less educated peers do not; rather, the more general capacity of well-organised and prosperous families to bring their children to a condition of education-readiness by the age of two or three makes a lot of difference. Children who have internalised the norms of turn-taking in conversation can learn and respond to what they learn at kindergarten, pre-school, and school in ways their deprived contemporaries cannot.

A government that wishes to get the biggest bang for its buck must be tempted to put its resources into improving the lot of the least fortunate in their first few years. The Labour government's 'Sure Start' programme has made a beginning in this direction; and the government's awareness that social mobility has slowed dramatically over the past two decades has recently put Sure Start on the Treasury's front burner. In the long run, such a programme will do more for HE than any directly targeted programme; but it is a *long* run. Getting pre-schoolers off to a flying start produces highly qualified applicants for university only 15 years later. Here emerges one familiar dilemma: what to do about modestly under-qualified 18-year-olds in the meantime, whether to encourage them into higher education and equip HEIs with the necessary staff and other resources for a certain amount of remedial pre-higher education, or to find another route into post-secondary education for the 18-year-olds, perhaps by way of Modern Apprenticeships. That neither route does much for the more dramatically under-equipped 40% below the government's targeted 50% is something not discussed here; and the problem of the young people below that, who remain unemployable at a time of full employment, is as obdurate as ever.

The Sure Start programme reflects every Labour government's concern with social mobility. Social mobility for these purposes is defined in terms of the odds on a child born to one social and income quintile fetching up in a different quintile in their middle years; perfect mobility would mean that the destination class was statistically independent of the starting class. Statistical randomness is not causal randomness. *Something* determines which direction a child goes in, some combination of raw intelligence, inclination, energy and simple luck, or the absence of these. Even with perfect social mobility, these would determine the fate of individuals. How far we are from perfect social mobility, however, is illustrated by the disheartening graph on which many commentators have dwelt: it traces the fates of children from the lowest income quintile and the highest measured IQ quintile at age three as compared with those from the highest income quintile and lowest measured IQ quintile. By the age of 11, the downward trajectory of the measured IQ of the poorest children crosses the upward trajectory of the measured IQ of the richest.

From the standpoint of higher education this concern with social mobility cuts across other goals. One is national prosperity. It is not obvious that the quest for a higher GDP is wholly consistent with a quest for greater social mobility so defined. It is obvious enough that social mobility and prosperity *may* go hand in hand, since wasting unused talents is precisely that—a waste; recruiting the able from no matter what social background is an obviously rational policy. It does not follow that intrusive measures to ensure that intelligent, energetic, and successful parents cannot pass on their advantages to their children will promote economic dynamism. There are, in principle, innumerable ways to secure that there is no statistical relationship between parental success and children's performance; most would be cruel or counter-productive or simply mad. Finding ways of increasing social mobility that do not leave the already advantaged feeling that they are being sacrificed to the undeserving is a major problem. The equality that comes from levelling down is equality, but it is not likely to feature high levels of prosperity.

Nor is the search for prosperity obviously consistent with an alternative understanding of the quest for equality which defines it in terms of reducing income differentials; one real novelty of New Labour policy has been its relative unconcern with equality thus defined, as distinct from equality-as-social-mobility. There has been some serious enhancement of the incomes of the very worst off, but no attempt to reduce the gap between the highest and median incomes. In general, New Labour has accepted the post-1970s consensus that a low tax, lightly regulated economy is more likely to lead to prosperity, and that the widening inequality of pre-tax income is a small price to pay for steady growth; greater friendliness towards the really badly off has not been matched by an attempt to reduce differentials throughout the income hierarchy. 'Access' is not surprisingly a key concept for such a government; what is imagined is equal access to a race that will differentiate the competitors on their merits. It is not usually stated as baldly as this, because the breach with more communitarian understandings of equality in education would be too marked, but it is evident that what one might call the R.H. Tawney view, that the purpose of education is to allow everyone to share in the richness of a common culture, would be thought to be hopelessly old-fashioned.

The motivation for New Labour's wish for continued growth in HE has been essentially economic. Although HE has many benefits, such as lengthening the life span of its beneficiaries and delaying the onset of senility as well as promoting toleration and adaptability to change, these have not featured in the government's arguments for an expanded HE sector. Nor has the government that created a department of 'Culture, Media and Sport' often sounded as though its members had read Coleridge, Mill, Leavis and Raymond Williams on the subject of culture.[1] What the two Labour governments have thought is that a higher proportion of young people attending HEIs is vital for a productive economy. Where French workers are more productive on an hourly basis than even American workers, British workers lag some 40% behind the French and Americans and 25% behind German workers. This is a very old story.

The empirical basis for the belief that expended HE will do anything to change the situation is debatable.[2] It is certainly true that the HE 'premium'—the difference in lifetime earnings between someone with a degree and someone with two A levels and no degree—is larger than in other countries. On the other hand, there has been no correlation between increases in the age-participation ratio and improvements in productivity or GDP growth. It is at least possible that employers use the possession of a degree as a marker for the qualities they seek—persistence, tidy-mindedness, ability to learn, and biddability—and that education beyond A level is irrelevant to actual productiveness. The ambition also reveals further dilemmas. The government is committed to two rather different views, both of them plausible, but likely to be in competition for public funding.

One is that a (generally) educated workforce is more productive than an unedu-cated one; the other that the future lies with economies that get scientific advances to market faster than their competitors. The first focuses on undergraduate education— and raises many questions about what level and what kind of education is good for productivity—while the second focuses on scientific research, and on graduate and post-doctoral training—and raises questions about how far 'blue skies' research is good for an economy as compared with deftness in turning other people's blue skies research into industrial applications. That suggests that there are three competitors in the field: basic HE to produce a competent workforce, applied research to improve the technological base of the firms for which this workforce will work, and the basic research that provides—eventually—something to apply.

This all breeds many tensions: between HE and pre-school; between expenditure on mass undergraduate education and expenditure on research both 'blue sky' and 'industry friendly'; there are tensions between taxpayers, who want low taxes and the HE workforce, whose pay has dropped dramatically below that of their white-collar peers; and there are tensions between both of these and students in HE, who want a fee-free education and maintenance grants as generous as those their parents enjoyed in the 1960s. New Labour's turning away from the pursuit of equality in the traditional sense—reducing income differentials—is not popular with Labour traditionalists, and this sets up further tensions when it comes to discussing what an egalitarian HE system might look like: one thought is that it should be savagely meritocratic, the other that it should be biased towards the provision of good basic HE, with a substantial element of affirmative action. No system in the world has resolved these tensions; the British— more exactly the English and Welsh—HE system is more agonised than most (the Australian and New Zealand systems being partial exceptions) only because it is highly centralised, and responsibility for finding answers can be laid squarely at the door of ministers. This is why there was a Dearing Report: ministers wanted not only advice but a screen.

2. The Dearing Report

The Dearing Committee was established under a Conservative government and reported under a Labour one. By the time it was set up in May 1996, it was overwhelmingly likely that the next government would be a Labour one; it was also clear that neither party relished the prospect of having to formulate a policy for HE ahead of a general election. A bi-partisan agreement to set up the committee was a neat way of kicking into the long grass difficult issues about access, diversity of mission and funding. Compared with its predecessor, the Robbins Report of 1963, the Dearing Report was less elegant, less aspirational, less committed to the idea that the promotion of liberal and humane values was the central task of university education. It was also vastly informative, as at 1700 pages it should have been.

The Commission was charged to consider not only higher education in the traditional sense, but 'lifelong learning' as well. It was required to imagine a world in which increasing numbers of students attended some form of HEI, although the report observed that it was already the case that 60% of the population would in the course of a lifetime have some exposure to higher education, even if most would have it in an FE College or through the Open University. The whole post-secondary sector fell beneath its gaze, and it calculated that that embraced some 2.8 million students, the majority of whom were not traditional school-leaver pupils, but mature students, a majority of them women, and many or most engaged in post-secondary learning as a part of their working lives.

It would be foolish to say that the Dearing Report had no effect on government policy, but it had less than was anticipated. Its greatest break with the past was its advocacy of charging students tuition fees, and the government did introduce tuition fees. But the government did it on a different basis from the one suggested by the Report, and did what the Report advised against by removing the last vestiges of the system of maintenance grants and providing all public support for living costs in the form of loans. The Report advocated a uniform tuition fee equal to around 25% of the average cost of a degree course, to be paid by everyone after graduation, so that students at expensive institutions or studying expensive subjects would be accepted on academic merit and not ability to pay; the government decided to impose a means-tested fee, payable upfront, which meant that a quarter of all students paid nothing. This violated the principle behind the Dearing proposal, which was that all students should contribute something—indeed, the same thing—when they could, and that means-testing should be reserved for the maintenance grant.

For those who had to pay fees, the fact that there was no loan to cover the fee meant they were dependent on the good will of their parents for the money. For an unknown number, this was a real problem. As to the destination of the fee income, the Report wanted to ensure that when students in work repaid their fees, the money would be directed only towards HE; the government made no such provision, and in fact the Treasury cut provision for HE by almost exactly the sums raised by the tuition fees. The Report urged the government to take a serious look at requiring substantial contributions from better-off parents; the government did no such thing, and in the 2003 White Paper made it a near-absolute principle that 18-year-olds were independent of their parents. Between the semi-implementation of the Dearing Report and the Clarke White Paper, the predictable consequence was that students whose parents could and did support them incurred only a limited amount of debt, while those whose parents could not or would not, incurred a lot. The financial innocence of 18-year-olds meant in addition that many of those who incurred the largest debts incurred them at high interest rates by running up credit card bills and bank overdrafts.

The decision to ignore parental contributions remains unfathomable. A government that has been accused of financing public expenditure by stealth taxes ought consistently to have regarded parental contributions of the sort that the US HE system exacts from better-off parents as a perfect stealth tax. Moreover, the proposition that young people are at 18 independent of their parents is not merely false, but most strikingly false of just those young people whose parents are best able to contribute. The offspring of human beings go through a more protracted upbringing than those of other primates, and within the human race, the offspring of higher social classes go through a more protracted process of upbringing than those of lower social classes.

Moreover, the people best able to pay are also most highly motivated to do so. The higher social classes readily see HE both as an investment in a future career and as something that is interesting in the present and life-enhancing in the long run. Still, there is a difficulty in all this that defies simple analysis. Britain was a relatively highly taxed country until the 1980s, and is now much less so; starting rates of tax have gone down from 33% to 22%, and top rates from 83% to 40%. On the face of it, governments, both Conservative and Labour, have offered the electorate a bargain; the government would take less of the electorate's income in tax, but the electorate must get used to paying for some of the services they had previously enjoyed 'free'. The inverted commas make the obvious point that paying taxes and receiving services is not very different from not paying taxes and buying the same services. The main difference is that in general, one pays smaller annual amounts of tax over a long period and receives particular services, whether health care, educational or other, over a short period. The difficulty, in Britain as in every other country where this implicit bargain has been offered, is that the electorate is both tax averse and eager to receive for nothing the services it received 20 years ago in exchange for higher rates of tax. This is a subject not to be pursued here. The important fact from the perspective of hard-up HEIs is that parental contributions have an advantage that almost every other funding device lacks: they produce money up front.

What provoked the setting up of the Dearing Committee was a funding crisis, a slow-motion crisis perhaps, but a crisis nonetheless. In 1992, the then Minister of Education, Kenneth Baker, had at a stroke doubled the proportion of young people going to university by relabelling the former polytechnics universities. This was welcomed by the ex-polys, who had for years wished to be emancipated both from the control of local authorities and from the academic tutelage of the CNAA. They may also have hoped that they would be funded at the same rate as the older universities.

They found themselves exchanging the frying-pan for the fire; they made no money by the move and found themselves forced to compete with universities whose research capability and teaching expertise at least looked rather better on paper than did theirs. Both before and after 1992, the 'old' and 'new' universities—post-1992 universities should perhaps be called 'new-new' to distinguish them from the post-Robbins 'new' or 'Plateglass' universities—were funded at very different levels. To take two extreme examples, the turnover of Imperial College London is around £40,000 per enrolled student. That of the University of Greenwich is about £8,000 per FTE, and £5,500 per enrolled student; that of the University of Central Lancashire barely £4,000 per enrolled student. The LSE does no natural science, and could to that extent be said to be working from a lower cost base than Central Lancashire; but its turnover is about £13,000 per student. The explanation of the differences is irrelevant to our present concerns—although it is obvious enough that having medical schools, doing a lot of research in the life sciences, and doing a lot of research in any area whatever puts up the costs; and being able to charge high fees to overseas students on graduate courses enables an HEI to cover some of the expense. What is not irrelevant is that the effect of unifying the HE sector was not to make the ex-polys better off but to erode the position of the pre-1992 universities.

There were two pressures; one came from the Treasury, which had for a long time held what one might parody as the Gertrude Stein view that 'a course is a course is a course'; this meant that there was pressure from the ultimate source of the block grants that the funding council (Hefce) handed to HEIs to reduce the unit of resource down to the level that reflected the price at which the cheapest supplier of a course would supply it. The other came from HEIs themselves, which were ready to expand their intakes at a very low cost. The post-1992 universities had done this throughout the 1980s, and over a decade had reduced their funding per student to some 75% of what it had been in 1980. The 'old' universities had contrived to hold the line, and were no worse off at the end of the 1980s than at the beginning. Between 1990 and 2002, however, the combined sector lost 35% of the unit of resource it had enjoyed in 1990.

Expanding numbers on the cheap is rational in the short term and irrational in the long term. A given estate and workforce can in the short term secure extra income without incurring greater expense. The teaching grant from Hefce was determined by the number of students and the courses they took, more bottoms on the seats meant more income, and in lecture-based courses, the impact of the marginal bottom on overall costs was slight. There was also a real and intended cut in resources; the 1% per annum cut in real terms imposed by the Conservatives and continued under Labour as so-called 'efficiency gains' made not a great deal of sense when imposed on organisations running as lean a system as is imaginable by anyone unwilling to contemplate a drop-out rate of more than 50% along the lines of the American community college.

The effect of the shrinking unit of resource is not easily measured. According to universities themselves, the standard of student performance is steadily rising. Although such claims are often met with unkind remarks about 'dumbing down', it is not impossible that they are correct, or that something is happening that is not obviously dumbing down—what one might call 'dumbing up' or 'dumbing into the middle'. We will return to that thought at the end of this essay; first, we should complete this glance at the provocation for and effect of the Dearing Report. Universities old and new very much dislike redundancies; they are not much happier about closing departments and redeploying staff. But staff salaries are the largest part of their budgets. Under pressure, the two things that give are student–staff ratios and what is broadly called 'the estate'. Maintenance will be deferred even if some glamorous new buildings are erected, and over time a backlog builds up that nobody knows what to do about; JM Consulting estimated in 2001 that the total backlog in HE was of the order of £8 billion in deferred maintenance and modernisation. The deficiency was some £5 billion in teaching premises and £3 billion in the research estate.

The worsening of the student–staff ratio takes a variety of forms, and has a variety of consequences. One is that HEIs become frightened of employing new academic staff, in spite of Sir Keith Joseph's 1988 legislation that enables them to dismiss rather easily staff who were appointed after the passage of the Bill. The anti-dismissal ethos is perverse in that universities will not let newcomers start on their careers in case they have to sack them later. If every intending husband or wife who understood the risk of divorce decided against marriage, there'd be few weddings. Since students need teaching, the temptation is to increase the number of adjunct faculty—'scholar gypsies' as they are wryly known in the United States. The other coping mechanism is to reduce the amount of time that each member of faculty needs to spend on reading and grading student work. This is most easily achieved by reducing the amount of individual written work that a student has to produce, making written work do double duty by assessing every piece of written work a student produces, substituting multiple choice tests for essay-style examinations, and so on.

3. Fees and beyond

The hurried decision to introduce tuition fees and maintenance loans, together with the tightening of the regulatory and inspection regime throughout education set the 1997 Labour government at odds both with the HE profession and with students. In the nature of the case, it is not easy to know—yet—what internecine struggles went on within the machinery of government after these decisions. It is clear enough that the Treasury, the Department of Trade and Industry (DTI) (and within it the OST), the DfES (formerly, and briefly, the Department of Education and Employment), and Hefce had and continue to have different visions of what policy should achieve. The process of channelling money to HEIs, not only through Hefce, but also through the plethora of funding councils that draw their resources from the DTI and the OST, is calculated to enrage a tidy-minded Treasury official, and rightly so. The post-1997 Treasury, even more than Mrs Thatcher's Treasury, likes to operate by agreements with departments; they promise performance and the Treasury in effect purchases their services with an implicit threat that lacklustre performance will be penalised in future spending rounds. The multi-channel distribution of public funds to HEIs frustrates that.

It is a safe conjecture that the Treasury would prefer a method of distributing HE funding that allowed it to direct the OST and DfES to direct money towards the destinations that the treasury approves of. In particular, Hefce has a policy of spreading small amounts of support thinly over the not very deserving that the Treasury would not follow if it were able to direct the funding as it chose. The beneficiaries and losers within the present system are not hard to pick out, save that all HEIs are to some extent losers when the Treasury fears that what it regards as 'its' money will not end up where it wishes, and therefore behaves ungenerously. At all events, the Treasury appears to have three aims; one is part of its social mobility—or 'an end to social exclusion'—agenda, and is directed towards opening the so-called elite universities to a wider constituency. This policy aim has few implications for public expenditure; in the short-run loans and grants have much the same impact on public borrowing. It does suggest that the Treasury, or the Chancellor personally, may have been unenthusiastic about the increase in tuition fees proposed in the White Paper of January 2003, and passed into law during 2004.

A second aim is to make universities 'business-friendly', and to make SMEs—small and medium enterprises—university aware; that is to ensure that SMEs take advantage of whatever scientific work their local universities are doing and that universities are active in seeking out SMEs to whom they can do some good. The achievement of this aim does not raise questions about sending funding in the right direction. So-called 'third stream funding' is ear-marked for the encouragement of the kind of science that will not do well at the hands of Hefce and the funding councils, but which will do a lot of good to particular sections of industry. Research into the packaging of pharmaceuticals, for instance, will get nobody a Nobel Prize, but it makes an enormous difference to the safety of drugs, their shelf-life, and the profits of their manufacturers. The only question about it is how much public funding is needed to promote the changes in culture identified as needed in the Lambert Report.

The third aim is to sustain world-class university research in the natural sciences. World-class quality is an awkward property to measure, and the Treasury has not found it easier than anyone else. International measures tend to concentrate very heavily on the combined quality and quantity of research in the natural sciences. By those standards, Britain does quite well; unsurprisingly, the science-heavy Cambridge is well ahead of Oxford, but both are in the top ten globally: Cambridge at fifth and Oxford at ninth, with Imperial College at 17th and UCL at 20th. The science-bias of the rankings is emphasised by the absence of the London School of Economics, which in UK rankings is in the 'magic 5', of Oxbridge, UCL, Imperial and the LSE. But the Treasury is anxious to protect the standing of Oxbridge, Imperial and UCL, all of which are expensive institutions to maintain as global competitors.

This, however, causes a familiar problem. It is politically very difficult to argue simultaneously that the overriding priority for HE is the opening of doors to students from previously under-represented backgrounds—which implies a strategy of cheap and cheerful basic HE up to BA and BSc level—and that the overriding priority is the preservation of world-class science—which implies a strategy of diverting resources into the sciences and out of the humanities, into research and out of undergraduate teaching, and into the top four, five, or ten institutions and away from those that specialise in access. Throw the Lambert Report into the mix, and one has the makings of policy overload, as blue skies research in the traditional universities competes with applied, non-research led business friendly science in the access-oriented universities of the class of '92.

4. 'Top-ups,' successes, failures, and the future

One of the strangest political phenomena of recent years has been the extreme difficulty a Labour government with a majority of 165 has had in pushing through an increase to a maximum of £3,000 in the tuition fee that students have to pay. The increase is very substantial—from a predicted £1,175 a year in 2006 to £3,000. The increase looks even more dramatic when applied to the three years of most courses: from £3,750 to £9,000. In terms of the impact on students while they are on course, it is much less alarming, since the repayment is deferred until students have graduated and are in work in the way the Dearing Report suggested and that the Scots system implemented. Less prosperous students continue to have the wind tempered by some means-testing of the fee liability, and less prosperous ex-students benefit because the repayment threshold has been raised so that students start to repay only once they are earning £15,000 a year; the rate at which payment is made remains 9%, taken as a surcharge on income tax. This is not the place to adjudicate the major unresolved argument: on one side are those who think that poorer students suffer from 'debt-aversion' and that students from non-traditional backgrounds contemplating higher education will suffer what the Americans term 'sticker shock'—will look at the nominal figure of the debt they will incur over a three-year course and will turn away; and on the other are those who point out that even with the 9% surcharge to cover their tuition fees, graduates today face a lower tax environment than their parents 20 years ago.

The argument that these proposals sparked off between the universities specialising in access and those aiming to maintain an international research reputation is also something we cannot expect to resolve here. As the turnover figures above suggest, there is something of a paradox about the post-1992 universities' hostility to increased tuition fees. A university turning over £4,500 per enrolled student could—if it charged the maximum and the students turned up—make an extra 55% per student, even after returning £300 a head in bursaries; a university turning over £30,000 per student will make 8% extra per head. On the face of it, the universities which make almost all their money from tuition fees and grants need the extra fee income more than their more expensive peers which make a much higher proportion of their income from research grants of all kinds.

The paradox dissolves when one reflects that if anyone suffers from sticker shock at the sight of a fee of £3,000 a year, it will be the students attending the post-1992 universities. What the universities who are unhappy at the proposal for flexible fees and a cap at £3,000 really fear is a collapse in enrolments if they put their fees up to the same level as their more expensive competitors—and severe discontent from their faculty if they do not charge the maximum and are therefore unable to do anything about academic salaries. The research-intensive universities have supported the increase in tuition fees not so much because the increased income will make a great deal of difference in the first instance, but because the fact of the change suggests that in a fairly short time, the cap will be lifted and universities will be allowed to charge whatever the market will bear.

In any event, from the point of view of the research-intensive universities—and to a lesser extent everyone else—the deficit in the unit of resource for teaching is less important than the deficit in public funding for research overheads, and by the same token for the laboratory and technical resources required for decent science teaching. If the figure of an £8 billion deficit for the system as a whole is right, the extra £1 billion a year that the tuition fee increase represents will not go a long way towards repairing the decay in estates; it allows for some stabilisation of the situation but not a lot for repairing the backlog. This is why the less visible but more important aspect of government funding is the Treasury's proposed doubling over five years of public funding for scientific research, together with enough of an injection into Third Stream funding to ensure that there will be no competition between blue-skies research and industry-friendly applied research.

Indeed, the one group of people who stand to prosper from recent initiatives are scientific researchers in the half-dozen top universities. The Treasury has since 1999 put pressure on everyone, from the universities to the funding councils to the charities who pay for a lot of medical research to adopt a 'Full Economic Costing' methodology for charging for and paying for research. If universities were selling research for something like 35% less than it really cost to do it—by overworking staff, running down buildings, and running equipment into the ground—they were operating non-sustainably, and it was time they stopped. Conversely, if government departments were refusing to pay the full cost of the research they were commissioning, they were as guilty as the researchers, and needed to be stopped as well. This appears to have been the Treasury view. The logic, however, is not wholly favourable to universities other than the very best; there will not be an immediate boost of 35% to the research budget nationally, and therefore not the budgets of every last university. What there will be, if the Treasury succeeds is 'less but better'.

The noise of campaigners for and against top-up fees, and the associated noise surrounding the proposal to set up an Office of Fair Access to encourage universities to take more students from underrepresented backgrounds, may give the impression that Higher Education is an unmitigated disaster. In fact, much of what the government has tried to do it has succeeded in doing, though at a price that may turn out to have been too low in one sense and too high in another. The government has wanted to expand HE without undue expense. Since 1997, the numbers in HE have moved up steadily rather than jumped, but they have moved up, both because demography has favoured expansion as increasingly large cohorts of school-leavers have come through the system, and because the wage premium for graduate level qualifications has—surprisingly—not been eroded by expansion. There were around 1,650,000 students in 1997–8, and 2,025,000 in 2002–3, with some 260,000 students graduating in 1997 and 274,000 in 2003. Unit costs per student have remained almost flat.

The increase in student numbers masks some interesting divergences, however. In 1992, rather more men than women entered higher education; since then, the number of male entrants has dropped by some 14% and the number of women has risen by the same percentage.

All discussion of expansion raises the question whether 'more means worse'. Those who think it does have not been very good at putting their case coherently, and I end with two thoughts about how they might put it more persuasively. The case for suggesting that more has not meant worse is very simple; numbers have risen and so has the percentage of students getting 'good'—that is, 2.1 and better—degrees. The validity of this as a measure of quality is contentious. There is undoubtedly a certain amount of sharp practice going on, as universities put pressure on their faculty to pass students who ought not to be passed, and examiners are more generous at the margin than they used to be. It seems unlikely that there is a great deal of it, though any at all is too much, of course. However, it was never true that a lower second from a poly-technic represented a striking intellectual achievement, and it seems wrong to make a tremendous fuss about standards after 1992, let alone to complain that New Labour has conspired to wreck standards.

Why might this produce something other than dumbing down? It is not implausi-ble that the financial pressure has produced a process of 'dumbing into the middle' by, in essence, making teachers produce predictable, manageable, easily mastered modules, examined in predictable and easily mastered ways. This will very likely produce better informed students than less tightly structured systems of instruction would do. Whether they are better 'educated' in some more qualitative sense is beyond the scope of this essay. Dumbing into the middle was reinforced by the QAA. The QAA is a response to a difficulty with assessing the quality of educational outputs that has no plausible solution.

The difficulty is that there is no accepted test of the quality of what is produced. Final examinations give a snapshot of what an institution thinks about its graduating students, but examiners may be self-deceived, they have an interest in presenting their students as 'successes', no matter what they think in their heart of hearts, and the management of their institutions have a vested interest in passing off their own students as 'above average'. There are no 'purchasers' for the final product in the way in which there are purchasers for motor cars, and the ambivalence of employers about the quality of the education their graduate recruits have had is evidence only of the wish of employers to have someone else pay the costs of training their employees. Absent a decisive estimate of the quality of the product, the temptation is to inspect the process of production.

That this is a very indirect way of achieving what is wanted is obvious enough. Whatever one thinks of Beethoven's Late Quartets, it is unlikely that a meticulous examination of the processes of composition would reveal anything illuminating. The Labour governments' concern with value for money has been such that all aspects of education have been subjected to continuous and intrusive inspection regimes, and HEIs have suffered rather less at their hands than have schools and FE colleges. However, there is an interesting feature of the attempt to square a concern for academic freedom—not a feature of the regime in primary and secondary schools—with a desire that uniform best practice shall prevail. It means that what began as a 'teaching quality assessment' turns into a 'quality assurance assessment'.

To raise questions about exactly *what* is taught, and *how well* gets perilously close to infringing on academic freedom. However most people feel less troubled by the question whether a faculty has in place efficient bureaucratic procedures that allow it to know whether it has delivered what it has said it would deliver. In principle, though not in practice, a department could announce that it was its intention to deliver complete drivel, and as long as it spelled out what that drivel was, by what means it was to be handed out, and how the efficiency of its delivery was to be assessed, it would be eligible for an excellent rating. But although the Quality Assurance Agency has had no tendency to increase the amount of complete drivel taught to undergraduates, and may have done something to eliminate the worst 10% of provision, it has promoted 'dumbing into the middle'. This is because the obvious way to meet the QAA's requirements is carefully to spell out course requirements, so that both teachers and taught know exactly where they are, moment by moment and week by week. This means that the standard performance by a modestly competent and attentive student is somewhere within the 2.1 envelope. The process replaces 'teaching' by 'course delivery', but it is not obvious that this is uniformly a disaster.

There are two more gloomy points to be made. There is one group of persons for whom more has certainly meant worse and that is the academic faculty. Salaries have kept pace with inflation since 1979, while white collar salaries in general have risen at around 3% a year compound in real terms. Given the extraordinary productivity of HE—there are no other service industries that can boast of producing an improved product at 40% lower unit cost—it is a curious state of affairs. Not surprisingly, low salaries have brought with them a decline in social status.

Finally, there is one thing to be said for the proposition that more means worse more generally. For students who would otherwise not have gone into HE at all, more has meant better; they would have had less education and probably to a lower level in qualitative terms, and in those terms more undoubtedly means better. Nor should we worry that what can be taught to 35% of the age cohort is different from what could be taught to a carefully selected 7%; that is no more surprising than the fact that a large field in a Sunday morning fun run is spread out more widely than the finalists in the Olympic 100 metres. What is worrying is the triumph of narrowly utilitarian standards, as though the only criterion of intellectual excellence was to send young people out into the world ready to make money by whatever legal means they could. And that has gone along with a certain duplicity about what exactly it is that we are offering the young. The participants in the Sunday morning fun run know very well that they are not Olympic stars; a government that cannot bring itself to acknowledge that introductory business studies is not as intellectually demanding nor as fulfilling as really understanding the plays of Aeschylus—or Fermat's Theorem—may have met high standards in caring for public finances, but has debased the intellectual currency. And doing that is not a response to unavoidable dilemmas, but a betrayal of the ambitions of the Labour movement.

Acknowledgements

I am grateful for the comments of two referees. I would have been more grateful if they had not offered diametrically opposed advice; one advised me not to touch the piece, the other thought it needed some recasting and lots of references. I have done a little recasting, and note 2 suggests some further reading.

Notes

1. Some of them must have read Raymond Williams, *Culture and society* (London, 1958, Chatto & Windus) or Richard Hoggart, *The uses of literacy* (London, 1957, Chatto & Windus); but not much seems to have rubbed off.
2. The by-now-classic text is Alison Wolf, *Does education matter?* (London, 2002, Penguin Books). For those who wish to dig deep, *Oxford Review of Economic Policy*, 20(2), Summer 2004 (Oxford, Oxford University Press) cannot be bettered, especially the article by Ewart Keep and Ken Mayhew, 'The economic and distributional implications of current policies on higher education'.

Note on contributor

The author is Warden of New College, Oxford, a professor of political theory, a frequent contributor to *The Times Higher Education Supplement*, and the author of *Liberal Anxieties and Liberal Education*, 2000.

Lifelong learning and the Labour governments 1997–2004

Richard Taylor

Introduction

Historically, there has been an affinity between the Labour Party and education as a central part of the welfare state, but it has been policy in the schools sector that has normally been dominant.[1] It is true that there has been a nagging concern over the years with the perceived inadequacy of vocational and applied science education and training at post-school level, especially in the 'intermediate' sector, but this has rarely assumed major policy importance nor has it often resulted in the past in significant policy innovation. Indeed, as Tony Jowitt has observed recently, it is arguable that even the Labour Government's 2003 White Paper on 'Skills' (as discussed below) fails to address the fundamentals because it does not confront the structural deficiencies of the education system, in particular its class-based nature (Jowitt, 2003).

Similarly, higher education in general, and in particular *part-time* higher education, adult education and lifelong learning, have rarely had a high profile with Labour. On the other hand, there has been an attachment in the Labour tradition to certain aspects of the 'adult education movement', especially the Workers' Educational Association (WEA) and the residential adult colleges (Fieldhouse, 1996; Ball & Hampton, 2004).

There was thus in the lifelong learning community what might be described as, at best, cautious optimism for the New Labour government in 1997. The Prime Minister's proclaimed priority for 'education, education, education' was buttressed significantly as far as lifelong learning was concerned by the appointment as Secretary of State for Education of David Blunkett, who had – and still has – a real enthusiasm for adult education and lifelong learning and particularly for access, community education and liberal education. Blunkett had wide experience of FE and adult education, and had been a prominent advocate of such work in Sheffield and the wider Yorkshire region in his roles in Sheffield City Council. He had, for example, been supportive of the foundation of Northern College, the residential adult education college at Wentworth Castle, near Barnsley (Taylor, 2004).

The views of commentators and analysts on Labour's record have varied from the dismissive – Labour's education policy has been little more than Thatcherism dressed up in Labour clothes (Power & Whitty, 1999)—through the hostile—Labour's emphasis upon human capital perspectives has been unwarranted and damaging (Coffield, 1999a, 1999b)—to those who have had at least a partially positive view of the Government's lifelong learning achievements (Tuckett, 2000; Fryer, 2004; Fullick, 2004).

This paper thus has several purposes: first, to discuss the ideological underpinnings of Labour's lifelong learning policy in the period in question; second, to delineate the main developments in lifelong learning; and third, to assess how far the 'cautious optimism' of 1997 has been justified.

Labour's ideology of lifelong learning

According to Tony Blair, speaking in 1999:

> The old dispute between those who favour growth and personal prosperity, and those who favour social justice and compassion, is over. The liberation of human potential – for all the people, not just a privileged few – is in today's world the key both to economic and social progress. In economic terms, human capital is a nation's biggest resource. (Blair, 1999 in Rentoul, 2002)

It was this integration of the economic (human capital) orientation and the liberal, social justice imperative that was embraced with such enthusiasm by David Blunkett in his much quoted Foreword to the Government's first major policy statement on Lifelong Learning, *The Learning Age* (DfEE, 1998).

> Learning is the key to prosperity. ... Investment in human capital will be the foundation of success in the knowledge-based economy of the twenty-first century. ... To achieve stable and sustainable growth, we will need a well-educated, well-equipped and adaptable labour force. ... We need the creativity, enterprise and scholarship of all our people.
>
> As well as securing our economic future, learning has a wider contribution. It helps make ours a civilised society, develops the spiritual side of our lives and promotes active citizenship.

The emphasis upon human capital arguments has characterised Labour's post-compulsory educational policy since 1945 (Bocock & Taylor, 2003a, 2003b). But never has it been so prominent as in the recent context. There is an acknowledgement in policy and political circles that developed societies are becoming 'knowledge societies' where a high level of, largely transferable, skills for the bulk of the workforce is a *sine qua non* of economic competitiveness in an increasingly globalised world order (Scott, 1995; Coffield, 1999a, b; Barnett, 1997, 2000).

Labour has thus been insistent on the importance of both the *expansion* of post-compulsory education and its key roles in vocational and professional training of the existing and future workforce. As Lindsey Paterson has observed, this has been combined with a strong meritocratic motivation (Paterson, 2003). Citing Blair's election speech in 2001 in his Sedgefield constituency, Paterson argues that New Labour's ideology is both meritocratic—Blair's aim is to create 'a meritocratic Britain where people can get to the highest level their talents take them' (Blair, 2001) – and neo-liberal. In this latter respect his 'liberal instincts incline him to competitive individualism, real partnership between public and private, and using the State only where necessary but—unlike the New Right—certainly where necessary' (Paterson, 2003, p. 173).

This *sounds* fine, from a social democratic perspective: but Thatcher too had no qualms about using the State, rather the reverse. Paradoxically, the neo-liberalism of the 1980s resulted, despite the rhetoric, in a significant shift to centralised control in education as in much else. More importantly, though, what has New Labour used the State *for*? Certainly Labour has not seen fit to introduce any measures that might curtail employers' 'freedoms' in relation to workforce education and training provision. In 1999, Ewart Keep noted that the Government was reluctant to 'enforce employer support for Lifelong Learning, despite evidence that a significant body of employers (perhaps up to one-third) are making little attempt to promote education and training of their workforces' (Keep, 1999). Little has changed since then. Nor has the taxation system been used for educationally redistributive purposes for any aspect of lifelong learning. Of course, these policy orientations relate to a much wider politics than education: a central plank of New Labour's electoral and ideological stance has been to engage with and reassure employers, and to rid the Labour Party of the 1980s image of a high taxation, bureaucratic party, run essentially by the trade unions (Coates, 2003).

What New Labour *has* used the State for is to take forward what Stephen O'Brien has termed its agenda of 'centralist progressivism' (O'Brien, 2000). Essentially, this embodies the 'Third Way' idea (Giddens, 1998) whereby New Labour has brought together market principles and social democratic emphases upon equality of opportunity.[2] As will be discussed in the section below, since 1997 Labour has consistently emphasised the importance of education generally, and in the context of a transformed, globalised economy, the centrality of lifelong learning. The 1997 Manifesto, for example, stated Labour's 'vision' in which 'a Britain equipped to prosper in a global economy of technological changes' (Labour Party, 1997, p. 3) would take full advantage of the perceived linear relationship between high quality education, including at its heart vocationally oriented lifelong learning, increased wages, greater productivity, and enhanced economic competitiveness.

Of these twin themes—lifelong learning for vocational skills, and for wider, liberal purposes—there is no doubt that the economic, human capital imperative has been dominant: lifelong learning policy can be caricatured, in Roger Boshier's phrase, as 'human resource development (HRD) in drag' (Boshier, 1998, p. 4). Certainly, 'much of the policy interest in lifelong learning is in fact preoccupied with the development of a more productive and efficient workforce' (Field, 2000b, p. viii). This is not the whole story, however: ideological stances, particularly in the amalgam of Labourism, are rarely that monolithic and straightforward. There is an accompanying commitment in New Labour's policy to what can be characterised as a marketised welfarism. This is clearly in significant contrast to neo-liberal Thatcherism, and is a position held broadly by those in the heart of government (Rentoul, 1997; Rawnsley, 2000).

Bob Fryer is quite correct in drawing attention not only to *The Learning Age* and its advocacy of broader lifelong learning perspectives, but to Blunkett's own commitments and achievements in this respect—'establishing major national task forces and subsequent strategies on adult literacy and numeracy, on skills for employment, on citizenship, on neighbourhood renewal and social inclusion ... support [for] trades union learning and adult and community learning' (Fryer, 2004, p. 38). However, the whole thrust of the Labour Governments' policy has been market oriented. This is not only the case in the persistent emphasis upon human capital arguments, as outlined, but also in the development of a terminology and conceptual framework that sees the whole complex of lifelong learning in terms of 'stakeholders', and audits and accountability criteria[3] (Coffield, 1999a, b; Taylor, 2000; Taylor *et al.*, 2002; Selwyn and Goddard 2002). The rhetoric, and to an extent the practical implementation, of lifelong learning policy geared towards liberal education, widening participation, citizenship education and the like, have continued to accompany these human capital themes as something of a leitmotif.

Whatever the viability of this overall ideological stance, Bob Fryer is surely right when he draws attention, in the context of 2004, to the 'apparent faltering support of the current Government for lifelong learning and social inclusion ...' (Fryer, 2004, p. 40).

To what extent this attempted ideological amalgam has been either coherent or successful in its objectives, to what extent the 'cautious optimism' in 1997 of the lifelong learning community has been justified, will be returned to in the concluding analysis. I turn now to the main elements of New Labour's record in lifelong learning development in the years since 1997.

The legislative and policy record[4]

Whatever else, the Labour Governments of 1997 to 2004/5 have presided over a period of unprecedented change in the post-compulsory sector. Much of this change is intimately related to broader political and constitutional change, not least the process of devolution to the constituent parts of the UK, and in the still embryonic 'regionalisation' of England. There is, thus, a new landscape for lifelong learning in the UK.

Leaving aside developments in Scotland, Wales and Northern Ireland, which fall outside the scope of this paper,[5] what have been the main landmarks? At the risk of over-schematising the sprawling complex of development in this field since 1997, I believe there are three distinct though related areas: the commissions and committees established by the Government to enquire into the various aspects of lifelong learning and post-compulsory education; the policy papers and legislative bills and acts from Government; and the new structures and cultures of lifelong learning provision.

In relation to the commissions and committees, the three most important have been the Dearing Report on higher education (which was of course established by the previous Conservative government—with Labour's positive agreement – primarily to remove the tricky issues of university funding from the political agenda during the election campaign) (Watson & Taylor, 1998); the Kennedy Report on further education; and the committee under Bob Fryer's chairmanship with the specific brief of recommending policy development in lifelong learning.[6] Significantly, all these took place and reported in the early years of the Labour Government's first term of office.

In 1998, David Watson and I concluded our book on Dearing and Lifelong Learning by drawing attention to four 'big ideas' which, we argued, underpinned the Dearing vision: 'the contribution of higher education to lifelong learning'; 'a vision for learning in the twenty-first century', involving developments in credit and qualifications frameworks, ICT, work experience etc; 'funding research according to its intended outcomes'—that is, moving away from the hierarchical and élitist culture of the Research Assessment Exercise; and 'a new compact between the State, the institutions and their students'—the stakeholder concept, involving 'a 'deal' whereby institutions retain their independence and gain increased security in return for clearer accountability', and includes *inter alia* a recognition that learners should contribute to the costs of their learning (Watson & Taylor, 1998, pp. 152–153).

The Dearing Report, despite its length and somewhat establishment aura, was in reality a radical document. In one respect at least though, as far as lifelong learning is concerned, it was a major disappointment: Dearing explicitly rejected an equitable funding structure for part-time, mature students (see Main Report, 20.11).

The Kennedy Report on further education was a very different document – shorter, punchier, more accessible—and generally welcomed by the field, and by those in the Labour Party who were advocates of Further Education and widening participation. As Leisha Fullick points out, the Report 'contained a strong message—we know how to widen participation, now we need to make it happen' (Fullick, 2004, p. 16).

Bob Fryer's committee was similarly positive. Addressing itself to Blunkett's clear commitment to lifelong learning, its first report set out 'the broad approach and key principles that should underpin a new strategy and the second ... advocated detailed policies to promote the creation and support of learning cultures' (Fryer, 2004, p. 38).

These three reports have much in common: as noted, they were all produced in the early years of the Labour Government and they were all positive and optimistic about the prospects for lifelong learning as a central part of Labour's change agenda. And they were all produced under the aegis of a Secretary of State committed to the development of lifelong learning. Arguably, the groundwork for a development programme was thus laid by 1998.

Subsequently, the Labour Government has taken a series of 'often radical and progressive steps to raise the levels of skill, qualifications and general learning in the workforce and in the community at large' (Fullick, 2004, p. 3). The Green and White Papers *The Learning Age* and *Learning to Succeed* led to what is perhaps the most important potentially of these innovations, the creation in 2000 (The Learning and Skills Act) of the Learning and Skills Council (LSC). David Blunkett called this 'the most significant and far reaching reform ever enacted in relation to post-16 learning in this country' (cited in Fullick, 2004, p. 14). The LSC, absorbing the former Further Education Funding Council and the Training and Enterprise Council structure, was created as a single non-departmental public body responsible for the whole range of all publicly-funded post-16 education and training – except, as ever, for higher education. It came into being 'in an atmosphere of almost euphoric goodwill generated by the Blunkett vision and commitments' (Fullick, 2004, p. 15). The importance of all aspects of adult learning was writ large in its aims and objectives. The LSC had primary responsibility for delivery on two of the three key targets affecting adult learners set by the Government, and a significant role in the third. (The three targets concerned are, in summary, the achievement by 2010 of a participation rate in higher education of 50% of the 18–30 age cohort, in which the LSC's role in providing pathways and facilitating partnerships between FE and HE over such innovations as Foundation Degrees was seen as crucial; improving the basic skills levels of 1.5 million adults between 2001 and 2007, with a 'milestone' of 750,000 by 2004; and reducing by at least 40% by 2010 the number of adults in the workforce who lack NVQ2 or the equivalent, with 1 million adults achieving Level 2 between 2003 and 2006.)

The tasks facing the LSC were formidable, and the barriers to their achievement even more so. It inherited a field of almost impenetrable complexity – 'a bureaucratic minefield' as *Learning to Succeed* described it. It was expected to act on the repeal of the old Schedule 2, to clear away the 'bureaucratic clutter of the TECs' and to avoid the mistakes of the FEFC (Fullick, 2004, p. 15).

There has been confusion over the responsibilities *within* the LSC between the national body and the bureaucracy based at Coventry, and the 47 local LSCs; and there have been understandable difficulties caused by the predominance of a 'TEC culture' in the new body (c. 80% of LSC staff came from a TEC background). There have also been problems over the LSC's actual remit, however, and thus over its *external* relationships. The DfES (and the Government more generally) have been unwilling to surrender policy control to the LSC—over the skills agenda, quality issues, and FE reform, for example.

One of the results has been the perception of LSC complexity experienced by FE Colleges and, particularly, the voluntary sector. Another has been the lack of clarity over the LSC's role in relation to the Regional Development Agencies (RDAs), and the Learning Partnerships.

The RDAs were founded in 1998, and have wide-ranging responsibilities for the regional economy and employment issues. This clearly has major implications for adult learning. A good example of the labyrinthine complexity of the bureaucratic structure is the fact that 'the Government's own flagship regeneration initiative, the Neighbour-hood Renewal Strategy, has its regional dimension delivered through neither the RDAs nor LSCs but through the Government Offices for the Regions' (Fullick, 2004, p. 18).

The developing regional agenda – far broader than lifelong learning of course – has resulted in yet further complexity, with the RDAs assuming functions, partially or in whole, that objectively would seem to belong to the LSCs. For example, the 2002 Spending Review White Paper announced that from April 2003 pilots would operate in one or two regions so that budgets for adult learning are pooled between local LSCs and RDAs. If the regional agenda develops significantly, possibly into a more fully devolved regional system, then such increased roles for the RDAs—or more likely some successor body with greater explicit powers—may well eventuate.

The purpose here is not to delineate the full range of these bodies' remits and performance, but rather to demonstrate the inherent complexity, and in some respects incoherence, of our current context. Of course, these patterns of complexity and change are neither new nor restricted to the areas discussed here: Marx and many analysts since have recognised that inevitable, unrelenting, unending change is endemic in modern capitalist societies.

However, part of the problem with lifelong learning structures under Labour has been both the proliferation of agencies and initiatives in the field *and* the degree of overlap between directly educational concerns and those of cognate areas in a policy context which has lacked coherence or a broad political strategy. Thus, the DTI has strong interests in employment and training issues; the Department of Health has a direct role in education for the huge number of employees in the general health field (see, for example, the developing National Health Service University headed, signif-icantly, by an experienced adult educator, Professor Bob Fryer); and the Treasury has interests, not only in the funding regimes and systems, but in enhanced skill levels and thus productivity in the workforce. There are thus competing bureaucratic 'power interests' adding greatly to the complexities noted.

Within the post-compulsory structures there are further layers of organisation, not yet alluded to:[7] these include Learning Partnerships (now numbering 104 and with the role of bringing together for liaison both statutory providers such as FE Colleges, Connexions/Careers Services, and schools, and voluntary and other bodies such as HE institutions, trade unions, faith communities, community education groups and so on); Local Strategic Partnerships (single bodies bringing together different parts of the private and public sectors, community and voluntary services and intended to be yet another Government body to produce coherence (Fullick, 2004, p. 27) and which have a very wide remit including a number of adult learning functions, such as the Neighbourhood Renewal Scheme); and of course Local Authorities (which, despite the attack on their powers in the 1980s years of Conservative governments, adminis-ter a range of services that are of key importance to adult learning, including social services, libraries, museums and youth and community services).

There have been other lifelong learning initiatives too, not least the ILAs (Individ-ual Learning Accounts) which, until their sudden termination because of evidence of quite widespread fraud and corruption, were regarded by the Government as important in developing education and training in the workforce. They were seen as a means of enabling individual employees to gain access to funding for their own choice of education and training, and were symbolic of New Labour's concept of the individual's right to choose, as a 'consumer', the form and location of their learning. However, in an authoritative and empirically based study, John Payne concluded in 2000 that ILAs were likely 'to produce contested and contradictory outcomes' (Payne, 2000).

As if these complexities were not formidable enough, little account here has yet been taken of higher education, which has remained very largely separate from the other parts of the lifelong learning sector, but is a key constituent element for adult learners, particularly in the light of its rapid expansion since the 1980s[8] (Scott, 1995; Barnett, 1997, 2000; Coffield & Williamson, 1997; Watson & Taylor, 1998; Slowey & Watson, 2003). Depending on definitions, approximately 35% of learners in higher education are part-time, and over 40% mature students.

Elsewhere in this journal, higher education since 1997 is analysed comprehensively. Here, it is sufficient to note that, although the Dearing Report and various government policy papers, including most importantly the Higher Education Act that passed through the legislative process in 2004, give *some* profile to lifelong learning, the strong emphases have lain elsewhere – the 18–21 cohort, research excellence, knowledge transfer *et al.* – despite the large numbers of lifelong learners in the system (Watson & Taylor, 1998; Slowey & Watson, 2003). Moreover, the older universities' traditional concerns with adult learning in the liberal and social purpose moulds have been largely superseded by more vocational and professional concerns (Fieldhouse *et al.*, 1996; Bocock & Taylor, 2003a; Osborne, 2003).

I have argued elsewhere that historically the Labour Party's higher education policy, reflecting the party's overall ideological complexion, has been characterised by a variety of often conflicting perspectives (Bocock & Taylor, 2003a). Since 1997, although this contestation has been more muted, there has been a series of ideological tensions in higher education policy. All these considerations apply in full measure too to the lifelong learning dimensions of higher education (Watson & Taylor, 1998).

Some major policy themes in lifelong learning since 1997

Within this structure of complexity several common themes in lifelong learning policy can be identified. Here, I discuss briefly three of the most important: the skills agenda; widening participation; and civic or social purpose education. Of course these are by no means the only key themes—other important thematic policy areas include literacy and numeracy, linked to 'basic skills', disability and ICT. Others are looming large for the next few years, not least the demographic trend and the expected increase in lifespan. Nevertheless, the three noted have been quite central to the Governments' concerns since 1997.

As noted at the outset of this paper, the Labour Governments since 1997 have been consistent in the high priority they have given to the skills agenda, based on the strong belief that, as Tony Blair put it in classic human capital terms, 'Education is the best economic policy we have' (Blair, 1998, p. 9). The Skills White Paper of 2003/04 represents perhaps the culmination of several legislative enactments in this area since 1997 (and is linked too to the reforms of the Careers Service, targeted workplace training initiatives, and the reform of Further Education). The White Paper outlines, for the first time, a comprehensive range of proposals to enhance the skills levels of adults, especially those with low skills levels for employability. The main provisions include entitlement for adults to free learning to acquire Level 2 qualifications, the designation of ICT as the third basic skill alongside literacy and numeracy, reform of fees and funding arrangements in various ways, and the introduction of a new Adult Learning Grant for full-time learners studying for Level 2 qualifications (and for young learners seeking a Level 3 qualification). Encouragingly, the Paper recognises the wider benefits of learning arguments, including the importance of adult and community learning.

However, as Alan Tuckett, the Director of the National Institute for Adult Continuing Education, and others have noted, the Government retains its policy of encouraging, as opposed to making mandatory, employers' investment in training. The outlook on this front is not good, and there is little evidence of change in employer attitudes and thus practices (NIACE, 2004). The Government 'has persisted with the same mix of voluntary strategies for securing employer investment that has failed for a decade. ... We can no longer afford to indulge the ignorance of those firms that won't invest in the capacity of their people' (Tuckett, 2000).

The White Paper envisages a major shift not only in the levels of training achieved for large numbers of employees and learners, but also in the *culture* of the work context. Relying as it does on voluntarism there must be scepticism over whether these targets can be met. What is crucial, as Fullick notes, is that the infrastructure of adult education support must be protected and enhanced as a core part of the strategy: 'better advice and guidance, outreach and confidence-building strategies of all kinds focussing on the needs of individuals rather than "skills for employability" *per se*' (Fullick, 2004, p. 11). There remains little incentive for most of those adults with low skills who are in employment; and, as noted, there is a confusing complexity of agencies and structures for both individuals and employers to negotiate.

The White Paper thus exemplifies much of Labour's record on lifelong learning: long on rhetoric and vision but, to date, rather short on delivery, or even viable structures for delivery. Advances on the skills agenda have undoubtedly been made but achievement to date is only modest. For example, whilst learning *opportunities* for employees have increased, the *actual increases* in both 'on and off the job' training are slight (Spilsburg, 2004). On the other hand, there have been areas of specific, tangible progress: the success of the Union Learning Fund initiative, the lifting of the age cap on Modern Apprenticeships, the experience of the Employer Training Pilots, and the 'resurgent confidence' of the Construction Industry Training Board; and, as Alan Tuckett has observed, the 'new Level 2 entitlement will not come cheap (and) it is some achievement to preserve the budgets overall for such work' (Tuckett, 2003a). Finally, as is discussed below, the White Paper does link the skills agenda to 'both economic and social needs' and, in that sense, is 'genuinely strategic' (McNair, 2003).

An analogous mixture of rhetorical advocacy, some achievement but essentially modest progress applies to the second thematic area, widening participation. This has been a high profile policy objective for New Labour across all sectors, from the outset, and encompasses all the ideological motivations discussed above: increasing skills levels in the workforce, enhancing a meritocratic and open educational culture, and an attachment to socially egalitarian structures and processes defined in a particular, New Labour, way.

Within a context of rapid expansion—especially in higher education (Scott, 1995; Barnett, 1997, 2000, 2003; Watson & Taylor, 1998)—there has been an insistence that more people from 'currently under-represented' groups should be encouraged to engage in post-compulsory education. One of the most prominent of Labour's targets is to achieve 50% participation of 18–30 year-olds in higher education by 2010. In higher education as across other sectors, the participation rates of those in what have been defined traditionally as the working class have remained relatively static—and low. However, as Bahram Bekhradnia notes, this general statement has to be treated with care: the social class patterns in Britain have changed markedly since the 1960s and 1970s, when nearly 90% of the population fell into such categories—the figure is now nearer 40% (Bekhradnia, 2003, Section 5). Nevertheless, the point remains that with as great a level of relative inequality as before, the numbers participating from those lower in the socio-economic scale, irrespective of the changes in occupation and the wider culture, continue persistently to be under-represented—as successive HEFCE and UCAS surveys have shown.

Of course, the absolute numbers participating have increased as a result of the expansion, but the expansion has occurred very largely through increases in the levels of participation from the higher socio-economic groups: 'more of the same', to put it crudely. As far as higher education is concerned, this same pattern is discernible, in broad terms, in most late capitalist societies (Scott, 1995; Watson & Taylor, 1998; Schuetze & Slowey, 2000; Slowey & Watson, 2003).

So, *widening* participation in addition to *increasing* participation has been only partially achieved. Numerous funding initiatives have been introduced: in higher education, for example, substantial funds have been in effect 'top-sliced' from the Funding Council's budget to support widening participation development, both through 'premium funding' and regional innovative widening participation development (HEFCE, for example, 1998, 1999a, b, 2000a; Taylor, 2004/5 (forthcoming)). And structures and review processes have been put in place, not least through the provision for a new Office for Fair Access (OFFA) in the 2004 Higher Education Act.

The position over adult participation in learning generally, across all sectors, is if anything even less encouraging. The 2004 NIACE survey of adult participation found that, in 2004, the 'total of adults reporting that they are currently learning (19 per cent) is the lowest of any year since 1996, ... and the combined totals of current and recent learners show a sharp reverse of the growth seen in the late 1990s.' Moreover, 'between

1996 and 2004 the learning divide widened, with participation rates falling among all but the highest socio-economic groups, and participation among the poorest (DEs) declining from 26 per cent to 23 per cent' (Aldridge & Tuckett, 2003a, p. 22).

There are three other aspects of widening participation policy to draw attention to here, as far as lifelong learning is concerned: the differential emphasis upon younger as opposed to older learners; widening participation in relation to institutional hierarchy; and the *purposes* of widening participation as Labour sees them.

The overwhelming emphasis of Government policy is upon younger learners in higher education, the 18–30 age cohort, and primarily the 18–21, 'standard' full-time students. 'The Government's concern with widening participation and fair access is really very largely a concern with young, largely full-time, traditional students. It barely touches on the question of lifelong learning and the increasing number of mature students who participate in education throughout their working lives' (Bekhradnia, 2003, section 27). Such students are now, in reality, barely a majority in higher education—or arguably a *minority* depending upon how calculations are formulated (Watson & Taylor, 1998; Slowey & Watson, 2003; Fullick, 2004). Why then does Labour continue to have this skewed emphasis? I would argue there are primarily two reasons: the first is that the 'human capital' perspective emphasises the potential contribution of more skilled young people in the workforce (and holds that there is a greater return on investment as, other things being equal, young people clearly have a longer span of working life); and the second is cultural – that is, virtually all senior policy makers, whether politicians or civil servants, have their university education at the standard age and almost always at one of the élite universities, more often than not Oxford or Cambridge. Their assumptions about higher education are conditioned accordingly.[9]

The second point is that the institutional locations of those who can be described as widening participation learners are predominantly in 'lower status' universities and colleges. Moreover, from 2003, the Government's main vehicle for boosting working-class participation in higher education is through Foundation Degrees, by definition sub-degree programmes with a strongly vocational orientation (HEFCE, 2000b). Whilst HEFCE has insisted, in my view rightly, that all higher education institutions should have a widening participation strategy and practice, it is clear that the élite 'Russell Group' universities, for example, will construe this in meritocratic terms: that is, that widening participation strategy will be focused on ensuring that the 'best' students are recruited and that admissions policies are 'fair' (Bekhradnia, 2003). There are strong arguments to support this policy: leading 'research' universities *should* be recruiting the best students, judged on academic criteria. However, such an approach is hardly conducive to the social policy objective of *widening* participation.

Finally, the Government's overriding purpose in widening participation policy is, in common with all aspects of lifelong learning policy, to enhance the skills levels in the workforce through vocational training. There is a seemingly apolitical merito-cratic motivation here: the implicit belief that what matters about widening participation is enabling the most able individuals to gain appropriate training and education. What this perspective omits, *inter alia*, however, is any realisation that there is a need to enable more and different learners to have access to a liberal and critical education; nor does it allow any collective or community notion of education – it assumes an entirely individualistic (and 'marketised') frame of reference (Taylor, 2000; Delanty, 2001; Taylor *et al.*, 2002).

None of this is surprising: but it must at least raise questions over how far, if at all, Labour's widening participation agenda can be regarded as either radical or emancipatory.

This leads on to the third of the themes specified: that of Labour's policy in relation to civic or social purpose education. Adult education has had a long association with emancipatory, social purpose education, from Mansbridge and the early pioneers of liberal education in the modern period through to socialist and community educators (Harrison, 1961; Jepson, 1973; Fieldhouse *et al.*, 1996, 1977; Wallis, 1996; Jennings, 2002). There are certainly 'Mansbridgean overtones' in Blunkett's Foreword to the *Learning Age* with its assertion of adult education as invaluable in its own right; and there has been a persistent reiteration – usually *sotto voce* – of such values in subsequent documents. Significantly, the Skills White Paper recognizes the interrelationship between vocational learning and broader, liberal education and advocates a unified approach, incorporating the wider benefits of learning.

It is true, too, that some Labour initiatives, such as the Neighbourhood Renewal programme, break new ground in the development of community approaches to lifelong learning. Perhaps inevitably, delivery structures are complex and overly bureaucratic with ultimate control of a highly devolved programme being retained centrally. Nevertheless, the funding is on a large scale (£900 million over the first three years), and the targeted and innovative initiatives effective with some very disadvantaged communities.

All these, and other similar ameliorative aspects of Labour's policy, do not however contradict the essential ideological drive of lifelong learning policy. In the early section of this paper I outlined this framework. Both this, and the record in practice, show that the policy is geared to human capital perspectives, within a particular version of meritocratic expansion and marketised welfarism. Far from being a transformative agenda for social democratic change, lifelong learning policy thus aims for the incorporation of an increasing number of learners into the existing free market culture thereby, it is argued, producing beneficial, wider social effects – reducing alienation, improving social cohesion and so on.

Indeed, the language of class and social change, the common currency of Labourism in the past (Miliband, 1972), has been replaced by categories of inclusion and exclusion, with an emphasis upon the individual rather than the collective, and within what is assumed to be a permanent and unchallengeable free market, capitalist economy and society (Readings, 1996; Coffield & Williamson, 1997; Taylor *et al.*, 2002).

Conclusion: prospects for Labour's lifelong learning policy

The 'cautious optimism' in 1997 about prospects for lifelong learning development under Labour reflected the general catharsis felt by many at escaping from the long years of Thatcherism. There was an inevitable sense of relief, if not euphoria. And, in the first two years or so, there was a flurry of energy and commitment in the field: even the more jaded had some sense of a 'bright new dawn'. Inevitably, again, such moods do not last. Reality intrudes. What then is the level of success and achievement of Labour in this field, reflecting over seven years?

To begin with, New Labour's lifelong learning policy is not merely Thatcherism with a new spin, as Paterson has argued convincingly (Paterson, 2003). There have been real, tangible advances in both legislative enactment and learner entitlement, across all sectors – some of which I have drawn attention to in this paper – and motivated by that particular New Labour ideological mix of meritocratic, individualistic idealism, laced with at least a little egalitarianism in a framework of marketised welfarism.

However, as Crowther, Martin and Shaw point out, whilst there is 'nothing intrinsically wrong with meritocracy … there certainly is when it masquerades as equality' (Crowther *et al.*, 2000, p. 175). And it is clear that *meritocracy* was by far the dominant emphasis in this context.

In many ways, the achievements of Labour since 1997 have much in common with Labour's overall perspective in this field since 1945: a policy which focuses upon post-school education and training as a means of modernising and making more efficient the existing mixed economy, capitalist system, introducing measures of meritocracy into social and economic structures, and using such educational provision to build consensual social cohesion (Bocock & Taylor, 2003a, b). The differences in the period since 1997 are primarily twofold: the *scale* of the expansion and the centrality afforded to such developments, given the conceptualisation of the 'knowledge society' and its education and training requirements; and the particular ideology of New Labour generally, with its embrace of 'Third Way' perspectives on both economic and social issues marking a sharp ideological break with 'old Labour'.

Not that a Conservative government would have put in place *radically* different policies. According to Tim Boswell, MP, a former Conservative Junior Minister of Education in the 1990s, 'we would not have done *that* much which was different' (Boswell, 2004). In his view the main problems with New Labour's policy were that it lacked flexibility, was overly bureaucratic and centralised, and that it failed to engage sufficiently with business culture or understand the nuances of *local* differences and priorities. Overall, though, the Conservatives were not fundamentally hostile to Labour's policy or its effects: such criticisms as there were, were essentially second order.

Because of this context and ideology, however, Labour's lifelong learning policy has fallen far short of the aspirations of many practitioners in the field in 1997: it has not been *transformative* (see, for example, NAGCELL, 1998 and 1999). At base, as McCaig has pointed out, New Labour has 'sought to offer opportunities for the individual to improve his or her occupational prospects periodically in response to the new demands of the knowledge-based economy' (McCaig, 2001, p. 191). Those who understand the conflicted history of the Labour Party since its inception will not find this unduly surprising. The Party has always been a coalition of disparate ideological strands, although under 'old' as under 'new' Labour it is the pragmatic right, laced with varying types of social democracy, that has predominated. The majority Labour ideology has never been 'transformative' in any socialist sense (Beer, 1959; Nairn, 1965; Pelling, 1965; Miliband, 1972; McKibbin, 1974; Howell, 1976; Warde, 1982; Newman, 2002).

There has been little acknowledgement by Government of the importance of voluntary organisations and of socially purposeful learning (and this could be construed as a significant encroachment, by default, upon the idea and practice of 'democratic education' embodied in voluntary sector agencies, such as the Workers' Educational Association (Tuckett, 2003b)). However, to re-emphasise the point, Labour, even in 1945, has never embraced notions of radical social change in that, or any other, sense. As John Saville has written rather sourly, even this reforming government in 1945 left 'the fundamental structure of society ... untouched ... [and] then it [was] only a matter of time before the normal processes of capitalist development' reasserted themselves and eroded any modest advances made (Saville, 1993, p. xxxiv). If this is true of 1945 to 1951, it is hardly surprising that Labour's achievements in the lifelong learning field from 1997 to 2004, as elsewhere in the social and domestic policy arena, whilst real and valuable, have been ameliorative rather than radically transformative. New Labour, despite its differences with Labour's traditional ideology and perspective, remains as ever not a reformist party but a party of modest social reform (Miliband, 1972; Coates, 1974, 2003).

And modest social reform will not produce, despite all the glossy rhetoric of New Labour, major change. Unless and until Labour confronts the structural inequality that has characterised society for many years, and continues unchecked, no fundamental advance is possible. Gross inequalities of wealth and power in the economy and in social and political structures will continue to manifest themselves in education as elsewhere.

What we have, then, has been predictable but modest advance. This is neither negligible nor unimportant, but it has not been a socially transformative phenomenon. It may be argued that, given the history and nature of Labourism, this is hardly surprising. This is a fair point: but the rhetorical claims of New Labour in its early years implied strongly that such changes would result from its policy agenda.

There are, in practical terms, arguably two main ways in which lifelong learning policy can be developed: through pressing for greater learner and local involvement, a reduction in bureaucratic complexity, and an advocacy of both the benefits and the centrality of broad, socially purposeful education; and through a re-engagement, largely outside the formal frameworks, with (often new) voluntary, social movements engaged with issues of social and political importance. In the end, lifelong learning is a dynamic social process not primarily because people want and need more skills training—through this is always an important element—but because they want to learn, socially and collectively, to enrich their lives and the lives of those around them. Hopefully, this will contribute to the creation of transformative social processes, and lifelong learning has potentially a role to play in this politics.

Acknowledgement

I am grateful to Janet Coles for her preliminary work on sources for this article.

Notes

1. Even this has to be qualified, however. As Jean Bocock and I have argued, education in the UK and Europe does not occupy the absolute policy centrality that it enjoys in the USA (Bocock & Taylor, 2003a).
2. O'Brien provides a useful taxonomy of terms associated with this twin track approach. Thus, 'economic progressivism' encompasses such terms as diversity, choice, efficiency, pressure/accountability, market, business values, league tables, and so on; whereas 'social progressivism' correspondingly refers to such terms as support, partnership, democratic choice, fairness, equality of opportunity, guidance, entitlement, democratic process and so on (O'Brien, 2000, Appendix 1, p. 11).
3. All this of course applies in differing degrees to all the more advanced economies of western Europe (see, for example, Osborne & Thomas (Eds), 2003).
4. This section draws on Fullick, 2004 and I acknowledge here the debt I owe to her excellent overview analysis of the whole, complex lifelong learning sector.
5. However, several commentators and academics based in parts of the UK other than England have argued that devolution has resulted in a more radical and desirable pattern of lifelong learning development in their 'devolved' context (for example, Paterson, 2003).
6. The formal titles of these committees were: the Dearing Report: National Committee of Inquiry into Higher Education, 1997; the Kennedy Report: Learning Works: Widening Participation in Further Education, 1997; the Fryer Reports: the National Advisory Group on Continuing Education and Lifelong Learning, 1998 and 1999 (the two Reports were entitled: Learning for the Twenty-first Century, and Creating Learning Cultures: next steps in achieving the Learning Age).
7. For a good overview summary of these and other bodies see Fullick, 2004, p. 24ff.
8. Numbers of students in UK higher education have risen from approximately 200,000 in the early 1960s to just under 2 million in 2002 (see Slowey & Watson (Eds), 2003).
9. There is much truth in the following exchange from the 1980s' BBC TV series, *'Yes, Prime Minister'*.

    Sir Humphrey (Cabinet Secretary): 'There really is a funding crisis in the universities, Prime Minister.'

    Prime Minister: 'What, *both* of them?'

Notes on contributor

Richard Taylor is Professor of Continuing Education and Lifelong Learning and Director of the Institute of Continuing Education at the University of Cambridge. He was, from 1991 to 2004, Professor of Continuing Education at the University of Leeds, where he was head of the School and, from 1999 to 2003, Dean of the Faculty of Business, Law, Education and Social Sciences. He has been secretary of the Universities Association for Continuing Education (UACE) and is currently chair of the National Institute of Adult Continuing Education (NIACE). His research interests are in the policy, politics and historical context of adult education, lifelong learning and higher education both in the

UK and worldwide. He is the author or co-author of numerous journal articles and 12 books, the most recent being (with David Watson) *Lifelong Learning and the University: a post Dearing agenda*; and (with Jean Barr and Tom Steele) *For a Radical Higher Education: after Postmodernism.*

References

Aldridge, F. & Tuckett, A. (2004) Business as usual? a report on adult participation in learning, *Adults Learning*, 15(9), 22–23.

Ball, M. & Hampton, W. (Eds) (2004) *Northern College: the first 25 years* (Leicester, NIACE).

Barnett, R. (1997) *Higher education – a critical business* (Buckingham, SRHE and Open University Press).

Barnett, R. (2000) *Realising the university in an age of super complexity* (Buckingham, SRHE and Open University Press).

Barnett, R. (2003) *Beyond all reason: living with ideology in the university* (Buckingham, SRHE and Open University Press).

Beer, S. (1959) *Modern British politics* (London, Allen and Unwin).

Bekhradnia, B. (2003) *Widening participation and fair access: an overview of the evidence* (Oxford, Higher Education Policy Institute).

Blair, T. (1998) cited in *The learning age: a renaissance for a new Britain* (London, HMSO).

Blair, T. (1999) Oxford Romanes Lecture, Oxford University, 2 December, cited in Rentoul, J. (2002) *Tony Blair: Prime Minister* (London, Time Warner), 507.

Blair, T. (2001) *Tony Blair's first keynote speech of the campaign, Sedgefield*, www.labour.org.uk.

Bocock, J. & Taylor, R. (2003a) The Labour Party and higher education: the nature of the relationship, *Higher Education Quarterly*, 57, 220–238.

Bocock, J. & Taylor, R. (2003b) The Labour Party and higher education: 1945–51, *Higher Education Quarterly*, 57, 249–265.

Boshier, R. (1998) Edgar Faure after 25 years: down but not out, in: J. Holford, P. Jarvis & C. Griffin (Eds) *International perspectives on lifelong learning* (London, Kogan Page), 3–20.

Boswell, T. MP (2004) in conversation with Richard Taylor, 1 April.

Byrne, B. (1999) *Social exclusion* (Buckingham, Open University Press).

Coates, D. (1974) *The Labour Party and the struggle for socialism* (Cambridge, Cambridge University Press).

Coates, D. (Ed.) (2003) *Paving the Third Way: the critique of parliamentary socialism, a 'socialist register' anthology* (London, Merlin Press).

Coffield, F. (1999a) Breaking the consensus: lifelong learning as social control. Inaugural Lecture, University of Newcastle.

Coffield, F. (1999b) Why is the beer always stronger up north? *Studies of Lifelong Learning in Europe* (London, Policy Press).

Coffield, F. (2000) *Differing visions of learning society*, Research Findings 2 (London, Policy Press).

Coffield, F. & Williamson, B. (Eds) (1997) *Repositioning higher education* (Buckingham, Open University Press).

Crowther, J., Martin, I. & Shaw, M. (2000) Turning the discourse, in: J. Thompson (Ed.) *Stretching the academy: the politics and practice of widening participation in higher education* (Leicester, NIACE), 171–185.

Delanty, G. (2001) *Challenging knowledge: the university in the knowledge society* (Buckingham, SRHE and Open University Press).

Department for Education and Employment (DfEE) (1998) *The learning age: a renaissance for a new Britain* (London, HMSO).

Field, J. (2000a) Governing the ungovernable: why lifelong learning policies promise so much yet deliver so little, *Educational Management and Administration*, 28, 249–261.

Field, J. (2000b) *Lifelong learning and the new educational order* (Stoke-on-Trent, Trentham Books).

Fieldhouse, R. (1977) *The WEA: aims and achievements* (Syracuse University Press, USA).

Fieldhouse, R. and associates (1996) *A history of modern British adult education* (Leicester, NIACE).

Fryer, B. (2004) The Northern College from Thatcherism to 'New Labour': a personal reminiscence, in: M. Ball and W. Hampton (Eds) *Northern College: the first 25 years* (Leicester, NIACE).

Fullick, L. (2004) *Adult learners in a brave new world: lifelong learning policy and structural changes since 1997*, a NIACE policy discussion paper (Leicester, NIACE).

Giddens, A. (1998) *The third way* (Cambridge, Polity Press).

Harrison, J.F.C. (1961) *Learning and living* (London, Routledge).

Higher Education Funding Council for England (HEFCE) (1998) *Widening participation in higher education: funding proposals*, paper 98/39 (Bristol, HEFCE).

Higher Education Funding Council for England (HEFCE) (1999a) *Widening participation: special funding programme 1998–99, outcome of bids*, Report paper 99/07 (Bristol, HEFCE).

Higher Education Funding Council for England (HEFCE) (1999b) *Widening participation in higher education: funding decisions*, Report Paper 99/24 (Bristol, HEFCE).

Higher Education Funding Council for England (HEFCE) (2000a) *Widening participation in higher education*, Report Paper 00/35 (Bristol, HEFCE).

Higher Education Funding Council for England (HEFCE) (2000b) *Foundation degree prospectus*, Paper 00/27 (Bristol, HEFCE).

Howell, D. (1976) *British social democracy* (Beckenham, Croom Helm).

Jennings, B. (2002) *Albert Mansbridge: the life and work of the founder of the WEA* (Leeds, Leeds Studies in Continuing Education).

Jepson, N. (1973) *The beginnings of university extension* (London, Michael Joseph).

Jowitt, T. (2003) in *Adults Learning: Skills Special*, 14, 6.

Keep, E. (1999) Employer attitudes towards adult learning, *Skills Task Force* research paper 15 (London, DfEE).

Labour Party Manifesto (1997) Labour Party, John Smith House, London.

McCaig, C. (2001) New Labour and 'Education, education, education', in: S. Ludlam & M. J. Smith (Eds) *New Labour in government* (London, Macmillan), 184–201.

McKibbin, R. (1974) *Evolution of the Labour Party 1910–1924* (Oxford, Oxford University Press).

McNair, S. (2003) Analysis, *Adults Learning: Skills Special*, 14, 10.

Miliband, R. (1972) *Parliamentary socialism* (second, revised edition) (London, Merlin Press).

Nairn, T. (1965) The nature of the Labour Party, in: P. Anderson & R. Blackburn (Eds) *Towards socialism* (London, Fontana and New Left Books).

Newman, M. (2002) *Ralph Miliband and the politics of the new left* (London, Merlin Press).

National Institute for Adult Continuing Education (NIACE) (2004) *Learning and training at work surveys* (Leicester, NIACE).

O'Brien, S. (2000) New Labour, new approach: exploring tensions within educational policy and practice, *Education and Social Justice*, 2(1), 18–27.

Osborne, M. (2003) University continuing education in the UK, in: M. Osborne & E. Thomas (Eds) *Lifelong learning in a changing continent* (Leicester, NIACE), 463–485.

Osborne, M. & Thomas, E. (Eds) (2003) *Lifelong learning in a changing continent* (Leicester, NIACE).

Paterson, L. (2003) The three educational ideologies of the British Labour Party 1997–2001, *Oxford Review of Education*, 29, 165–186.

Payne, J. (2000) The contribution of individual learning accounts to the lifelong learning policies of United Kingdom government: a case-study, *Studies in the Education of Adults*, 32(2), October.

Pelling, H. (1965) *Short history of the Labour Party* (Oxford, Oxford University Press).

Power, S. & Whitty, G. (1999) New Labour's education policy: first, second or third way? *Journal of Education Policy*, 14, 535–546.

Rawnsley, A. (2000) *Servants of the people: the inside story of New Labour* (London, Hamish Hamilton). Paperback edn. (2001) (London, Penguin Books).

Readings, B. (1996) *The university in ruins* (Harvard, Harvard University Press).

Rees, G. & Fevre, R. *et al.* (1997) History, place and the learning society: towards a sociology of lifetime learning, *Journal of Educational Policy*, 12, 485–498.

Rentoul, J. (2002, paperback edn.) *Tony Blair: Prime Minister* (London, Little, Brown).

Saville, J. (1993) Introduction, in: J. Fryth (Ed.) *Labour's High Noon: the government and the economy 1945–51* (London, Lawrence & Wishart).

Schuetze, H. & Slowey, M. (Eds) (2000) *Higher education and lifelong learners: international perspectives on change* (London, RoutledgeFalmer).

Scott, P. (1995) *The meanings of mass higher education* (Buckingham, SRHE and Open University Press).

Selwyn, N. & Gorard, S. (2002) Exploring the 'new' moral and technological imperatives of lifelong learning, paper presented at the Cardiff conference *Demoralisation: Morality, Authority and Power,* Cardiff University.

Slowey, M. & Watson, D. (Eds) (2003) *Higher education and the lifecourse* (Buckingham, SRHE and Open University Press).

Spilsburg, D. (2004) *The learning at work surveys* (London, IFF Research Ltd).

Taylor, R. (2000) Concepts of self-directed learning in higher education: re-establishing the democratic tradition, in: J. Thompson (Ed.) *Stretching the academy: the policies and practice of widening participation in higher education* (Leicester, NIACE).

Taylor, R. (2004) Creating Northern College, in: M. Ball & W. Hampton (Eds) *Northern College: the first 25 years* (Leicester, NIACE).

Taylor, R. (2004/5) Widening participation in British higher education: underlying agendas, *Studies in the Education of Adults* (forthcoming autumn 2004/spring 2005).

Taylor, R., Barr, J. and Steele, T. (2002) *For a radical higher education: after postmodernism* (Buckingham, SRHE and Open University Press).

Tuckett, A. (2000) You've got to admit it's getting better, it's getting better all the time: lifelong learning and widening participation, *Times Educational Supplement.*

Tuckett, A. (2000, 10 May) Why don't employers pay their way? *Guardian.*

Tuckett, A. (2003a) Commentary, *Adults Learning* Skills Special, 14(11), 6.

Tuckett, A. (2003b) Making it different—voluntary movements, democratic diversity and adult learning, *Albert Mansbridge Memorial Lecture* (Leeds, University of Leeds).

Wallis, J. (Ed.) (1996) *Liberal adult education: the end of an era?* (Nottingham, University of Nottingham Continuing Education Press).

Warde, A. (1982) *Consensus and beyond: the development of the Labour Party strategy since the Second World War* (Manchester, Manchester University Press).

Watson, D. & Taylor, R. (1998) *Lifelong learning and the university: a post-Dearing agenda* (Brighton, Falmer).

New Labour and teacher education: the end of an era

John Furlong

Introduction

> I have always said that education is this government's top priority. The teaching profession is critical to our mission ... this Green Paper sets out the governments' proposals to improve the teaching profession ... [It represents] the most fundamental reform of the teaching profession since state education began. (Tony Blair in DfEE, 1998, p. 5)

The Green Paper Tony Blair was referring to, *Teachers: meeting the challenge of change* (DfEE, 1998), was issued by the first New Labour Government just one year after they came to office. It has remained *the* key policy document on the teaching profession throughout both periods of office and, as the Government moves towards the next general election, it is still central to their thinking with many of its principles incorporated in future policy plans (DfES, 2004). In the Green Paper, the Government set out their vision for the modernisation of the teaching force with the development of what they called a 'new professionalism'.

> The time has long gone when isolated, unaccountable professionals made curriculum and pedagogical decisions alone without reference to the outside world. Teachers in a modern teaching profession need:
>
> - To have high expectations of themselves and of all pupils;
> - To accept accountability;
> - To take personal and collective responsibility for improving their skills and subject knowledge;
> - To seek to base decisions on evidence of what works in schools in this country and internationally;
> - To work in partnership with other staff in schools;
> - To welcome the contribution that parents, business and others outside schools can make to its success; and
> - To anticipate change and promote innovation.
>
> (DfEE, 1998, para. 13)

As I will argue in this paper, this 'new professionalism' marks the final completion of a 30 year shift from the 'individualised professionalism' of the past to new forms of 'managed' and 'networked' professionalism. For New Labour, the aim has been to establish forms of professionalism that accept that decisions, about what to teach and how to teach and how to assess children, are made at school and national level rather than by individual teachers themselves. This in turn, I will argue, has had major implications for teacher education. Re-modelling professionalism remains a key objective, but the move away from a concern with individual professional formation means that teacher education is now no longer seen as an important site for achieving that objective. After many years of being at the heart of national policy, teacher education, and particularly initial teacher education, is, in policy terms, being returned to the back waters. In this sense, it is the end of an era.

Re-forming teacher professionalism—a Conservative agenda

Over the last 30 years, the nature of teacher professionalism, what it means to be a teacher, has been a central area of concern for successive governments. During the 1970s, the prevailing image of teacher professionalism was of teachers possessing a high degree of autonomy justified by their expertise. It was widely accepted that their role included the freedom to decide not only how to teach but also what to teach and assess pupils on, and that they had a particular responsibility for curriculum development and innovation. It was this autonomy that was fundamentally challenged by Prime Minister James Callaghan when he initiated 'the great debate' on education, in 1976 (Callaghan, 1976). Although he did not actually mention the term, Callaghan's focus was on the nature of teachers' professionalism and particularly their individual and collective autonomy.

> I take it that no one claims exclusive rights in this field. Public interest is strong and legitimate *and will be satisfied.* (Callaghan, 1976, p. 332, emphasis added)

A great deal has happened in education over the intervening years but, interestingly, Callahan's concern with the nature of teacher professionalism has remained a constant for governments whatever their political hue. New Labour's Green Paper and its aspirations for a 'new professionalism' were therefore only the last in a long line of attempts to challenge, change and to refocus the nature of teaching as a profession.

Another constant, at least throughout the Conservative years (1979–1997), was that teacher education, and particularly initial teacher education, was seen as a key instrument for altering the nature of teacher professionalism. As I myself wrote in 2001, reflecting on the 25 years since Callaghan's intervention:

> It may be a false assumption but it nevertheless has been assumed that one way of changing the nature of teacher professionalism is to change the structure and content of initial teacher education. As a result, the period has seen initial teacher education and training move from being a relative backwater in terms of educational policy to a position of key strategic significance. (Furlong, 2001, p. 118)

As has been well documented elsewhere (Adams & Tulasiewicz, 1995; Wilkin, 1996; Furlong *et al.*, 2000; Mahony & Hextall, 2000; Whitty, 2002), the Conservative years saw government intervention in initial teacher education on an unprecedented scale. And as most commentators agree, the fundamental aim of the reforms that were instituted was to reconstruct the nature of teacher professionalism. Those in higher education, with their focus of theory and critique, were seen as associated with more traditional forms of professionalism prioritising individual knowledge, autonomy and responsibility (Hoyle & John, 1995). What was needed, therefore, was to wrest control of the system from higher education and to develop a more practically based form of preparation with an emphasis on training rather than education.

As in all areas of the public sector, in order to achieve reform, a new style of managerialism was introduced (Hood, 1991; Hughes, 2003), led jointly by a reformed inspectorate (Ofsted) and the newly established Teacher Training Agency (TTA). Ofsted was charged with the inspection of teacher education using ever more detailed lists of criteria and the TTA was charged with managing the system and linking funding to publicly available performance data. In addition, in order to increase market competition, the TTA was required to promote school-centred initial teacher training schemes (SCITTs) where consortia of schools themselves became providers of courses with no necessary involvement of higher education. During the early and mid-1990s, the work of the TTA and Ofsted was consistently confrontational with those in higher education, and by the end of their period in office, Conservative administrations had developed a system of initial teacher education that was highly centralised and highly responsive to government policy initiatives. As Furlong *et al.* (2000) demonstrated through their national surveys of change in English initial teacher education during the 1990s, despite the resistance of those in higher education, by the end of the period, the majority of teacher education in England had indeed become a largely school-based affair, with an emphasis on the achievement of practically based competences or 'standards'. In the course of just 15 years, the system had been moved from one of diversity and autonomy to a 'command economy' with unanimity and central control (Furlong, 2001). Similar, though less extreme moves took place within continuing professional development (CPD). The agenda for CPD courses was increasingly centrally defined and focused on short-term practical training. Those teachers who wished to undertake more sustained, academically based study through, for example, a Masters degree, increasingly had to fund their professional development themselves.

But why was teacher professionalism of such significance for the Conservatives, why did it become such a battleground and what relevance did that have for New Labour who followed them? To answer such questions, we need to place their policies on teacher education in a broader context.

The Conservative reforms of the 1980s and 1990s were based on both neo-liberal and neo-conservative principles. The key to improving standards in schools (and indeed teacher education itself), it was argued, was the creation of quasi-markets (Le Grand & Bartlet, 1993). Quasi-markets would be, at one and the same time, more 'democratic' and lead to improved quality (Whitty *et al.*, 1993; Power *et al.*, 1994; Gewirtz *et al.*, 1995; Halsey *et al.*, 1997; Lauder *et al.*, 1999). In addition, neo-conservative elements within the party were insistent on a return to traditional values in education, arguing that the primary purpose of schooling was to induct young people into an established cultural heritage as embodied in traditional school subjects taught in traditional ways (Hillgate Group, 1989).

However, successive Conservative administrations believed that teachers, and the 'liberal establishment' that supported them, were hostile to market principles and to traditional forms of teaching. Teachers were portrayed as wedded to outmoded, left-wing, collectivitist ideologies and to the principle of individual professional autonomy: the teacher's right to choose (Hillgate Group, 1989). Most important of all, teachers believed in 'progressive' educational ideas where knowing 'how to teach' was seen as more important than being an expert in 'what to teach'—in subject knowledge (Lawlor, 1990). And the source of these ills that were infecting successive generations of teachers was teacher education and training. More than any other group in the now vilified 'educational establishment', university and college departments of education were singled out as being the most pernicious in their influence (O'Hear, 1988). If a generation of teachers was to be raised who would support the new Conservative world, then the reform of teacher education and training was of paramount importance.

But what is interesting, and perhaps clearer in retrospect than at the time, is the continued importance given in this vision to the contribution of individual teachers. Conservative educational policy certainly fore-grounded the importance of markets, but individual teachers remained key players: it was individual teachers who operated the new markets; it was individual teachers who needed to be experts in the subjects defined by the National Curriculum; and, crucially, it was individual teachers who still decided *how* to teach. Rather than being de-professionalised by the Conservative reforms as some have argued (Ozga, 1995), I would agree with McCulloch (2001) that the policies aimed at a 're-professionalisation'. This was necessary because the individual teacher was still inscribed as an essential actor within the system: he or she had to be competent and confident in their specialist subject knowledge but sensitive to the demands of the market, particularly as it was mediated through parental choice.

The re-formation of teacher professionalism at the level of the individual was therefore essential in the achievement of the Conservative vision.

What is significantly different with the coming of New Labour has been the progressive moving away from this concern with teachers as individuals. As I will argue below, increasingly the site for reform has shifted from individuals to the state and, to a lesser degree, to schools. The state has taken a much more assertive role in defining how to teach as well as what to teach; the result has been the establishment of what I would term a more 'managed' professionalism. And schools have become the focus of what can be characterised as 'networked markets' (Reid *et al.*, 2004) with new opportunities for a minority of senior teachers for forms of 'extended professionalism' (Hoyle, 1974). This in turn has led to a downgrading of the significance of teacher education as a key site for policy intervention. But before we look at New Labour's teacher education policy in detail, we need to understand something of their broader educational project and the role of teacher professionalism within it.

Enter New Labour

There has been a considerable debate within the educational literature as to whether or not New Labour's 'third way' policies represent a continuation or even an extension of what the Conservatives began (Demaine, 1999; Power & Whitty, 1999; Docking, 2000; Mahony & Hextall, 2000; Gewirtz, 2002). The reason that there has been such debate, I would suggest, is because there has been both continuity and change. From the beginning, there was a new vision, or at the very least a new rhetoric, but to a significant degree that was assembled by building on much that the Conservatives had achieved. As Newman (2001) states:

> The third way attempted to forge a new political settlement by drawing selectively on fragments and components of the old, and reconfiguring these through the prisms of a modernized economy, a modern public service and modern people. (p. 46)

Modernisation, as Newman stresses, has been *the* core concept for New Labour; it is seen as essential because of the massive changes overtaking society.

> Modernization is situated in a number of structural forces—globalization, competition, and meritocracy—that are collapsed into a single unifying theme. Globalization occupies a special place at the core of these series of narratives that construct an imperative to change. (Newman, 2001, p. 48)

Giddens (2000) makes a similar point when he states that the primary purpose of 'third way' politics is to restructure social democratic doctrines 'to respond to the twin revolutions of globalisation and the knowledge economy' (p. 162).

And in that modernisation project, education has been seen as of crucial significance and has remained so throughout both periods of office (DfES, 1997; DfEE, 2001; DfES, 2004). Raising educational standards has been one of the government's key priorities because at one and the same time education is seen as being able to create economic growth in the flexible, knowledge-based economies of the twenty-first century, and to promote social inclusion by creating pathways out of poverty. As the

Government stated in their Green Paper issued shortly before they began their second term in office:

> Education ... is seen not only as key to developing equality of opportunity, but also to enabling the nation to prepare for the emergence of the new economy and its increased demands for skills and human capital. (DfEE, 2001, paras 1.1–4)

But how is that modernisation to be achieved? New Labour's approach to public service reform has had many points of continuity with the previous Conservative regimes. In particular, there has been a continued focus on market mechanisms and the forms of new managerialism associated with them. The neo-liberal critique of the public sector has been accepted as largely correct and there has been a new 'realism' about the necessity of markets; in the words of Giddens (2000) 'There is no known alternative to the market economy any longer' (p. 164). Labour has therefore retained an emphasis on competition as a lever both for ensuring greater efficiency and quality in the delivery of services and as a means of securing innovation. It has also continued with the forms of new managerialism developed under the Conservatives that are necessary for the maintenance of such markets, though new managerialism is now presented as an entirely natural, rational and common sense response to inevitable forces beyond the control of any individual state (Newman, 2001; Hughes, 2003). As a consequence, New Labour has reinforced many of the core principles of previous Conservative government market-based reforms in education including:

> per capita funding for schools; the devolution of school budgets; differentiation between types of schools; promotion of selection in some areas; use of school performance league tables; setting of narrowly defined attainment targets, and the instruments of school inspection. (Reid *et al.*, 2004 p. 253)

At the same time, however, there has also been a recognition that markets alone cannot achieve all that is necessary. Again, as Giddens states, 'Modernizing social democrats are not believers in laissez-faire. There has to be a newly defined role for an active state, which must continue to pursue social programmes' (Giddens, 2000, p. 7).

This notion of an 'active state', intervening in market mechanisms to ensure that they deliver the modernising agenda, has been profoundly important for New Labour and has taken two distinctly different forms; these in turn have had quite contradictory implications for the nature of teacher professionalism.

On the one hand there has been the promotion of collaborative networks and partnerships between schools and between other 'partners' (businesses, community groups, statutory and non statutory services), in order to raise standards. This, Reid *et al.* (2004) characterise as the development of a 'networked market'; market competition retains its core position but is overlaid with incentives to encourage the most successful schools to work collaboratively with their less successful neighbours to improve their performance in relation to national targets. For this strategy, the emphasis is very much at the school level and a wide range of initiatives has been based on this principle. The most notable are Education Action Zones (EAZs), Sure Start, Beacon schools, and the Networked Learning Community initiative supported through the National College for School Leadership (NCSL). All of these initiatives take the school as the basic unit for locally based policy intervention and are based on an explicit networked market philosophy. As we will see below, these initiatives have implications for an extended notion of professionality (Hoyle, 1974), matched by appropriately extended notions of teacher education, especially in terms of CPD.

However, although such a strategy has been rhetorically extremely important for New Labour in claiming to modify some of the negative impacts of markets, in reality it has only been the minor strand in the management of the teaching profession; the opportunities for an extended professionalism offered by local networking are, by definition, limited to a minority of schools and a minority of (usually senior) teachers within them. For the majority of teachers, far more significant in the management of their day-to-day lives has been a very different sort of market intervention: intervention by the government in the detailed processes of teaching and learning itself.

In an attempt to ensure that schools improve, the Government developed what they called their 'high challenge, high support' strategy (DfEE, 2001). First, they set ambitious targets.

> Our education system will never be world class unless virtually all children learn to read, write and calculate to high standards before they leave primary school. We have therefore given top priority to a national strategy to achieve this goal, setting ambitious national targets for 2002: that in English 80 per cent and in mathematics 75 per cent of 11 year olds should meet the standards set for their age. These targets are staging posts on the way to even higher levels of performance. (DfEE, 2001, 1.15–16)

They then devised prescriptive strategies that involved intervening in the detailed processes of how to teach, based on evidence of 'what works'. In their first term of office they did so with the development of their primary literacy and numeracy strategies, and in the second term of office by the extension of this approach to the Key Stage 3 strategy. As the current DfES website demonstrates, there is now a huge enthusiasm on the part of the Government to intervene in the detail of educational processes with advice on all aspects of teaching and the day-to-day running of schools (there are, for example, over 2000 model lesson plans that can be downloaded, an intervention that would have been unthinkable a generation ago). And all of these moves have been accompanied by a new enthusiasm for large-scale, publicly funded research that will 'tell us (government) what works and why and what types of policy initiatives are likely to be most effective' (Blunkett, 2000, para. 63). As Andrews (1998) states:

> New Labour shares with new managerialism the obsession with achieving outcomes at the micro level, on the principle of 'what matters is what works' where 'delivery, delivery, delivery' is the name of the game. (p. 18)

These two strategies of a networked local market, where schools as institutions become a key vehicle for localised policy intervention, and increased government involvement in the processes of teaching and learning itself, mark, I would argue, a final and fundamental shift away from a concern with individual professionalism. The ball that was set rolling 30 years ago by Callaghan in his Ruskin speech has indeed run its course. In terms of official policy at least, individual teachers are no longer seen as key actors in the educational process and therefore the nature of individual professionalism is no longer a key policy priority. What have been the implications of this shift for policy on teacher education?

New Labour and initial teacher education

As I have already indicated, by the end of their period in office, Conservative administrations, through the work of the TTA and Ofsted, had developed a system of initial teacher education that was highly centralised and highly responsive to policy change. What the government and particularly the TTA had wanted in initial teacher education was a common system with common standards and procedures, no matter where or by whom the training was provided; by the end of the 1990s they had largely achieved it. It is important to recognise that, in terms of governance, the instincts of the Conservative and Labour governments have been identical. Throughout their period of office, New Labour have insisted on the maintenance of a competitive market in teacher education; as a result, they have continued to encourage competition with higher education, the main 'provider'. SCITT schemes (School Centred Initial Teacher Training led and managed by schools themselves) have continued to be encouraged, despite their overwhelmingly low ratings by Ofsted, and 'new routes' into teaching have been developed with the Graduate Teacher Programme (GTP) (an employment-based route, theoretically for older entrants), 'Teach First' (another employment-based route for 'high flying' new graduates wishing to experience teaching for a year or two), and the 'flexible PGCE' (a teacher education programme that can be taken on a flexible, part-time basis). Inspection and the publication of results also remain core parts of the management strategy. Following Giddens' line of argument that 'there is no alternative to markets', markets have been maintained as the first, and unchallengeable principle of management of the sector. However, by the end of the 1990s, when a command economy had been achieved, an additional policy agenda was also possible: intervention in the content of training itself.

Until 1996, the content of training had been only broadly prescribed. During the middle 1990s in particular, the most important influence on the content of training was 'the market' to which students were increasingly exposed, i.e. practice in schools. In sharp contrast, policies in the late 1990s sought to exploit the new control of the system to begin specifying the content of professional education in much more detail. Two strategies evolved. The first was the issuing of a new circular, Circular 10/97 (DfEE, 1997), which transformed the previously specified 'competencies' into more elaborate 'standards'. The second was the development of an 85 page National Curriculum for initial teacher education, specifying in very great detail the content that had to be covered by trainee teachers in English, mathematics, science, and information and communication technology (ICT). The English curriculum in particular was controversial with its insistence on whole class teaching and the detailed coverage of the teaching of reading through phonics. Both of these initiatives were begun well over a year before the 1997 general election but were carried through by the New Labour government with little change to the original plans. The transition was seamless and those in higher education who had anticipated that a change of administration would lead to a reduction in government control were disappointed. Indeed, the aspiration of the TTA at the time was that this would become the first step in defining the nature of teaching for *all* teachers. As Anthea Millett (Millett, 1997), then chief executive of the TTA, wrote in her covering letter introducing the new curriculum:

> The benefits of the standards and curricula extend beyond initial teacher training. I have no doubt that the new standards for the award of QTS will come to be seen as a landmark for serving teachers in making clear the expectations of them in this most demanding yet rewarding of professions.

And the Labour minister responsible, Estelle Morris, endorsed this view, explicitly recognising the link between such initiatives and her new Government's wider agenda within education. As she wrote in a letter to the TTA only six weeks after the election (Morris, 1997):

> Raising the standards we expect of new teachers in this way is clearly essential to delivering the government's commitment to raising pupil performance across the education system and in particular to delivering the major new literacy and numeracy targets.

In reality, the National Curriculum for initial teacher education, with its controversial specification of how to teach core subjects, was short lived. In retrospect, it now appears to represent the high point of previous neo-conservative thinking—using initial teacher education as a key vehicle in the bid to re-establish traditional methods of teaching. After five years in office, the Labour government issued new documentation (DfES/TTA, 2002) that abandoned the National Curriculum for teacher education, perhaps recognising that if teaching in general was to change, then more direct strategies of intervention were needed. This, I would suggest, was an important turning point and marked the beginning of the move away from seeing initial teacher education in itself as the main strategy for changing teacher professionalism. Instead of a National Curriculum for initial teacher education, the Government returned to a more general list of 'standards', covering three major areas, all relatively briefly (13 pages). These were: professional values and practice; knowledge and understanding; and teaching (planning, expectations and targets; monitoring and assessment; teaching and class management). However, the non-statutory 'hand book of guidance' that was also issued to give advice on how these standards might be achieved currently runs to 59 pages and is regularly updated. This 'non-statutory guidance' remains a key document in Ofsted inspections that have continued to be a major part of the machinery of the management of the system. As I indicated above, the maintenance of 'the market' remains the bedrock of public management.

Yet it is important to recognise that the twin strategies of defining 'standards' and the insistence on a range of different 'providers' has done more than maintain a market; together, they have also ensured that teacher education has now become narrowly functional; an entirely 'technical rationalist' enterprise. Technical rationality in education, as I have argued before (Furlong, 1991), creates the impression of disinterestedness and objectivity. It implies that there is a common framework for people, with fixed goals. In the words of Popkewitz (1987) it 'flattens reality and obscures the struggles which fashion and shape our world' (p. 12). One of the things that has been 'flattened' is the complexity involved in professional education; the current, school-based system is now widely accepted as largely unproblematic. Also flattened is any idea that higher education and schools might have different perspectives and different forms of knowledge to contribute to teacher education. Such a view has in the past been vehemently championed by those in higher education who see the need for student teachers to gain access to different forms of professional knowledge, some of which may be accessed through higher education and others through direct practical experience in schools (McIntyre, 1993; Furlong & Maynard, 1995). However, rather than recognising and encouraging partnership between 'complementary' contributors to professional learning, New Labour policies have insisted that all 'providers', whether schools, universities or now private consortia, are identical. All are capable of 'delivering' an effective 'training' in the technical list of standards that trainee teachers need to meet.

The acceptance by the TTA and, indeed, by the majority of 'providers', that the current system of school-based teacher education is unproblematic, that getting it 'right' is a technical matter (ensuring, for example, that there are the right number of school places for training, that teachers have the time they need for mentoring), this acceptance has allowed a considerable change in style on the part of the TTA. A new chief executive, Ralph Tabberer, appointed in 2000, was able to distance himself from the confrontations of the past and to develop a more consultative style. As he said recently 'it was very much about working with people, not picking a fight' (*Guardian*, 2004, p. 4).

Under Tabberer, the TTA today is the very model of 'third way' public management. It is consultative, though, following consultation, directives are issued that are binding and used as the basis for competitive assessment; and it has now developed a new interest in research and the development of evidence-informed practice. In initial teacher education it has also developed its own version of a networked market. At school level, there are designated 'Training Schools' and 'Partnership Promotion Schools' with additional funding for senior staff to network with other schools; as a result, these initiatives are providing opportunities for a small but élite group of teachers to develop new forms of professionalism as specialist, school-based trainers. And from 2001–2005, for 'providers' (universities, SCITT schemes, GTP schemes) there was the National Partnership Project, which gave project-based funding for groups of providers to work collaboratively on projects on a regional basis with a view both to increasing the capacity of schools to take students and to improving quality by sharing expertise across the system. Providers remained competitors, subject to Ofsted inspection, and in competition for the allocation of student numbers, but they were also being encouraged to network together so that quality overall was improved.

New Labour and Continuing Professional Development

If New Labour policy in initial teacher education has increasingly spoken to the managerialist tendencies of the government, then CPD policy, at least in its early years, spoke of something different. What the 1998 Green Paper argued for was the need to balance different sorts of training needs. There should be a balance between responding to:

> *National* training priorities focused on particular needs, which have been identified nationally, e.g. literacy, numeracy, ICT, headship training, special educational needs;
>
> *School* priorities emerging from school development planning to help schools reach their own targets and implement their post Ofsted action plans; and
>
> *Individual* development needs of teachers identified through annual appraisal. (para. 123)

The national needs were predictable enough and involved substantial support in the first term of office for the primary literacy and numeracy strategies and in the second term of office for the Key Stage Three strategy. Another major national initiative was the use of Lottery funding to support ICT training via the 'New Opportunities Fund'. Such initiatives were no different in character from those provided under previous Conservative regimes; most of the training offered was short term, highly practical and focused almost entirely on helping teachers meet government targets that it had set itself. As the 2001 Green Paper proudly claimed:

> Last year alone, for example, all 18,000 primary head teachers received a day's training on literacy, 38,000 teachers received additional phonics training, 25,000 teachers were trained in how to teach writing and 6,000 primary schools received intensive support in the teaching of numeracy. (DfEE, 2001, para. 5.27)

However the suggestion in the Green Paper that CPD policy should also pay attention to individually defined learning needs was of a profoundly different character. The Green Paper talked of opportunities for research, for sabbaticals, and for international exchange with up to 5,000 teachers a year having the opportunity for internationally based professional development of some sort.

> As in other professions, we believe that experienced and excellent teachers should have opportunities to undertake development or research work to extend and enhance their performance. We need to review the existing opportunities for study leave, sabbaticals and teacher researchers as a basis for establishing from 2000 a new national programme of scholarships to be open to teachers at all levels in the new professional structure with outcomes disseminated widely. (DfEE, 1998, para. 134)

This aspiration spoke to the more liberal interpretation of the much-heralded 'new professionalism'. Certainly, if teachers were now to take 'personal and collective responsibility for improving their skills and subject knowledge'; if they were to seek to 'base decisions on evidence of what works in schools in this country and internationally'; if they were to 'anticipate change and promote innovation', and if they were to help other schools and teachers improve by participating in a 'networked market', then it is clear that they would need a very different sort of CPD from that which had been made available under the Conservatives; one that developed their individual professionalism as well as their ability to work collectively.

However, despite the heady aspirations of early days in office, and in growing contrast to Wales and especially Scotland with the development of the Chartered

Teacher Scheme (http://www.ctprogrammescotland.org.uk/), much of this promise was unrealised. Sabbaticals and international exchanges were developed in only a very limited way and research scholarships (the Best Practice Research Scholarship scheme, BPRS) after providing opportunities for 1,000 teachers a year for three years were ended in the face of a crisis in educational funding in 2003–2004. The truth was that, vitally important as these initiatives were to the teachers that took part in them (Furlong & Salisbury, 2005), they were always only designed for a small minority. And even more importantly, the investment in individual teachers' professional development did not sit well with the Government's strongly managerialist tendencies. As Reid *et al.* 2004 have commented:

> Teacher training formats have not developed along the road of customisation, but rather have remained standardized upon the model of teacher as curriculum deliverer. Similarly, CPD opportunities have been closely tied to government strategies. The focus has not been on equipping teachers with the skills to engage in professional self-development, to develop evidence-based practice, to run educational teams, to innovate or facilitate, but rather to prepare a generation of teachers as technicians or deliverers of set strategies. (p. 263)

In 2004, the DfES gave up the struggle of trying to reform the large and unwieldy CPD system and passed responsibility for it to the TTA; how they respond to that challenge will not be apparent until after the next general election.

Conclusion

There is, therefore, I would suggest, substantial evidence to support the claim that during their two terms of office New Labour forged a policy on teacher education that was distinctively different from the Conservative administrations that preceded them. Like the Conservatives, they have seen the maintenance of a competitive market as essential for the governance of the system. But beyond that, they have significantly moved away from a concern with individual professional formation. This is evidenced in their turning away from a concern with the content and structure of initial teacher education as a key site for intervention; it is also evidenced in their record on CPD, where the early rhetoric has been largely unrealised.

As I have argued, individual professional formation is seen as far less critical than it was, especially at the level of initial training. In the lives of young teachers, the state now provides far greater guidance than ever before in the definition of effective teaching, learning and assessment in both primary and secondary schools. And at more senior levels, opportunities for extended professional development are increasingly focused on and achieved through the school as an institution. And such developments provide a new twist in the long-standing arguments about the 'de-professionalisation' or 're-professionalisation' of teachers since the Thatcher revolution that I referred to above (Ozga, 1995; McCulloch, 2001). For new teachers, their professionalism is increasingly externally defined; it is a form of 'managed' professionalism. And for those senior teachers willing to take on roles in the new networks that are being established around schools, there are real opportunities for extended professionalism. But whereas in the past, extended professionalism was achieved at the individual level (by, for example, taking a Masters' course), today those opportunities are nearly all played out within the institutional context of the school.

But if individual professional formation has not been the Government's main priority in managing the teaching force, what has? Here we must return to their own targets, which they set themselves in relation to the teaching profession: reducing teachers' administrative workloads, developing the role of teaching assistants to support curriculum delivery, and introducing new pay and performance management systems. These policies, termed 'workforce remodelling', have all been major preoccupations. And in the field of teacher education, rather than worrying about the content of training, they have been primarily concerned to ensure that there are enough qualified teachers to meet the ambitious targets they set themselves for staff–student ratios, particularly in primary schools. As a result, supply has been a major preoccupation and numbers have indeed increased substantially over both terms of office, with some 25,000 additional teachers in post now compared with five years ago. In order to achieve this, recruitment to initial teacher education has risen dramatically by 50% to over 40,000 a year (Clarke, 2004). This has in turn put significant strain on the system, especially in terms of ensuring that there are sufficient schools willing to participate in the training of these new numbers (hence the TTA's ongoing concern with school capacity). It has also led to the introduction of a whole range of new financial incentives for trainees (bursaries, 'golden hellos') and the pursuit of new routes into teaching. The Graduate Teacher Programme scheme in particular has expanded rapidly with now some 6,000 places available for this work-based training route.

In the run up to the next general election, a number of those close to the government (Bentley, 2003; Hargreaves, 2003) have pointed to the urgent need, if the profession is to meet the challenge of modernisation, for the government to move away from its 'command economy' approach to managing the teaching profession; it needs, once again, to invest in teachers' personal professional learning if they are individually and collectively going to respond to the challenges of teaching in a rapidly changing world.

However, recently, the Labour Government have set out their vision for the future of education over the next five years, assuming they are returned to office (DfES, 2004). And rather than respond to this plea, what the five-year strategic plan does is to confirm the moves we have already seen. Initial teacher education is displaced as a prime site for intervention; the only references to it concern issues of supply with the promise of a substantial increase in the Graduate Teacher Programme. Far more significant is the promised extension of workforce re-modelling 'to bring in a yet wider range of adults, working in and beyond the classroom' (para. 35). Both of these initiatives will further confirm schools as *the* key site for professional formation, though as always working within tightly prescribed national standards.

We are also promised significant changes in CPD with both a school-led and government-led dimension. At school level, a greater emphasis on 'classroom observation, practice, training, coaching and mentoring' (para. 35) is proposed. Appraisals are to become 'teaching and learning reviews' with personal professional development matched to these, school identified, needs. And teachers will be expected to offer coaching and mentoring to other teachers where they have the teaching and subject skills from which other teachers can benefit. At the same time, a re-branded Teacher Training Agency (now to be called the Training and Development Agency for Schools) will have a critical role in setting national benchmarks and 'encouraging' schools to work in appropriate ways.

A New Labour third term would therefore consolidate the changes that we have seen. What they believe they have confirmed in their first two terms of office is that real change in teacher professionalism is unlikely to be achieved by changing teacher education alone. Indeed, the five-year strategic plan (DfES, 2004) seems to write teacher education out almost entirely as a policy concern. New policies seem to shift the centre of gravity even further away from education and training, to targets, to teaching and assessment guidelines, and to support for ever more elaborate forms of networking. And while those in higher education may breathe a sigh of relief that they are no longer the object of what, from their point of view, felt like unwanted attention or even obsession, such complacency would be misplaced. This move away from seeing teacher education as a key concern in policy development means that the Government have won in their struggle to reduce teacher education to an unproblem- atic, technical rationalist, procedure. Being at the heart of Government policy over the last 30 years may have been uncomfortable for many of us, but at least there was an arena in which to engage. In this sense, the end of the era is to be regretted.

Notes on contributor

John Furlong is Professor of education at the University of Oxford and is Director of the Oxford University Department of Educational Studies. From 2003–5 he was also President of the British Educational Research Association.

References

Adams, A. & Tulasiewicz, W. (1995) *The crisis in teacher education: a European concern?* (London, Falmer Press).

Andrews, G. (1998) Shifting to the Bright; in search of the intellectual left, in: A. Coddington & M. Perryman (Eds) *The Modernizers' dilemma: radical politics in the age of Blair* (London, Lawrence & Wishart).

Bentley, T. (2003) Introduction, in: D. Hargreaves *Education epidemic: transforming secondary schools through innovation networks* (London, Demos).

Blunkett, D. (2000) *Influence or irrelevance: can social science improve government?* (London, Department for Education and Employment), reprinted in *Research Intelligence*, 71, March 2000, 12–21).

Callaghan, J. (1976) *Towards a national debate*. Reprinted in *Education*, 22 October, 332–333.

Clarke, C. (2004) *Speech at the launch of the TTA Corporate Plan Launch*, 29 March.

Demaine, J. (1999) *Education, policy and contemporary politics* (London, Macmillan).

DfEE (1997) *Teaching: high status, high standards* (Circular 10/97) (London, DfEE).

DfEE (1998) *Teachers: meeting the challenge of change*. Green Paper (London, DfEE).

DfEE (2001) *Schools: building on success*. Green Paper (London, DfEE).

DfES (2004) *Five year strategy for children and learners* (London, DfES).

DfES/TTA (2002) *Qualifying to teach (professional standards for qualified teacher status and require-ments for initial teacher training)* (London, DfES/TTA).

Docking, J. (2000) *New Labour's policies for schools: raising the standard?* (London, David Fulton).

Furlong, J. (1991) Reconstructing professionalism: ideological struggle in initial teacher education, in: M. Arnot & L. Barton (Eds) *Voicing concerns: sociological perspectives on contemporary educa-tion reforms* (Wallingford, Triangle Books).

Furlong, J. (2001) Reforming teacher education, re-forming teachers: accountability, professional-ism and competence, in: R. Phillips & J. Furlong (Eds) *Education, reform and the state: 25 years of policy, politics and practice* (London, Routledge).

Furlong, J. & Maynard, P. (1995) *Mentoring student teachers: the growth of professional knowledge* (London, Routledge).

Furlong, J., Barton, L., Miles, S., Whiting, C. & Whitty, G. (2000) *Teacher education in transition: re-forming teacher professionalism* (Buckingham, Open University Press).

Furlong, J. & Salisbury, S. (2005) The best practice research scholarship scheme: an evaluation, *Research Papers in Education* (forthcoming).

Gewirtz, S. (2002) *The managerial school* (London, Routledge).

Gewirtz, S., Ball, S. & Bowe, R. (1995) *Markets, choice and equity* (Buckingham, Open University Press).

Giddens, A. (2000) *The third way and its critics* (Cambridge, Polity Press).

Guardian (2004) Qualified success, *Education Guardian* 7 September, 2–3.

Hargreaves, D. (2003) *Education epidemic: transforming secondary schools through innovation networks* (London, Demos).

Halsey, A.H., Lauder, H., Brown, P. & Stuart Wells, A. (Eds) (1997) *Education: culture, economy and society* (Oxford, Oxford University Press).

Hillgate Group (1989) *Learning to teach* (London, The Claridge Press).

Hood, C. (1991) A public management for all seasons? *Public Administration*, 69, 3–19.

Hoyle, E. (1974) Professionality, professionalism and control in teaching, *London Education Review*, 3(2), 13–19.

Hoyle, E. & John, P. (1995) *Professional knowledge and professional practice* (London, Cassell).

Hughes, O. (2003) *Public management and administration: an introduction* (Basingstoke, Palgrave Macmillan).

Lauder, H., Hughes, D., Watson, S., Waslander, S., Thrupp, M., Strathdee, R., Simiyu, I., Dupuis, A., McGlinn, J. & Hamlin, J. (1999) *Trading in futures: why markets in education don't work* (Buckingham, Open University Press).

Lawlor, S. (1990) *Teachers mistaught: training theories or education in subjects* (London, Centre for Policy Studies).

Le Grand, J. & Bartlet, W. (1993) (Eds) *Quasi-markets and social policy* (London, Macmillan).

McCulloch, G. (2001) The reinvention of teacher professionalism, in: R. Phillips & J. Furlong (Eds) *Education reform and the state: 25 years of politics, policy and practice* (London, Routledge).

McIntyre, D. (1993) Theory, theorizing and reflection in initial teacher education, in: J. Calderhead & P. Gates (Eds) *Conceptualising reflection in teacher development* (London, Routledge).

Mahony, P. & Hextall, I. (2000) *Reconstructing teaching: standards performance and accountability* (London, RoutledgeFalmer).

Millett, A. (1997) *The implications for teacher training of the government's Green Paper – Teachers: meeting the challenge of change* (London, TTA).

Morris, E. (1997) *Letter to TTA, 26 June* (London, DfEE).

Newman, J. (2001) *Modernising governance: New Labour, policy and society* (London, Sage).

O'Hear, A. (1988) *Who teaches the teachers?* (London, Social Affairs Unit).

Ozga, J. (1995) De-skilling a profession: professionalism, deprofessionalisation and the new mana-gerialism, in: H. Busher & R. Saran (Eds) *Managing teachers as professionals in schools* (London, Kogan Page).

Popkewitz, T. (1987) Ideology and social formation in teacher education, in: T. Popkewitz (Ed.) *Critical studies in teacher education* (Lewes, Falmer Press).

Power, S., Fitz, J. & Halpin, D. (1994) Parents, pupils and grant maintained schools, *British Educational Research Journal,* 20(2), 209–226.

Power, S. & Whitty, G. (1999) New Labour's education policy: first, second or third way? *Journal of Education Policy,* 14(5), 535–546.

Reid, I., Brain, K. & Comerford Boyes, L. (2004) Teachers or learning leaders? Where have all the teachers gone? Gone to be leaders everyone, *Educational Studies,* 30(3), 251–264.

Whitty, G. (2002) *Making sense of education policy* (London, Paul Chapman).

Whitty, G., Edwards, T. & Gewirtz, S. (1993) *Specialisation and choice in urban education: the city technology college experiment* (London, Routledge).

Whitty, G., Power, S. & Halpin, D. (1998) *Devolution and choice in education: the school, the state and the market* (Buckingham, Open University Press).

Wilkin, M. (1996) *Initial teacher training: the dialogue of ideology and culture* (London, Falmer Press).

Reinventing 'inclusion': New Labour and the cultural politics of special education

Derrick Armstrong

Introduction

Special education is rarely seen as a contentious area of public policy, except perhaps by those families whose lives are directly touched by it and those professionals and administrators with responsibility for managing this resource-hungry sector. Special education is generally seen as a charitable, humanitarian concern rather than as a politically constructed domain that defines the nature and limits of 'normality'. Thomas and Loxley (2001) point out that the discourse of special education is deeply ingrained and it is one which has led to generosity becoming the hallmark of educational funding. Throughout its history, this humanitarian discourse has been a significant factor in securing additional resources for children who have experienced serious failure within the mainstream education sector, or who have been excluded altogether from that system. Yet, beneath the surface of this humanitarian consensus there have always been rumblings of dissent and the 'dark side' of special education as a system of regulation and control of troublesome populations is one that has been widely exposed and critiqued by sociologists (Ford, *et al.*, 1982; Tomlinson, 1982; Armstrong, 2003a), historians (Pritchard, 1963; Hurt, 1988; Copeland, 1999), psychologists (Galloway & Goodwin, 1987; Sigmon, 1987), parents (Murray & Penman, 1996, 2000; Murray, 2004) and by disabled people (Mason & Rieser, 1990).

It is, of course, easy to oversimplify the nature of special education, both as a humanitarian resource and as a system of control. Recent developments in this field, in particular, are suggestive of the complexity of the system and of the discourses underpinning it. In this respect, much has been made of the inclusive 'third-way' philosophy of New Labour. In special education, this philosophy is represented in terms of policy goals of the integration of children with special needs in mainstream schooling, of the provision of high quality education for all, and of a responsibility shared by all teachers for children with special needs. Yet, as will be argued in this paper, the New Labour vision of inclusion is one that reconstructs inclusion within the traditional framework of special education and in so doing reinforces its traditional purposes. This involves a conceptualisation characterised by what Slee (2001a, p. 117) has described as 'a deep epistemological attachment to the view that special educational needs are produced by the impaired pathology of the child'.

I begin this article by outlining the key features of New Labour's early Green Paper on special and inclusive schooling, *Excellence for all children* (DfES, 1997a), which provided the framework upon which policy has subsequently been developed. I will then look more closely at three key initiatives on inclusive education introduced by the New Labour government over its two terms of office: the 2001 Revised Code of Practice (DfES, 2001a); the Special Educational Needs and Disability Act (HMSO, 2001); and the SEN Strategy, *Removing barriers to achievement* (DfES, 2004) which aims to bring special educational services under the broader strategy of child protection. In the third section of this paper I will argue that, despite the rhetoric of 'inclusion' in which these policies have been cloaked, it would be quite misleading to represent 1997 as a turning point for 'inclusive education'. The statistics on the identification, statementing and placement of children with special educational needs during the period of New Labour's term of office do not suggest any radical transformation of the social practices of inclusion/exclusion. Indeed policy on inclusion is characterised by incongruities with the broader, reconceptualisation of educational values in terms of the values of performativity, uncritical notions of 'academic standards' and the role of education as a producer of human capital. This model of inclusive education is one that has allowed the recreation of the special educational industry under the banner of 'inclusion'. What is distinctive about New Labour policy on inclusive education, however, is how the language of inclusion has been mobilised as a central normalising discourse of governance. State intervention is advanced in pursuit of technical 'solutions' to social exclusion as a moral rather than as a political problem.

Year zero—the end of ideology and beginning of an inclusive society?

Robin Alexander (2003), writing in the *Times Educational Supplement*, argued that, for Tony Blair and New Labour, 1997 represented 'year zero' in education: 'The strategy is part of a political world view in which history and enlightenment began in 1997'. The 'enlightenment' of educational policy was grounded in the school-effectiveness and school improvement movements. The language of individual pupil needs was ostensibly rejected and replaced by a policy focused upon failing schools and the actions required to transform institutional failure into success and by this means into individual pupil achievement. The White Paper *Excellence in Education* (DfEE, 1997a) set out the broad agenda of the government as it started upon an educational 'crusade'. Emphasis here was placed upon the improvement of 'standards' and the accountability of schools, setting out six policy principles:

- Education will be at the heart of the government.
- Policies will benefit the many, not just the few.
- The focus will be on standards in schools, not the structure of the school system.
- We will intervene in underperforming schools and celebrate the successful.
- There will be zero tolerance of underperformance.
- Government will work in partnership with all those committed to raising standards.

Shortly after publication of this document the government brought out its consultation paper *Excellence for all children—meeting special educational needs* (DfEE, 1997b) which signalled its commitments to improving the quality of education for children with special educational needs.

The relationship between these two documents is of course important, with the latter being firmly embedded in the philosophy of the former, as David Blunkett, the first New Labour Secretary of State for Education, made clear in his Foreword (p. 4), 'There is nothing more important to the Government than raising the standards children achieve in our schools'. Yet, he was also to maintain that this vision of school improvement and rising standards was, at least for children with special educational needs, 'an inclusive vision' (p. 4). What he wanted to know was why it was that mainstream schools were identifying 18% of their children as having special educational needs and almost 3% of children had statutory statements of special educational needs which set out additional special educational provision that they required. For Blunkett, this said something very telling about the quality of education being provided within the mainstream school sector and this led him to argue for the benefits of high expectations and standards being established in the mainstream sector with the implication that many more pupils with special educational needs would benefit from an inclusive system of education: 'Where all children are included as equal partners in the school community, the benefits are felt by all. That is why we are committed to comprehensive and enforceable civil rights for disabled people. Our aspirations as a nation must be for all our people' (DfEE, 1997b, p. 5).

Blunkett went on to set out the six principles underpinning the strategy. First, there would be high expectations for all children, including those with special educational needs. Second was the promotion of inclusion of children with special educational needs within mainstream schooling wherever possible. This would not only involve the removal of barriers to participation but also a redefinition of the role of the special school in terms of a network of specialists. A place was to remain for special schools but this place was one that was itself framed by the broader objective of educational inclusion. Moreover, the somewhat sterile debates about the 'integration' of children with special educational needs into mainstream schooling were to be overridden by an emphasis not merely upon the educational advantages of inclusion but also of the social and moral benefits of this policy. Third, a commitment was given to providing parents of children with special educational needs with effective services from the full range of local services and voluntary agencies. The fourth principle was concerned with ensuring value for money which would mean 'shifting resources from expensive remediation to cost-effective prevention and early intervention' (p. 5). This, he argued, would entail a review of the statementing procedures for special educational needs. Local education authorities were by this time spending one-seventh of their budget (£2.5 billion) on special education and the costs of statementing, in particular, had been rising quite staggeringly during the earlier part of the 1990s. Fifth, Blunkett promised to boost opportunities for staff development in special education. Finally, he stated an expectation that in the future provision locally would be based on 'a partnership of all those with a contribution to make' (p. 6).

This was a document claiming very explicitly that change *would* happen. The target setting agenda of the first term of the New Labour government has been well documented, as have some of the spectacular failures to meet the targets set. This document was no exception with a total of 31 policy targets being set, with an implementation date of no later than 2002. Yet, in practice some of these specific targets were achieved with greater success than others. Targets, as New Labour came to recognise, are a hostage to fortune. In the setting, if not in their realisation, they do suggest a dynamic programme of transformation. However, such a transformatory agenda may be characterised by the rhetoric of change rather than by any substantive transformation of values and practices. Of more interest is the rationale that underpinned those targets. The document certainly adopts the language of 'inclusion', yet, despite so doing, its focus is entirely upon individual pupils' needs and improving the efficiency and cost-effectiveness of systems for managing those needs. Thus, the targets that are set out in *Excellence for all children* are grouped into eight sections which can be summarised as follows: improving efficiency to reduce expenditure; maximising parental involvement and therefore responsibility; refining early assessment procedures to reduce statementing; encouraging integration of children with special educational needs in mainstream schools; improving national and regional planning and support for children with special educational needs; training teachers and support staff; maximising interagency collaboration; and building teacher skills and support systems for managing pupils with emotional and behavioural difficulties. Nowhere does the strategy talk about the barriers that create educational disadvantage; nowhere does it talk about the institutional and social discrimination experienced by pupils from certain minority groups (e.g. children of Caribbean heritage and children of Irish heritage, to name but two); nowhere does it talk about the principles of an inclusive society and the role of education as a tool of social policy for supporting social cohesion and inclusion. The list could go on. Policy, as Tony Booth (2000, p. 91) has forcefully argued, 'remains locked into a response to difficulties in learning experienced by children and young people which predates the Warnock Report of 1978'. The rhetorical emphasis upon mainstream schools as the point of delivery for special educational support was hardly new. Given the continuing reliance upon special schools for the more disabled and troublesome pupils the reality did not represent such a radical departure from the past as it was claimed to be. The replacement of a discourse of individual failure by a discourse of school failure based upon the promotion of academic excellence for those identified as having special educational needs did little to challenge the underlying conceptualisation of individual deficits.

This basic approach remained unchanged as a torrent of policy documents and legislation for special education flooded from Westminster. All of this strengthened the rights of children with special educational needs to a mainstream education but said little about the nature of that education, other than the promotion of the universal mantras of 'high expectations', 'standards', 'school improvement'. Thus, for instance, while *Meeting special educational needs—a programme for action* (DfEE, 1998), which set out the strategy for achieving the objectives of the earlier Green Paper, strengthened the rights of children and parents to mainstream schooling, there was little recognition of the wider social barriers to inclusion that inhibited inclusion within the environment of mainstream education. Again, those barriers that were recognised were merely those of low expectations and standards. The wider context of discrimination, segregation and exclusion, some of which was promoted by the very policies of 'inclusion' themselves, were at best unanalysed and more commonly ignored.

Policy, policy, policy!

Despite concerns about the level of sophistication underpinning New Labour's approach toward inclusive education, the Green Paper on special education and inclusion did give rise to a number of significant initiatives in furtherance of the broad policy objective of making educational opportunities more widely available to disabled children and young people. Indeed, the extent of policy intervention by this government in the field of special and inclusive education far outstrips that of any previous government. However, in this second part of the paper I want to look in detail at three initiatives that highlight both the interventionist trend and the substantive thrust of policy in this area: the Special Educational Needs Code of Practice (DfES, 2001a); the 2001 Special Educational Needs and Disability Act (HMSO, 2001); and New Labour's most recent Strategy for SEN, 'Removing Barriers to Achievement' (DfES, 2004).

A new code of practice

The 2001 Code of Practice was not in itself new. It revised an existing Code of Practice on the Identification and Assessment of Special Educational Needs introduced by the previous Conservative government in 1994. The 1994 Code of Practice arose out of the 1993 Education Act which made a number of significant amendments to the landmark 1981 Education Act. The latter had introduced the statementing procedure for children with special educational needs, but was perhaps more renowned for its introduction of the notion advanced by the Warnock Report (DES, 1978) of a continuum of special educational need. At the time, this conceptualisation of special educational needs, rejecting as it did the idea of categories of handicap based on individual deficits, was widely seen as promoting a charter for the integration of children with special educational needs into the mainstream sector. In retrospect, such claims were massively overstated. Not only were there significant 'let-out' clauses in this legislation (and in the Warnock recommendations that underpinned it) but, in practice, the subsequent difficulty in specifying what constituted a 'special educational need' led inexorably to a growth in statementing and special school placements as this meaning was negotiated in practice by powerful pressure groups and Local Education Authorities struggled to manage and restrain the professional judgements that had been empowered by the 1981 legislation. The 1993 Education Act made provision for a Code of Practice on the identification and assessment of special educational needs to be introduced which would direct attention towards early assessment and intervention rather than at the far more costly statutory assessment procedures. This Code of Practice (DEE, 1994) introduced a five stage procedure ranging from initial classroom monitoring at stage 1 to statutory assessment at stage 5 and created the new role in each school of the Special Educational Needs Co-ordinator, or SENCO. SENCOs were to have special responsibility for the school-based elements of the procedure and in particular for individual education plans (IEPs) which were to include information on such things as short-term targets, teaching strategies, special resources, review dates, etc.

In 2001 a revised Code of Practice was introduced by the Labour government (DfES, 2001a). This replaced the five stage assessment process with two pre-statutory stages: 'School Action' and 'School Action Plus'. The former is to be initiated where there is evidence of poor progress linked to emotional and behavioural difficulties, sensory or physical problems, or communication difficulties, despite the child having received normal differentiated learning opportunities in the classroom. The action to be taken is to be specified in an Individual Education Plan. School Action Plus involves a request for help from external services and follows upon continued lack of progress on the part of the child, despite the measures taken at the School Action stage. Whereas, in the past, a referral of a child with special educational needs to outside agencies generally resulted in a statement of special educational needs and, frequently, placement in a special school, the procedures introduced by the Code of Practice were designed to avoid this by ensuring a clear record of assessment, intervention and review at each stage. By implementing such procedures it was intended to avoid the crisis management of children who experience difficulties with learning.

One of the major impacts of the Code of Practice has been to give greater responsibility to mainstream schools and to ordinary classroom teachers for pupils with special educational needs. Yet, teachers may be encouraged to represent different sorts of issues under the banner of special educational needs simply because the Code provides a convenient system for organising the management of pupils who experience difficulties with learning and behaviour in their schools. Deeper seated problems such as bullying and discrimination can easily be reconstructed under the procedures of the Code as individualised learning and behaviour deficits. In this way, the Code may perpetuate long-standing and institutionally embedded practices such as racial and gender stereotyping which lead to distortions in the gender and racial profiling of special educational needs (Armstrong, 2003b).

Revisions to the Code of Practice introduced by New Labour have done nothing to address these disturbing features associated with the 'distribution' of special educational needs. Indeed, it could be argued that in some respects these features have become more damaging with the emphasis placed upon a rhetoric about children's involvement in decision-making. Thus, the revised Code of Practice (*Section 3:2*) states that:

> Children and young people with special educational needs have a unique knowledge of their own needs and circumstances and their own views about what sort of help they would like to help them make the most of their education. They should, where possible, participate in all the decision-making processes that occur in education including the setting of learning targets and contributing to IEPs, discussions about choice of schools, contributing to the assessment of their needs and to the annual review and transition processes. However, there is "a fine balance between giving the child a voice and encouraging them to make informed decisions, and to overburdening them with decision-making procedures where they have insufficient experience and knowledge to make appropriate judgements without additional support."

The purpose of this involvement is made clear in the following section where we see the same series of assumptions about 'accessing voice' and the value of children's voices to professional decision-making that characterised the original Code of Practice. Thus *section 3:3* maintains that:

> ... the principle of seeking and taking account of the ascertainable views of the child or young person is an important one. *Their perceptions and experiences can be invaluable to professionals in reaching decisions.* (My italics)

Absent from this discussion of inclusion is any reference to the protection of children's rights against the discriminatory practices that may arise from the process of assessment itself.

The apparently 'inclusive' principle of children's involvement in decision-making continues under the new Code of Practice to be subordinated to the practical value of the child's involvement for those professionals who are managing the child's learning, emphatically asserting the purpose of the Code, not as a tool of empowerment for children but rather, as a mechanism for channelling troublesome voices into safe waters. At root, the rhetoric of inclusion is based upon the assumption that to be 'just' the education system must accommodate children whose individual disadvantages place them at risk of exclusion. It palpably fails to appreciate how the language of 'special educational needs' is a socially constructed response by adults to troublesome behaviour that is located in wider-reaching social inequalities. In other words, ironically, it fails to appreciate how the language and policies of inclusion, as presently represented in educational policy, are part of the problem and not part of the solution.

The 2001 Special Educational Needs and Disability Act

At first sight, at least, a much wider reconceptualisation of special educational needs is suggested by the 2001 Special Needs and Disability Act (HMSO, 2001). Part I of this Act applies specifically to special educational provision and is concerned with relatively minor 'tweaking' of previous legislation: for example, requiring local education authorities to provide and advertise parent partnership services and tightening up the workings of the Tribunal system to reduce delays. Part II of the Act, however, extends the power of the Disability Discrimination Act (1995) to education, ensuring that discrimination against disabled students is unlawful. Thus, a duty is placed on schools not to discriminate against disabled pupils, either in the provision of education and associated services or in respect of admission to and exclusion from mainstream schooling. Moreover, schools are required to have regard to the Disability Rights Commission Code of Practice when identifying the 'reasonable steps' they must take to avoid discrimination. Section 316 of the Act states that a child who has a statement of special educational needs must be educated in the mainstream school unless this would be incompatible with: a) the wishes of the child's parents; or, b) the provision of efficient education for other children (HMSO, 2001). 'Mainstream education cannot be refused on the grounds that the child's needs cannot be provided for within the mainstream sector' (DfES, 2001b). However, the fact that mainstream education can be refused on the grounds that the educational interests of other children would be adversely affected by the presence of a disabled child continues a qualification on inclusion that has a long legislative history.

Government policies on special education have historically shied away from linking special educational needs to the politics of disability. For this reason, the linking of special educational needs with disability issues by New Labour in the 2001 Special Educational Needs and Disability Act is significant. This has been a position advocated for many years by the Disabled People's Movement (Oliver, 1996; Barton & Oliver, 1997; Oliver & Barnes, 1998) but it is one that in the past has been largely ignored by politicians and professional agencies working with children in educational settings.

For disability activists, there have been two broad arguments in favour of conceptualising inclusive policies in education in the context of society. The first of these has focused upon the ways in which disability, including learning difficulty, is a social construction, created by the social relations and power structures in society. On this argument, impairment does not of itself give rise to disadvantage and social exclusion. Physical and mental impairments are factors reflective of the diversity of the human condition. What turns diversity (and therefore impairments) into disabilities is the way in which people are disadvantaged and mistreated because of those differences. Special education, and particularly segregated special educational institutions, belongs to the social relations of oppression through which people are disabled. The second strand of argument advanced by disability activists has been that the struggle against the disabling features of social life should focus upon removing the barriers that disabled people face in accessing participation in social life. These barriers include those barring physical access to social spaces as well as the discriminatory practices of public policy and private prejudice. These two aspects are inextricably linked and this has informed the writing of a new generation of disability activists and inclusive education theorists. Sadly, few lessons have been drawn by policy makers from this rich critical tradition.

The disability legislation introduced by New Labour has focused almost exclusively on issues of physical access to public spaces. Legislation in this area is, of course, to be welcomed and removing these physical barriers to access in many ways does represent an ambitious and difficult objective to achieve. On the other hand, the policy is one that implies a technical solution to the problem of how to achieve educational equity. It suggests that if only disabled people can physically access educational spaces the barriers to participation will be dissolved. At best this is idealistic and at worst disingenuous. The radical thrust of the argument of disability activists that disability is not a product of impairment but rather a social act of discrimination embedded in the power relations of society is muted by this legislation. The political concept of inclusion, and the wider social question that asks why discrimination and disadvantage are so embedded in the system, is lost in legislation that represents inclusion in terms of 'impairment friendly' schooling. Similarly there is no consideration of how the relations of power that support discrimination against disabled people can be transformed as a necessary basis for an inclusive society. Yet schooling, as Slee (2001b) has argued, was never really intended for everyone. 'The more they have been called upon to include the masses, the more they have developed the technologies of exclusion and containment' (p. 172). Special education, however, has been historically characterised by the pathologising of young people who are represented as troublesome. An analysis of the processes and mechanism of exclusion, such as that advanced from within the disability movement begins to unpack the 'disablement' of people on the basis of their impairments, social class, gender, ethnicity and their willingness, or not, to conform to state-imposed systems of child management. The most important contribution of the disability movement to the framing of debates about inclusive education has been to politicise disablement in terms of these broader processes of cultural representation and social exclusion. The disability legislation of New Labour however, fails even to acknowledge the politics of exclusion. A policy promoting inclusive education that remains constrained by the goal of assimilating those with impairments into mainstream schools without addressing the exclusionary character of a disabling society is doomed to reinforce the very exclusionary process that it seeks to overcome.

'Removing barriers to achievement': the government's strategy for SEN

The most recent New Labour initiative in support of inclusive schooling has been the Strategy for SEN, 'Removing Barriers to Achievement' (DfES, 2004). The significance of this strategy is that it contextualises special education within the broader policy initiative of the Green Paper *Every child matters* (The Stationery Office, 2003) and as such offers the most complete articulation of inclusive education policy within New Labour's wider ideological vision of the inclusive society. *Every child matters*, which had its origins in the Victoria Climbie Report (DOH/Home Office, 2003) speaks to a commitment to reform children's services to prevent vulnerable children 'falling through the cracks between different services' (p. 5) and the need to recognise that 'child protection cannot be separated from policies to improve children's lives as a whole' (p. 5). The Government's Strategy for SEN (DfES, 2004, p. 9) attempts to represent inclusive education within a similar framework of child protection by targeting attention toward four areas of activity which are seen as essential for the protection of vulnerable children in schools and the promotion of learning opportunities for children with special educational needs. These are:

- Early intervention—to ensure that children who have difficulties learning receive the help they need as soon as possible and that parents of children with special educational needs and disabilities have access to suitable childcare.
- Removing barriers to learning—by embedding inclusive practice in every school and early years setting.
- Raising expectations and achievement—by developing teachers' skills and strategies for meeting the needs of children with SEN and sharpening our focus on the progress children make.
- Delivering improvements in partnership—taking a hands-on approach to improvements so that parents can be confident that their child will get the education they need.

Pursuing this child protection model of inclusion, the Strategy for SEN locates special educational interventions within the broader context of social disadvantages experienced by young people whose origins lie within 'risk factors' associated with educational failure, community breakdown, parenting inadequacies, school disorganisation and individual and/or peer group difficulties. These risk factors have been widely proclaimed as giving rise to concerns for the welfare of young people across the domains of education health, social welfare and youth justice (Lupton, 1999; Bessant *et al.*, 2003). The risk factor model is one that has been instrumental in promoting an interventionist strategy of risk reduction to be delivered by cross-agency childhood services.

Dyson (2001, p. 103) has argued that notions of risk and resilience 'offer the sort of "hook" that is now needed … [for] "reconnecting" educational difficulty to wider issues in social and economic disadvantage'. This view is certainly shared by the Strategy for SEN (DfES, 2004, p. 8) where we are told:

> We have never been so well placed to deliver such a wide-ranging strategy to transform the lives and life chances of these children. The reform of children's services set out in Every Child Matters, with its focus on early intervention, preventative work and integrated services for children through Children's Trusts, will deliver real and lasting benefits to children with SEN and their families. And our commitment to reducing child poverty, investing in early years education and childcare and targeting support at areas of social and economic disadvantage will enable us to address the underlying causes of children's difficulties.

Thus it is maintained that we are historically now at a juncture at which an intervention strategy can transform the lives of children with special educational needs. This transformation is possible because child services have been integrated in ways that make early intervention and prevention capable of delivering real benefits. Moreover, such a strategy will have the significant impact of reducing child poverty because early intervention and support can now be targeted at areas of social and economic disadvantage, thus addressing 'the underlying causes of children's difficulties'.

Herein lay a set of important ideological claims. First, that poverty is the underlying cause of educational disadvantage. Second, that the effects of poverty can be transformed through social interventions aimed at those most at risk. Third, that we now have the technical skill and organisational structures to maximise the impact of such interventions. Implicit in the first two of these claims is a view that poverty is a consequence of the inadequacies of those individuals who are placed at risk by it. If this is not what is being claimed then what would be the purpose of intervening at the individual level rather than at the macro-economic level to reduce poverty and its effects? The third claim advanced in the quotation above maintains that elimination of the disadvantages of poverty can be achieved through early interventions with children because the technical skill exists to identify and target those most at risk. The reduction of poverty and disadvantage (as well, presumably, as its creation) is represented as possible through technical solutions aimed at the individual child.

Susser (1998) has argued that there are serious problems about extrapolating from factors identified at the group level to assessments of individual risk. Moreover, despite the apparent linkage between individual risk and social disadvantage, what this model proposes is a focus upon protecting those individuals who are at risk from the micro-social factors of 'disadvantaged' families, schools and communities that are correlated with risk. What is lacking in this approach is any theorisation of the ways in which risks are situated historically in cultural and social formations in relation to the construction and negotiation of individual identities as 'normal' or 'abnormal' and of how social power is exercised both in the social construction and academic theorisation of what constitutes risk (Armstrong, 2004). An illusion of scientific objectivity is also created which implies that these risks and the likelihood of their effect upon future behaviour can be measured and therefore controlled by appropriate early interventions.

Inclusion, governmentality and the interventionist state

Gillian Fulcher (1989) has argued that written policy is but one element of the policy–practice equation. Written policy may speak to social aspirations but it also gives voice to a political conceptualisation of social problems. Similarly, enacted policy reflects the implementation of policy aspirations but it also constitutes a continuing re-articulation and contestation of the meaning of policy as an expression of power, normalising views of how the world *is*, whilst at the same time marking the limits of power by the ambiguities of policy as practice. In this section of the paper I first consider what difference New Labour policies have actually made to the construction of children's educational experiences. Statistics are useful in this respect because they reveal the extent to which the old labels of 'special educational needs' remain active in defining the character of educational failure. Moreover, they point to the ways in which special education operates as a mechanism suppressing alternative cultural representations of disempowered identities. Second, I will explore the contradictions within the policy agenda of New Labour to suggest how these contribute to the reinvention of the special needs industry in inclusive education (Slee, 2001a). Third, I will discuss how New Labour's policies on inclusion reflect the processes and contradictions of governmentality in late modern societies.

Are more children included?

Looked at in its own terms, the successes of New Labour policy on inclusion have been limited. Statementing has in fact very slightly increased since the New Labour special educational strategy was set out in 1997. Between 1999 and 2003 a 1% increase to 250,500 pupils with statements of special educational needs in England was recorded (DfES, 2003a). Over the same period a similarly modest decrease of 1% (from 97,700 to 93,000) was recorded in the numbers of children receiving their schooling in special schools. Yet, these figures conceal more worrying indications of the failure of inclusive schooling to be realised. Apart from wide local variations in statementing and placement policies that have been a characteristic of the special education system throughout its history, there continue to be significant differences in statementing practice between the primary and secondary sectors (in 2003 2.4% of secondary school pupils having statements compared with 1.6% of primary pupils); and between year groups within each sector (e.g. in 2003, 53% of statements of special educational needs in England were held by children aged 11 to 15 year-olds compared with 37% held by children aged 5 to 10 years). Gender differences continue to show the most striking disparities with boys accounting for 71.7% and 77.9% of all statemented pupils in primary and secondary schools respectively in 2003. Differences between ethnic groups continue to be pronounced despite a long history of concern about discrimination and institutional racism (Blyth & Milner, 1996; Gillborn & Youdell, 2000), with travellers of Irish heritage and Roma/Gypsy children having the highest percentage of children with statements of special educational needs. In 2003 1% of primary schools still accounted for 10% of pupils with statements and 0.5% of secondary schools accounted for more than 10% of pupils with statements. School differences also suggest that little has changed since 25 years ago when attention was first drawn to this by a number of groundbreaking studies on school effectiveness (Rutter *et al.*, 1979). Interestingly, the extensive school effectiveness literature that followed Rutter's seminal study has largely focused upon government preoccupations with academic achievement rather than upon what is perhaps more illuminative from the standpoint of inclusive schooling, namely the social and affective dimensions of children's experiences of schooling.

The statistics suggest that very little has changed, not only over the last six or seven years, but over the last 25 years since the Warnock Report (DES, 1978) first advocated the abolition of categories of special educational need and movement toward a more inclusive system based upon a continuum of needs which were themselves significantly related to the quality of education being received. The much acclaimed technical ability to address the factors producing educational disadvantage by intervening with those individuals at an early age has it seems come to very little. More importantly, special education continues to fulfil its traditional function *vis-á-vis* the mainstream sector of containing troublesome individuals and depoliticising educational failure through the technologies of measurement and exclusion.

Is the education system more inclusive?

The policy contradictions of New Labour's approach to inclusion are striking and have been widely commented upon (Tomlinson, 2001; Armstrong, 2003a). Under the banner of inclusion, educational equality is being reconceptualised in terms of conformity to quite narrowly defined performance criteria, a definition that is designed to select, place value upon, and advance the opportunities of certain individuals. Yet such a utilitarian system of performativity inevitably promotes exclusion for those who do not meet the standard. In these circumstances, special educational needs continues to be a legitimating label for the failure of the system to address itself to the aspirations, dignity and human worth of so many young people. As Benjamin has argued that:

> For students who are not going to succeed in dominant terms, the standards agenda is instrumental in constructing barriers to their participation. Herein lies one of the most fundamental contradictions at the heart of New Labour's educational policy. (Quoted by Barton, 2003, p. 16)

Narrowly conceived performance criteria are central to the rhetoric of inclusion advanced by New Labour's education policy. Inclusion is a normative concept. Its colonisation, under the banner of academic opportunity and high standards for all, serves to normalise the values of individual responsibility for individual achievement. The policy of inclusion is aimed not at promoting equity whilst recognising and supporting the richness of social diversity, but at establishing narrow cultural parameters of normality to which all must have the opportunity to conform. The role of education as a mechanism of assimilation, ironically, but inevitably, constructs the role of inclusion as a disciplinary force, regulating the lives of those disabled by their lack of utilitarian value to the interests of an individualised society.

The narrative of inclusion that features so strongly in the social policy agenda of New Labour can be understood as a product of what Andrew Gamble (2000) has described as the attempt of governments in late modern societies to dominate what's left of the state in the face of the uncertainties of a highly marketised civil society, leading to fewer opportunities for citizen rights to be articulated and organised for within a public sphere. The freedom of citizens within the public sphere is squeezed between the market and the state. In education, the marketisation of services within a preferential system of private choices is balanced by a highly regulated system of state-organised prescriptive demands around standards and measures of performance, which leave little room for alternative educational values and goals to be formulated, debated and pursued.

This world, in which the public sphere is increasingly ordered and regulated by the state and the market, is a world from which certainty has disappeared and individuals lack the ability to control the flow of events. This tension between regulation and uncertainty has led to a situation described by Zygmunt Bauman (1990, pp. 182–183) where 'only the vigilant management of human affairs seems to stand between order and chaos'.

During the New Labour period, policy targeted on social prevention measures has increased significantly. In particular, policy has focused on children, parents, communities and schools that are seen as potentially problematic. Those not conforming to certain norms and values have become the subject of intensive state interventions aimed at correcting the social deficits that place children at 'risk'. What we see in this new policy is a widening of what constitutes legitimate sites of state intervention, based upon beliefs about the moral importance of early intervention and prevention and the technical possibilities that science creates for the policy maker and implementer.

State intervention in the governance of children, families, schools and communities who are deemed to be potentially problematic is legitimated on the basis of moral beliefs in pathologies of risk for which technical solutions of risk management can be specified under the ideological formulation of an inclusive society. The process of educational assessment is transformed from a formative and educative process into a risk management system. On the one hand, failure is conceptualised entirely in moral terms as the consequence of individual, family, community and/or school inadequacies. On the other hand, a technical solution to these moral deficiencies is proposed, which involves early identification of at-risk populations on the basis of risk factors 'known' to correlate with the likelihood of failure or anti-social behaviour in the future. Thus, the idea of inclusive education is used to justify the growth of surveillance and management of troublesome populations based on the assumption that special educational needs are an outcome of dysfunctional individuals and communities and that these individuals can be identified through an assessment process determined by experts (Rose & Miller, 1992). Nikolas Rose (1999, p. 134) has described this process as one in which 'The soul of the young person has become the object of government through expertise'.

Such regulation, however, has not been confined to the troublesome. Just as important is the establishment of criteria for what is 'normal'; and it is the values prescribing normality that in turn are used to define the parameters of an inclusive school, community and society and which encourage self-regulation. A process of governmentality is embedded in the moralisation of political values in terms of assumptions about the nature of 'inclusion' supported by technical judgements that masquerade as expertise. It is a masquerade because the 'science' which defines inclusion is decontextualised from the contested beliefs and values which give meaning and relevance to particular representations of normality and social order. Thus, the linking of the science of 'risk assessment' to 'inclusion' supports an anti-welfare rhetoric (Culpitt,

1999) that legitimises the redistribution of social resources into a privatised world of individual responsibility and risk management, replacing 'need' and equity as the core principles of educational and social policy (Kemshall, 2002).

Conclusion

New Labour has from the beginning of its first term pursued a vigorous agenda around the issues of social and educational inclusion. It is an agenda that has taken from the disability movement what were transformatory values drawn from a critique of the cultural politics of disability and reconstructed these in terms of the regulatory and normalising functions of the neoconservative state. At one level the inclusive policies of New Labour go no further than to redress the traditional deficit-driven discourse of special educational needs in the fashionable but illusionary language of inclusion. More perniciously, the discourse of children at risk within whose parameters the policy of inclusive education has been constrained represents a new assault on the public sphere of democratic practice. The contribution of New Labour's inclusive educational policy has been to forward a process of assimilation based upon an uncritical view of 'normality', itself structured by the values of performativity that legitimate state regulation and control. The risks to the self that are generated in the institutionally structured risk environments of the risk society are individualised (Kelly, 2001) and marshalled in support of policies of inclusion as mechanisms for managing the excluded. Thus, the meaning of inclusion has been colonised by political and moral values that articulate, sometimes imprecisely and ambiguously, the fears and desires of an increasingly authoritarian state.

Note on contributor

Derrick Armstrong is Professor and Dean in the Faculty of Education and Social Work at the University of Sydney. He is author of *Power and partnership in education: parents, children and special educational needs* (Routledge, 1995) and *Experiences of special education: re-evaluating policy and practice through life stories* (RoutledgeFalmer, 2003).

References

Alexander, R. (2003, September 19) For Blair 1997 is year zero, *Times Educational Supplement* (Friday Magazine, p. 11).

Armstrong, D. (2003a) *Experiences of special education: re-evaluating policy and practice through life stories* (London, RoutledgeFalmer).

Armstrong, D. (2003b) Partnership with pupils: problems and possibilities, *Association for Child Psychologists and Psychiatrists Occasional Papers*, 20, 39–45.

Armstrong, D. (2004) A risky business? Research, policy, governmentality and youth offending, *Youth Justice*, 4(2).

Barton, L. (2003) Professorial Lecture. Inclusive education and teacher education: a basis for hope or a discourse of delusion (London, Institute of Education).

Barton, L. & Oliver, M. (Eds) (1997) *Disability studies: past, present and future* (Leeds, Disability Press).

Bauman, Z. (1990) *Thinking sociologically* (Oxford, Blackwell).

Bessant, J., Hil, R. & Watts, R. (2003) *'Discovering' risk: social research and policy making* (New York, Peter Lang).

Blyth, E. & Milner, J. (Eds) (1996) *Exclusion from school* (London, Routledge).

Booth, T. (2000) Inclusion and exclusion policy in England: who controls the agenda? in: F. Armstrong, D. Armstrong & L. Barton (Eds) *Inclusive education: policy, contexts and comparative perspectives* (London, David Fulton).

Copeland, I. (1999) *The making of the backward pupil in education in England: 1870–1914* (London, Woburn Press).

Culpitt, I. (1999) *Social policy and risk* (London, Sage).

Department for Education (DfE) (1994) *Code of practice on the identification and assessment of special educational needs* (London, DfE).

Department for Education and Employment (DfEE) (1997a) *Excellence in education* (London, DfEE).

Department for Education and Employment (DfEE) (1997b) *Excellence for all children: meeting special educational needs* (London, DfEE).

Department for Education and Employment (DfEE) (1998) *Meeting special educational needs: a programme for action* (London, DfEE).

Department for Education and Skills (DfES) (2001a) *Special educational needs: code of practice* (London, DfES).

Department for Education and Skills (DfES) (2001b) *Inclusive schooling: children with special educational needs* (Statutory Guidance) (London, DfES).

Department for Education and Skills (DfES) (2003a) *Statistics of education: special educational needs in England: January 2003* (London, DfES).

Department for Education and Skills (DfES) (2003b) *Every child matters* (London, The Stationery Office).

Department for Education and Skills (DfES) (2004) *Removing barriers to achievement: the Government's strategy for SEN* (London, DfES Publications).

Department of Education and Science (DES) (1978) *Special educational needs: report of the committee of enquiry into the education of handicapped children and young people* (The Warnock Report) (London, HMSO).

Department of Health (DoH)/The Home Office (2003) *The Victoria Climbie Inquiry*. Report of an inquiry by Lord Laming (London, The Stationery Office).

Dyson, A. (2001) Special needs education as the way to equity: an alternative approach? *Support for Learning*, 16(3), 99–104.

Ford, J., Mongon, D. & Whelan, M. (1982) *Special education and social control: invisible disasters* (London, Routledge & Kegan Paul).

Fulcher, G. (1989) *Disabling policies: a comparative approach to educational policy and disability* (Lewes, Falmer Press).

Galloway, D. & Goodwin, C. (1987) *The education of disturbing children: pupils with learning and adjustment difficulties* (London, Longman).

Gamble, A. (2000) *Politics and fate: themes for the twenty first century* (Cambridge, Polity Press).

Gillborn, D. & Youdell, D. (2000) *Rationing education: policy, practice, reform and equity* (Buckingham, Open University Press).

HMSO (2001) *Special educational needs and disability act* (London, HMSO).

Hurt, J. (1988) *Outside the mainstream: a history of special education* (London, Routledge).

Kelly, P. (2001) Youth at risk: processes of individualisation and responsibilisation in the risk society, *Discourse: Studies in the Cultural Politics of Education*, 22(1), 23–33.

Kemshall, H. (2002) *Risk, social policy and welfare* (Buckingham, Open University Press).

Lupton, D. (Ed.) (1999) *Risk and sociocultural theory: new directions and perspectives* (Cambridge, Cambridge University Press).

Mason, M. & Rieser, R. (1990) *Disability equality in the classroom—a human rights issue* (London, Disability Equality in Education).

Murray, P. (2004) *Living with the spark: recognising ordinariness in the lives of disabled children and their families*. Ph.D thesis, University of Sheffield.

Murray, P. & Penman, J. (Eds) (1996) *Let our children be: a collection of stories* (Sheffield, Parents With Attitude).

Murray, P. & Penman, J. (Eds) (2000) *Telling our own stories: reflections on family life in a disabling world* (Sheffield, Parents With Attitude).

Oliver, M. (1996) *Understanding disability: from theory to practice* (London, Macmillan).

Oliver, M. & Barnes, C. (1998) *Disabled people and social policy: from exclusion to inclusion* (London, Longman).

Pritchard, D. G. (1963) *Education and the handicapped 1760–1960* (London, Routledge & Kegan Paul).

Rose, N. (1999) *Governing the soul: the shaping of the private self*, 2nd edition (London, Free Association Books).

Rose, N. & Miller, P. (1992) Political power beyond the state: problematics of government, *British Journal of Sociology*, 43(2), 173–205.

Rutter, M., Maughn, B., Mortimore, P., Ouston, J. & Smith, A. (1979) *Fifteen thousand hours: secondary schools and their effects on pupils* (London, Open Books).

Sigmon, S. B. (1987) *Radical analysis of special education: focus on historical development and learning disabilities* (London, The Falmer Press).

Slee, R. (2001a) 'Inclusion in Practice': does practice make perfect? *Educational Review*, 53(2), 113–123.

Slee, R. (2001b) Social justice and the changing directions in educational research: the case of inclusive education, *International Journal of Inclusive Education*, 5(2/3), 167–177.

Susser, M. (1998) Does risk factor epidemiology put epidemiology at risk? Peering into the future, *Journal of Epidemiology and Community Health*, Accessed online at: http://proquest.umi.com/pqdlink? (21 May 2002).

Thomas, G. & Loxley, A. (2001) *Deconstructing special education and constructing inclusion* (Buckingham, Open University Press).

Tomlinson, S. (1981) *Educational subnormality: a study in decision-making* (London, Routledge & Kegan Paul).

Tomlinson, S. (1982) *A sociology of special education* (London, Routledge & Kegan Paul).

Tomlinson, S. (2001) *Education in a post-welfare society* (Buckingham, Open University Press).

Race, ethnicity and education under New Labour

Sally Tomlinson

Introduction

The New Labour government came to power affirming a commitment to social justice and to education as a means to create a socially just society (Blair, 1997). In 1999 the Prime Minister asserted that 'nations that succeed will be tolerant, respectful of diversity, multi-racial societies' (Blair, 1999). The Conservative government had, between 1990 and 1997, virtually removed issues concerning racial and ethnic[1] inequalities in education from political consideration—outgoing Prime Minister Major asserting that 'policies must be colour blind ... and must just tackle disadvantage' (Major, 1997). Following their first election victory in 1997, New Labour was eager to affirm their view of a modern national identity which valued cultural diversity and recognised the citizenship rights of settled minorities and the inequalities they faced. Within a year, the new government had attempted to tackle a number of long-running grievances and inequalities. These included setting up a Social Exclusion Unit which would enquire immediately into the issue of school exclusion and truancy, particularly relating to black students; recognising in their first White Paper inequalities in achievement by different ethnic groups and lack of proper monitoring (DfEE, 1997); replacing the outdated Section 11 grant with an Ethic Minorities Achievement Grant;[2] making the first positive decision to offer Muslim schools state funding similar to that given to existing Anglican, Catholic, Methodist and Jewish schools; and announcing the setting up of an inquiry into the murder in 1993 of black student Stephen Lawrence (Macpherson, 1999).

However, by the second term it was becoming clear that the limited positive moves to alleviate ethnic inequalities in education were insufficient. Contradictions and conflicts due to hasty legislation were becoming more obvious and gaps between policy rhetoric and practical reality more evident, particularly between a rhetoric of 'inclusion' and a school system that increasingly separated different groups. Well before the government took office evidence had accumulated that 'choice' policies were increasing social and racial segregation (Gewirtz *et al.*, 1995; Tomlinson, 1997). Indeed, during the passing of the 1988 Education Act Lady Hooper, a Conservative Minister of State for Education, had concluded publicly that 'racial segregation may be a price to be paid for giving some parents the opportunity to choose' (Tomlinson, 1988, p. 108). Market policies in education continued to exacerbate a hierarchy of more and less desirable schools—the most desirable being less likely to be attended by minorities—and by 2004 a government committee felt able to assert that 'choice' policies in education had indeed led to the development of racially segregated schools (House of Commons, 2004). Punitive policies against 'failing' schools were creating new disadvantages for minorities. The failure to develop a curriculum which would educate all young people for a multicultural society had contributed to continuing ignorance and xenophobia between communities. Race riots in English northern towns in the summer of 2001 (Cantle, 2001); the events of 11 September 2001 in the USA; the 2003 war in Iraq; plus increased racism against refugees and asylum seekers, had moved political rhetoric away from support for addressing inequalities in a culturally diverse society towards new kinds of assimilationist policies (Back *et al.*, 2002). By 2004, even the Director of the Commission for Racial Equality was attacking multiculturalism as contributing to segregation and diverting attention from equality issues (Phillips, 2004).

This paper briefly notes policies affecting migration and minority experiences in Britain, noting that policies and legislation produced by the Home Office as well as the Department for Education and Skills, have affected the education of minorities. It then overviews some effects of policies of selection and diversity on minority students, examines the continuing attempts to improve the achievements of minorities and the facile comparisons made about the achievements of different groups, and considers the policies which have encouraged schools to rid themselves of students who interfere with the credentialing of others via various modes of exclusion. It notes the contradiction between declared intentions to offer a 'safe haven' to refugees (Home Office, 2002) and punitive policies towards refugees and their children, and considers some policies directed towards citizenship education and preparing pupils for 'positive participation in our ethnically diverse society' (Qualifications and Curriculum

Authority, 1999) despite the minimal attention given to the preparation of teachers for such a society.

Policies, Migration and Minorities

In the 2001 Census, nearly 8% of the UK population—4.6 million people—identified themselves as from an ethnic minority (ONS, 2003). The majority were British citizens, settled minorities originally from the Caribbean, Africa, India, Pakistan, Bangladesh, Hong Kong and China, and Cyprus. Patterns of settlement and original job opportunities meant that most minorities were living in London, Birmingham, Glasgow, Cardiff and other large cities and also in smaller northern English towns where, until the 1970s, there was employment in textile industries. By 2001, two London boroughs had more people who identified as ethnic minority rather than white, and census analysts have suggested that by 2011, Birmingham and Leicester will have non-white majorities. Minority groups have a younger age structure, some 43% of Bangladeshi and 35% of Pakistani groups being under 16 as compared with 20% of whites. It is becoming clearer that a future workforce will draw heavily on minority young people. During the 1990s, new patterns of migration were developing. An increase in temporary skilled migrant labour was encouraged by formalizing work permits. The Single European Act allowed more movement of EU nationals and there was an increase in transnational movement between countries. Civil wars in the 1990s brought in refugees and asylum seekers from Somalia, Sudan, Sri Lanka, Turkey, Bosnia, Kosova, Sierra Leone, Afghanistan and other places. There were some 110,000 applications for asylum in 2002 (of which two-thirds were refused) with much exaggeration given to figures in the tabloid media and much hostile publicity given to both accepted and illegal migrants.

The New Labour government had, from 1997, continued the avalanche of education-related legislation, policy initiatives, and advice which had characterised eighteen years of Conservative rule. There were two or more education bills and acts each year between 1997 and 2004—apart from 2003, a year blessedly free from legislation. Hundreds of Statutory Instruments, regulations and circulars accompanied this legislation and schools and Local Education Authorities spent countless hours preparing bids for policy initiatives. How all this activity affected the education of migrant and minority groups has not been subject to much rigorous research. A non-statutory policy consultation document on raising minority achievement (DfES, 2003a) depended heavily on a few academic studies and OFSTED monitoring (OFSTED, 1999; Gillborn & Mirza, 2000).[3]

The education of minority and migrant young people has been affected by Home Office legislation—a government response to the Stephen Lawrence Inquiry Report (Macpherson, 1999) being to introduce strengthened race relations legislation. The 2000 Race Relations (Amendment) Act requires public authorities to 'eliminate unlawful discrimination, promote equal opportunities and promote good race relations'. Local authorities must prepare Race Equality Schemes and all schools are required to have Race Equality Policies. This is an important measure that, for the first time, requires schools and Local Authorities to be pro-active rather than reactive in producing equality policies. The Commission for Racial Equality (CRE) has produced guidelines on the duties laid down in legislation. The schools inspectorate, OFSTED, which introduced a new framework for inspection in 2000, had not been particularly rigorous in inspecting for racial inequality to that date (Osler & Morrison, 2000) but now has a major role in monitoring the new legislation. However, other Home Office legislation has been more contentious. A White Paper (Home Office, 2002) outlined new policies for citizenship and nationality, followed by a Nationality, Immigration and Asylum Act in 2002 which required future British citizens to pass an English language and a citizenship test. The Act also proposed the building of 'accommodation centres' for asylum seekers which would provide separate schooling for the children, a move which has led to campaigns and arguments that such separate schooling could breach the children's human rights (Rutter, 2003).

The White Paper and 2002 legislation, although largely concerned with new migrations, was partly prompted by conflicts between white and Asian groups in the northern English towns of Bradford and Oldham in 2001. A Home Office sponsored report (Cantle, 2001) complained about the loss of 'community cohesion' and the school segregation of pupils, which was in fact the result of patterns of settlement, and 'white flight' over 30 years, exacerbated by school choice policies. One effect of Home Office legislation has been to conflate the problems of settled minority citizens, with those of new migrants. Home Secretary David Blunkett, commenting on the 2001 conflicts, referred to 'norms of acceptability ... those who come into our home ... should accept those norms', presenting long settled members of the Asian communities as visitors rather than citizens. It was noteworthy however, that politicians, alongside the general public, were quick to embrace the 'Britishness' of Amir Khan, a 17 year old College student from the neighbouring northern town of Bolton, who won a silver medal for boxing in the 2004 Olympics (Wainwright, 2004).

School diversity policies

New Labour post-1997 committed itself to continuing the Conservative policies of creating a diversity of schools, with market competition between schools fuelled by league table publication, school 'choice', the extension of a specialist school programme, and enhanced private funding and influence in education (Tomlinson, 2001; Chitty, 2004). While originally promising not to increase selection between schools, the remaining 164 grammar schools were retained, with the 1998 Schools Standards and Framework Act setting out a complex balloting procedure for parents to vote for change. The legislative requirements do in effect constitute discrimination against minority parents. In Calderdale, Yorkshire, the local Council estimated that 80% of Asian parents would not be able to vote.

A Beacon Schools programme, whereby schools were given money for recognised excellence, was initiated in 1998 and later expanded, as was an Academies programme whereby sponsors from private, voluntary and faith groups could establish new schools with running costs met by the State. The establishment of more faith schools was part of government policy, a White Paper in 2001 noting that ' over the past four years we have increased the range of faith schools, including the first Muslim, Sikh and Greek Orthodox schools'. This paper supported the view of the Archbishop of Canterbury's Council that more Church of England schools be established (DfES, 2001, p. 45). Government policy on faith schools has enhanced the contradictions inherent between inclusive education policies and separating pupils by faith. The 2001 White Paper, a precursor to the 2002 Education Act, reinforced the general policy of creating a diversity of schools—'a diverse system whereby schools differ markedly from each other in the particular contribution they chose to make but are equally excellent in giving their students a broad curriculum' (p. 38). It would seem to be important to know how these policies of diversity affect minorities.

By 2003 a hierarchy of schools was well established with around a thousand specialist schools in operation.[4] Overall there was private schooling for some 7% of pupils—who constituted some 26% of those staying in school to take A levels. Private schools have never provided information on numbers of British minority pupils attending, but there is some evidence from University applications that Chinese and Indian groups are more likely to use private education. For the majority of children in state-funded education, schools in many areas had become battlegrounds for parents anxious to get their children into desirable schools, but often these were defined as schools with low numbers of minority children (Gewirtz *et al.*, 1995). The government did, from the outset, recognise that the settlement of minorities in urban areas—40% of minority pupils attend schools in London, 18% in Birmingham and the west Midlands—meant that attention had to be paid to inner city schools. The urban schools most minority students moved into from the 1960s to the 1990s, although nominally comprehensive, had largely been schools for the working classes and had never been intended to prepare pupils for higher level academic work. A House of Commons Committee in 1995 had noted in 1995 the low performance in city schools 'which can propel a school on a downward slope, leading to a flight of more mobile parents' (House of Commons Education Committee, 1995, p. liv), and research during the 1990s demonstrated that school choice policies have tended to increase segregation in schools by social class and ethnicity (OECD, 1994; Ball *et al.*, 1996; Gillborn & Youdell, 2000).

The strongest evidence of the effects of this school diversity suggests that many white parents have continued to move their children away from schools with large numbers of minority pupils, while the emerging black and Asian middle classes adopt similar strategies to white parents, with expressed preferences for selective or private schools, or schools with low proportions of minority pupils (Noden *et al.*, 1998; Abbas, 2002). Choice continues to be more problematic for middle class and aspirant minorities. There is evidence that some black middle class parents are sending their children back to the Caribbean for secondary schooling, the young people then returning for College or University (Goring, 2004). Research by Noden and his colleagues showed that despite expressed preferences and high aspirations for their children, minority families were less likely to get their children into high performing schools. Even when minority students attend schools in predominantly white suburban areas and achieve well, they are still likely to report that they experience low teacher expectations and negative stereotyping (Smith, 2004). Schools which chose to become specialist sports schools are more likely to be located in inner cities and attended by minorities, and the examination performance of these schools is reported to be lower than in other specialist schools (Jesson, 2003). Research into the Beacon schools programme has suggested that students attending these better resourced schools feel more fortunate and successful than those at other schools, although the schools are supposed to spread their good practice. Sikh pupils at one West London Beacon school felt they had advantages over students in other schools and admired their (Sikh) Head of science who owned a Lexus car despite being not yet 30 (Hey & Bradford, 2004)!

Minority parents, especially African-Caribbean, have been enthusiastic for any forms of schooling that would seem to offer communities some measure of control over the education of their children.[5] The development of Academies has had some support. Parents in Brixton, South London, raised £4 million in sponsorship for an Academy, a plan given support by Nelson Mandela. Despite this, neither the local authority nor the government have been willing to buy the land required (Ward, 2004). However, there are no guarantees that these privately sponsored schools will admit pupils locally, especially in London. Other parents have demonstrated concern that Academies could easily be taken over by business or religious organisations—two already being sponsored by the Reg Vardy Foundation which promotes Christian evangelicalism, and creationism over evolution. One group of parents demonstrated their scepticism by putting their local school up for auction on the internet e-Bay auction site before it could be sponsored by this Foundation (Shaw, 2004). A Paper on *Transforming London secondary schools* (DfES, 2003c) promised that by 2006 there would be 290 specialist schools in London, including new schools, 21 Academies, 33 Extended Schools offering social and other services to families, 28 Training schools for teachers, 15–20 new sixth form Colleges. The paper also promised reductions in the achievement gap by class, gender and ethnicity. By July 2004 this had been overtaken by a government *Five year strategy for children and learners* (DfES, 2004), which asserted that there would be 200 Academies open or in preparation by 2010. It is unfortunate that the kind of long-term research, which during the 1980s was carried out by the now defunct Inner London Education Authority, has not been planned in order to monitor the effects of these proposed changes on minorities.

Excellence in cities

A well publicised and funded policy intended to improve the education of all children in cities was the Education Action Zone programme (EAZ's), initiated in 1998 with 73 zones in operation before their amalgamation into the *Excellence in cities* programme (DfEE, 1999) in 2004. The action zones were intended to combat urban disadvantage, and bring together schools, community and business influence to improve attainment. The Excellence in Cities programme was also intended to reassure inner city and outer estate parents, who could not 'take flight' that attention would be focused on attainment and behaviour. This programme was particularly aimed at minority parents, who for years had been vocal critics of the schools their children attended. In particular, the programme was to offer special programmes for gifted and talented children, provide more Learning Support Units for the disruptive and provide learning mentors for children. Although the DfES claimed in 2003 that these programmes had helped raise achievement in inner cities, research into the EAZ's was more equivocal (Power *et al.*, 2003) and the head of the schools inspectorate reported that the impact of the programmes had been 'variable' (Bell, 2003). One policy generally recognised as a success was the Sure Start programme, designed to improve the health, development and education of all children up to three years of age in areas of disadvantage. (DfEE, 1999). By 2003 some 486 Sure Start programmes were in operation, bringing together midwives, health visitors and play workers to offer services for some 300,000 children, and a Sure Start Unit was set up in the DfES. There is, as yet, no research exploring how this programme has impacted on ethnic minorities, although community workers in Tower Hamlets, London, noted that Bangladeshi mothers, while using Sure Start facilities, thought it was 'just a place for the children to go and play'.[6]

From 2001, in its second term of office, the New Labour government, having instigated a National Childcare Strategy linked to wider employment of women in its first term, gave more attention to child-care and children's services. In 2000 the torture and death of Victoria Climbie, an eight-year-old child of West African origin, led to a public inquiry into the failures of children's services, and in 2003 to the publication of a Green Paper *Every child matters* (DfES, 2003b). A Children's Minister, Margaret Hodge, was appointed to lead a Children's Directorate in the DfES and a Children's Act was passed in 2004 which required school, health and social services to work closely together. The Secretary of State for Education, speaking in September 2004 at a conference on childcare in London envisaged 'schools becoming community hubs, offering 'educare'—early years provision and health services' (Lepkowska, 2004, p. 10). However, the House of Commons Public Accounts Committee reported in September 2004 that many parents in deprived areas—where minority parents are more likely to live, were less likely to find or afford pre-school places (Public Accounts Committee, 2004).

Selective policies

Although in 1996 David Blunkett, then shadow secretary of state for education, promised no more selection under a Labour government, selection of pupils by schools continues to increase. Apart from the private sector, which selects by both income and by 'ability' in some schools, formal selection by an 11+ examination continues in 36 local education authorities. Under section 102 of the 1998 Education Act there is permitted 10% selection by 'aptitude' in all other schools, 6% of specialist schools being known to have taken up this option. There is selection by faith, and by covert selection by interviews and various other means in schools which are their own admission authorities (West & Hinds, 2003). Despite the plans for London schools, a majority of over-subscribed London secondary schools set entrance tests. Selection by mortgage, for those able to afford to move near to desirable schools, has been quantified by estate agents in Reading as £42,000 to be near a good primary school, £23,000 near a sought after secondary school (Garrett, 2003). The remaining 164 grammar schools have been allowed to increase their intake, equivalent to some eight more schools, and Hey and Bradford (2004) consider that Beacon schools are becoming 'reconstituted grammar schools'. The grammar schools predominantly educate middle-class children. Overall only 2% of children in selective schools are eligible for Free School Meals, compared to 18% nationally. In Birmingham 37.5% of children in comprehensive schools are on FSM, compared to 4% in the selective schools (Birmingham City Council, 2004).

Perhaps unsurprisingly, there is evidence that some minority parents are in favour of selection, in the hope that at least some of their children will have the benefit of superior resourcing and status in the remaining grammar schools. However children from minority groups have never done well in systems of selection. In the late 1980s Walford and Miller found that in the first City Technology College to be set up there were no students of Asian origin and only a few black students (Walford & Miller, 1991). In Birmingham in the 1970s only 1% of minority children attended the city's 21 grammar schools (Rex & Tomlinson, 1979). Twenty-five years later the remaining Birmingham grammar schools were 68% white, with 1% pupils of Bangladeshi origin, 3.2% African-Caribbean, 6.9% Pakistani and 14.4% Indian (Birmingham City Council, 2004). The city wards with the highest number of minority children had the lowest numbers selected for grammar schools. Abbas (2002), interviewing South Asian parents in Birmingham explained his respondents' support for selection partly because they 'viewed English education based in part on the residuals of a colonial education system experienced in Bangladesh, India and Pakistan'—where competition and selection was the norm. Additionally, as research has consistently documented (Tomlinson, 1984; Chen, 2004), economic migrants have always adopted 'middle-class' values towards education, whatever their class position. Education was and remains a necessity for economic mobility and to overcome disadvantage and discrimination. Abbas noted that the relative success in selection of the Indian group was due more to social class position and material advantages. Abbas also noted, in an analysis by religion, that Hindu and Sikh groups are more likely to do well in selective systems than Muslims. A study by Warren and Gillborn for Birmingham City Council Equalities Division (2004) documented minority parental anger and concern at what they saw as a distant and unresponsive education system.

Achievement issues

The relatively lower school achievements and examination performance of minority pupils became a major issue from the 1960s onwards, with a good deal of bitterness and frustration expressed by minority parents, who whatever their educational or economic background have always seen the need for their children to acquire educational credentials in order to obtain jobs or move into higher education. A large amount of research into ethnic achievements, documenting the lower attainments of African-Caribbean, Pakistani and Bangladeshi pupils in particular, has always been available to governments. Research during the 1980s and 1990s and into the 2000s has continued to find the same groups making less progress than other pupils, although attainments of all young people in public examinations rose considerably (Smith & Tomlinson, 1989; Demack *et al.*, 2000; Gillborn & Mirza, 2000). From 2002 information from the Pupil Level Annual Schools Census (PLASC) provided detailed information on performance at GCSE level by ethnic origin and gender, and also on the performance of smaller minority groups (DfES, 2003a). Osler and Vincent (2003, p. 17) pointed out that international studies have confirmed the importance of examining the intersection of ethnicity and gender in order to understand achievement. They noted that anxieties in England about 'boys' underachievement', were in fact about white male under-achievement, and the overall improvement in girls school performance masked the educational difficulties of significant numbers of girls from minority backgrounds.

The New Labour government did view the issue of minority achievement with concern, setting up a Unit in the Education Department to monitor achievements in 1997, (now an Ethnic Minorities Achievement Division) and providing money for local authorities with significant numbers of minority pupils with an Ethnic Minority Achievement Grant costing some £155 million annually. Every White Paper and document introducing new legislation since 1997 has included a section on raising standards and achievements of minorities. The White Paper preceding the 2002 Education Act noted that 'There are encouraging signs that standards have risen rapidly among some ethnic minority groups. However many pupils from ethnic minorities are not achieving as well as they could. It is unacceptable that, for instance, children of Caribbean, Pakistani or Bangladeshi backgrounds have been half as likely to leave school with 5 good grades at GCSE as children of some other ethnic backgrounds' (DfES, 2001, p. 24). Policies to improve the situation in 2001 included general strategies to improve learning, repeating strategies in the Excellence in Cities programme, with the addition of an 'Excellence Challenge' programme to encourage more young people into higher education, working more closely with the Inspectorate and the Teacher Training Agency, better monitoring of the EMAG grant, supporting teachers with second language speakers in their classrooms and recruiting more teachers from minority backgrounds—a recommendation with a long and unsuccessful history.

By 2003 the government was acknowledging that 'opportunities are unequal for many of the one in eight pupils who come from a minority ethnic background' (DfES, 2003a, p. 4), speculating on the reasons for differential performance between minority groups, and repeating in more detail proposals to improve the situation, including a more comprehensive English as an Additional Language strategy. The paper included a warning that if African-Caribbean pupils 'continue to be failed by the system' they will end up in the criminal justice system (p. 32). The system appeared to be failing over the following year, according to a 2004 research report on the educational experiences and achievements of black boys in London (London Development Agency, 2004). This research was sponsored by the Mayor of London, Ken Livingstone, and documented again the lower achievements of boys of African Caribbean origin in public examinations.

In attempting to explain the overall differential performance of different ethnic groups, especially Indian and Chinese pupils, who on a national level achieve more GCSE's than white pupils even when socio-economic status is taken into consideration, some facile comparisons are made between groups which have the effect, long noted in research, of pathologising black and Muslim students and families. The White Paper *Aiming high* (DfES, 2003a), for example, refers to the fact that 'many African Asian and Chinese communities developed after the Pakistani community, yet these young people have significantly better exam results' (p. 10). There is no recognition that a majority of Pakistani settlers came largely from rural backgrounds and parents undertook low skill low wage jobs, whereas the East African Asians (Indian) settling after expulsion from Kenya and Uganda in the 1970s, had higher educational and entrepreneurial backgrounds and rapidly achieved middle class status. Chinese families settling in the 1970s were also from more educated backgrounds (Chen, 2004). Patterns of settlement have ensured that overall Chinese children are more likely to attend schools with few other minorities (Burgess & Wilson, 2003). Both groups, as many white middle class parents do, make much use of private tutoring.

The *Aiming high* paper noted that in the PLASC census 28% of Caribbean secondary school pupils were recorded as having special educational needs, with schools more than four times more likely to exclude these boys, but made no comment about the long history of negative treatment of black pupils in the English educational system which has continued into the 2000s. The report by the London Development Agency's Education Commission (2004) referred yet again to the lower teacher expectations, unfair behaviour management practice, high levels of exclusion and an inappropriate curriculum, which research over forty years had documented, although the General Secretary of the National Union of Teachers rightly noted that blaming teachers for a complex situation was counter-productive. Shotte (2002), researching the school experiences of pupils relocated from the volcanic Caribbean Island of Montserrat from 1995, found that levels of performance and motivation, good in the Montserrat system, declined rapidly in London schools, with teachers and parents mutually misunderstanding each other in discussions of achievement, behaviour, language and curriculum. Both government and parents groups see the appointment of more black teachers as one solution to improving black achievements. In 2004 there were some 4% of teachers from black and other minority backgrounds in the teaching force.

Higher education

Those minority students who do achieve the required A levels or equivalent are increasingly well-represented in higher education, assisted by government policies which required institutions of Higher Education to widen access and participation for disadvantaged groups—included those disadvantaged by socio-economic position, ethnicity, or disability. Being female was less likely to be regarded as a disadvantage from the mid 1990s, when girls achieved equal numbers of undergraduate places in higher education—a move that resulted in differences in participation between girls from different social and ethnic groups being ignored. The 2004 Higher Education Act allowed Universities to charge up to £3000 for their courses, but all would be required to demonstrate to an Office for Fair Access that they had developed bursaries and other measures to encourage disadvantaged students. Research from the later 1990s indicated that Indian, Chinese and black African groups were well represented in higher education—African-Caribbean men, Pakistani and Bangladeshi women least well—the latter coming from the most disadvantaged backgrounds. Minorities were more likely to study part time and attend the new universities (Owen *et al.*, 2000). Minority students were less likely than white applicants to gain admission to traditional universities. Indeed, Shiner and Modood found that 'when applying to the old universities, there is strong evidence that minority candidates face an ethnic penalty. Institutions in this sector are more likely to select white or Chinese candidates from among a group of similarly qualified applicants' (Shiner & Modood, 2002, p. 228). In general applicants from ethnic minorities have to perform better than white peers to achieve places in old universities. How far applications and rates of success by various minority groups will be affected by new fee policies, is as yet unknown.

Exclusion and failing schools

Whether or not the New Labour government was aware that the development of an education market had further encouraged schools to get rid of pupils who disrupt the smooth running of schools and interfere with the credentialing of others, attention has been paid to the numbers of students, topping 12,000 in 1997, excluded from mainstream schooling. African-Caribbean pupils, previously removed and four times over-represented in the old category of special education known as 'educationally subnormal' (Coard, 1970; Tomlinson, 1982) and as 'emotionally and behaviourally disturbed' were, during the 1990s, candidates for removal into Pupil Referral Units and by straight exclusion (expulsion) from school on both a temporary and permanent basis. Gillborn had pointed out in 1995 that exclusions from school operate in a racist manner and deny a disproportionate number of pupils access to mainstream education. (Gillborn, 1995). Parsons (1999) pointed out that the media tended to emphasise the violence of excluded pupils and, since disproportionate numbers of students from African-Caribbean background are excluded, links between school exclusion, criminality and black students are assumed. Maud Blair (2001) who placed the issue in a broad social and historical perspective, in fact showed that black pupils were criticised and excluded from school more than white children who committed similar and often minor 'offences', and Osler and Vincent (2003) explored the complexities of inclusion and exclusion from education as they applied to girls from all social and ethnic groups. As part of a wider policy to tackle social exclusion, and following recommendations from the first report of the Social Exclusion Unit (1998), the government set targets for reducing exclusions and introduced Behaviour Support Plans and Behaviour Improvement Plans to be implemented and funded by local education authorities. Although numbers of children excluded dropped for two years they began to rise again by 2001, after which targets for reducing exclusion were dropped and an emphasis placed on full-time education outside mainstream class-rooms. The issue does not appear to be fully understood by government as one which creates much bitterness among black pupils and parents. The young people Maud Blair spoke to in her study were particularly angered by the negative racial stereotypes they felt schools and teachers attached to them (Blair, 2001), and Goring (2004) documented the very real fear that even middle-class black parents felt that their children would be excluded from school and denied mainstream education. OFSTED has noted that the standard of alternative provision is unsatisfactory and excluded pupils have poor standards of teaching.

A further policy that continues to disadvantage minorities has been the official targeting of schools, from 1993, as 'failing' and 'in need of special measures' on criteria applied by OFSTED. Schools move in and out of special measures, depending on whether their examination performance is thought to be improving, and some schools have been given 'Fresh Starts' with new headteachers and school names. Over the past ten years over a thousand schools have been identified as in need of special measures. The schools identified have been largely concentrated in deprived areas and, especially in London, attended by high proportions of minority pupils and second language speakers. A 'failing' school closed after a court case in 1995, Hackney Downs in London, had 80% of pupils of minority and refugee background, 70% second language speakers and a high proportion of children with special needs and in poverty (O'Connor *et al.*, 1999).[7] The press coverage of failing schools has always been derisory with blame attached to pupils, parents and teachers. The 'naming and shaming of schools' was officially abandoned by Labour in 1998, but in May 2003 Prime Minister Blair was still claiming that 'weak' schools which failed to reach exam targets would close. On current examination performance these are likely to be schools attended by minorities and refugee children.

Refugee children

Contradictory policies which claim to offer a safe haven to refugees (Home Office, 2002) while enacting 'tough' policies designed to placate an increasingly xenophobic electorate, do little to counter print media hostility to both economic migrants and asylum seekers, and affect the settlement and education of thousands of refugee children.[8] Conservative policies in the early 1990s restricting the welfare entitlements of asylum seekers were continued and extended by New Labour after 1997. Policies of dispersal of those awaiting decisions on applications mean that families and children are often housed in areas hostile to their presence. Refugee agencies report an increase in racist abuse and attacks and 'the majority of perpetrators of racist harassment are young' (Rutter, 2003, p. 141). All studies of refugee pupils' experiences indicate that a majority suffer racial harassment in school and in their neighbourhoods. Rather than developing policies which might encourage integration and acceptance of refugees, the Nationality, Immigration and Asylum Act of 2002 outlined increasingly punitive policies against asylum seekers, Part Two of the Act suggesting the setting up of accommodation centres, with sections 36–38 allowing for the separate education of asylum seeking children. One argument presented by the Home Secretary in defending this legislation was that some schools were overwhelmed by refugee pupils entering, despite evidence which indicated that schools and teachers taking refugee children were not complaining, and worked well with them, despite lack of funding. Allocation of funds per pupil, determined by an annual schools census, often miss out refugee pupils entering after the census, no aspect of the Ethnic Minorities Achievement Grant (see note 2) relates to work with refugees, and there is insufficient funding for any English as an Additional Language work (Refugee Council, 2000; Rutter, 2003). The Refugee Council has suggested a written education policy on support for refugee and asylum seeking children—two local authorities (Camden London, and Gloucestershire), having already prepared such local policies. Although the New Labour government has been strong on a rhetoric of partnership and sharing good practice, there has been a general reluctance to support the transfer of good practice between local authorities where issues of race, ethnicity and/or refugees are concerned.

Curriculum and language issues

Arguably, the most serious omission concerning the education of all young people in a multiethnic society concerns the failure of successive governments to encourage curriculum policies that would combat cultural ignorance, ethnocentric attitudes and racism. Despite Lord Swann's impressive report in 1985, which recommended a rethink of the curriculum to reflect the pluralist nature of society (DES, 1985), there was much antagonism to the idea that an Anglocentric curriculum needed to change. There was considerable government interference with the working groups set up to develop a national curriculum in 1988, Prime Minister Thatcher attempting to impose her views of traditional British history (Phillips, 1998), and documenting in her memoirs her irritation at any suggestion of multiculturalism or anti-racism (Thatcher, 1993). A Task Group set up to 'consider ways the national curriculum can broaden the horizon of all pupils as well as the particular needs of pupils from ethnic minority backgrounds' had its report censored (Tomlinson 1993), and the first Chair of the NCC reported that it was made 'starkly clear' to him by Conservative Ministers that any references to multicultural education would be unacceptable (Graham, 1993).

The New Labour government, while unafraid to take central control of curriculum delivery and assessment, was similarly reluctant to encourage curriculum changes to prepare all young people for life in a multiethnic society. The Macpherson Report on the murder of Stephen Lawrence included four recommendations on education, one of these being that 'consideration be given to the amendment of the national curriculum aimed at valuing cultural diversity and preventing racism, in order to better reflect the needs of a diverse society' (Macpherson, 1999). The Qualifications and Curriculum Authority responded with an assurance that the curriculum from 2000 would help young people to become 'healthy, lively, enquiring individuals capable of rational thought and positive participation in our ethnically diverse society' (QCA, 1999). However there has been little guidance to teachers on how to achieve this aim. David Blunkett, Secretary of State for Education until 2001, when he became Home

Secretary, encouraged the notion of citizenship education, appointing an advisory group, chaired by his old university tutor Bernard Crick to consider the teaching of citizenship and democracy (Crick, 1998). This group recommended that citizenship education should be mandatory in all schools, a recommendation which took effect from 2002. Figueroa has noted that the targets set for citizenship education do not include diversity, conflict resolution, international or global issues or gender and ethnic equality and anti-racism (Figueroa, 2003). As Home Secretary Blunkett continued his focus on citizenship, the Nationality, Immigration and Asylum Act required new citizens to take a citizenship oath and allowed for regulations on the testing of citizens on life in Britain and knowledge of English. A further report by Crick in 2003 recommended that those seeking citizenship should show measurable progress in a UK language—English, Welsh or Gaelic (Crick, 2003).

The promotion of policies to teach English to new citizens is somewhat ironic if the history of teaching English as a second language is examined. Teaching 'immigrant' children English was a major priority in the 1960s, and there was a consensus among policy-makers, educationalists and parents that children should be fluent in English (Tomlinson, 1983). Most local authorities that received Section 11 money for assisting minority children employed specialist language teachers and during the 1970s and 1980s bilingualism was researched, debated and encouraged. The end of Section 11 and the introduction of the Ethnic Minority Achievement grant in the 1990s, led to the dispersal of expert bilingual teachers. At the adult level, there is a shortage of teachers of English for Speakers of Other Languages (ESOL) and migrants other than refugees must live in the UK for three years before they qualify for free ESOL classes (Midgley, 2004).

Despite repeated assertions that teachers needed preparation to teach in a multiethnic Britain, during the 1990s many university and local authority courses for such preparation disappeared and student teachers are now less likely to have any preparation in the area than in the 1980s. The Teacher Training Agency produced guidelines in 2000 which noted that 'every trainee teacher needs to understand how to prepare all pupils to play a part in a culturally diverse democratic society which values everybody and accords them equal rights' but there is little advice on how to bring this about (TTA, 2000). The TTA is currently preparing an expensive web site for teachers in training to consult, in place of face-to-face courses. OFSTED, the schools inspectorate, has produced more useful guidelines on what is expected from schools, and has monitored developments on achievements, but there has been little evidence that government policy is guiding the various agencies towards a curriculum that might combat the racism and ignorance evident in the popular press and demonstrated in the increasing support for fascist political parties in the country.

Conclusion

The Conservative government preceding New Labour was still strongly attached to imperial views of a traditional British identity which rejected debate over cultural diversity and racial equality. The multicultural, anti-racist policies and practices in education that were slowly developing during the 1980s had more or less disappeared by the 1990s. The New Labour government initially appeared more aware that an education system incorporating some measure of social justice and equity, and responding to cultural diversity, was both a modern response to globalization, and also a more economically sensible way of preparing a future workforce (Tomlinson, 2004). The early recognition and attempts to redress long-running educational inequalities and strengthen race relations legislation signalled an intention to work towards a more democratic multicultural society less influenced by Britain's imperial past.

But good intentions and politics seldom mix, and as this paper has documented, contradictory policies in education, particularly market policies which encourage parents and students to compete for good schools and educational resources, and allow for the further segregation of social and ethnic groups, do not ensure justice and equity. Market reforms ensure winners and losers and although the life chances of some minorities may be enhanced, the majority remain in disadvantaged positions. Explanations for educational success or failure which criticise schools attended by minorities or hold particular communities or groups of students responsible for their low achievements are unacceptable given the history of discrimination and difficulties minorities have faced in incorporation into an education system designed for a white majority. Singling out a few students for a superior education does not raise achievement as a whole. Punitive policies towards refugees and asylum seekers have encouraged racism in the wider society. There have been no educational policies designed to counter a xenophobic nationalism exacerbated after 11 September 2001, which resulted in enhanced hostility towards Muslims and media-fed hostility towards economic migrants and refugees. Despite the introduction of citizenship studies, there has been no review of the National Curriculum to enquire whether it reflects Britain as a multicultural society. Exhortations to achieve well and obtain qualifications and skills are only of use to individuals if there are social and educational policies which aim for a secure and productive life for all members in the society. Market policies which legitimise inequalities will continue to exclude many of those belonging to minority groups and do little to advance social justice. The potential for continued disadvantage and new forms of exclusion of racial and ethnic minorities in national education systems, which affects their placement in a global economy, is becoming very obvious.

Notes

1. Groups are described in this article as racial or ethnic on the basis of characteristics attributed to them by others (Rex, 1986) and on self-assignment in the 2001 Census, (ONS, 2003). The major categories in the Census were White, Irish and White Other, Mixed, Asian or Asian-British, Black or Black British, Chinese, Other Ethnic Groups.
2. An Ethnic Minority Achievement Grant (EMAG—briefly EMTAG when Travellers children were added in 2001–2) replaced Section 11 of the 1966 Local Government Act, which provided extra funding for local authorities with significant numbers of New Commonwealth children.

3. The non-statutory consultation Paper *Aiming high: raising the achievement of minority ethnic pupils* (DfES, 2003) was intended as a statement of government policy towards the education of minority children. It has nothing to say about the education of all young people in a multi-ethnic society.
4. By 2003 some 173 schools specialised in arts, 18 in business, 4 in engineering, 157 in languages, 12 in computing and maths, 24 in science, 162 in sports and 443 in technology. It is government policy to increase numbers of specialist schools—a five year plan published in July 2004 envisages that all secondary schools will eventually specialise, despite the requirement that they all offer a 'broad and balanced curriculum' to all pupils.
5. There is a long history of black parents providing supplementary schools over which they had control.
6. Discussion with Sure Start worker.
7. A newly-built Academy—Mossbourne—sponsored by shipping freight businessman Clive Bourne, opened in September 2004 on the site of Hackney Downs school.
8. Numbers of refugee children are hard to establish. In January 2002 there were an estimated 82,000 refugee children in school, 70% in the London area. 'Refugee' has a defined legal status under a 1967 UN Protocol. 'Asylum seeker' is one who has crossed an international border to seek safety and is waiting for a decision to remain in the country.

Note on contributor

Sally Tomlinson is Emeritus Professor of Educational Policy at Goldsmiths College, London University and a Senior Research Associate in the Department of Educational Studies, University of Oxford. She has taught, researched and published in the area of race ethnicity and education for over 25 years. She is currently writing a book on *Race and education in Britain 1960–2004: a political history*.

References

Abbas, T. (2002) The home and the school in the educational achievements of south Asians, *Race Ethnicity and Education*, 5(3), 292–316.
Back, L, Solomos, J. & Shukra K. (2002) Challenge of unrest brings out Labour's true colours, *Times Higher Education Supplement*,14 June, 22–23.
Ball, S., Bowe, R. & Gewirtz, S. (1996) School choice, social class and distinction: the realisation of social disadvantage in education, *Journal of Educational Policy*, 11(1), 89–112.
Bell, D. (2003) Education Action Zones and excellence in cities, *Educational Review*, Vol 15 (London, National Union of Teachers).
Birmingham City Council (2004) *City Statistics.*
Blair, M. (2001) *Why pick on me: school exclusion and black youth* (Stoke-on-Trent. Trentham Books).
Blair, T. (1997) Speech to the 1997 Labour Party Conference (Brighton, October).
Blair, T. (1999) The Prime Minister's New Year speech given at Trimdon Community Centre (County Durham, Durham).
Burgess, S. & Wilson, D. (2003) *Ethnic segregation in England's schools. CMPO working paper 03/86* (Bristol, University of Bristol).
Cantle, T. (2001) *Building community cohesion* (London, The Home Office).
Chen, Yangguang. (2004) *The negotiation of equality of opportunity for emergent bilingual children in English mainstream classes* Unpublished PhD thesis (London, Goldsmiths College, London University).
Chitty, C. (2004) *Educational policy in Britain* (London, Palgrave-Macmillan).

Coard, B. (1970) *How the West Indian child is made ESN in the English school system* (London, New Beacon Books).

Crick, B. (1998) *Education for citizenship and the teaching of democracy in schools. Final report of the advisory group on citizenship* (London, Qualifications and Curriculum Authority).

Crick, B. (2003) *The new and the old, interim report. Living in the United Kingdom group* (London, Home Office).

Demack, S., Drew, D. & Grimsley, M. (2000) Minding the Gap: ethnic, gender and social class differences in attainment at 16, *Race Ethnicity and Education*, 3, 117–144.

Department for Education and Employment. (1997) *Excellence in schools* (London, The Stationery Office).

Department for Education and Employment. (1999a) *Excellence in cities* (London, The Stationery Office).

Department for Education and Employment (1999b) *Sure Start: a guide for trailblazers* (London, DfEE).

Department for Education and Science (1985) *Education for all: the Swann Report* (London, HMSO).

Department for Education and Skills (2001) *Schools: achieving success* (London, The Stationery Office).

Department for Education and Skills (2003a) *Aiming high: raising the achievement of minority ethnic pupils* (London, DfES).

Department for Education and Skills (2003b) *Every child matters (Green Paper)* (London, The Stationery Office).

Department for Education and Skills (2003c) *Transforming London secondary schools* (London, The Stationery Office).

Figueroa, P. (2003) Diversity and citizenship in England, in: J.A. Banks (Ed.) *Diversity and citizenship education: global perspectives* (New York, Jossey-Bass), 219–244.

Garret, A. (2003) *Top dollar to be top of the class,* The Observer (Property) 21 September.

Gewirtz, S., Ball, S. & Bowe, R. (1995) *Markets, choice and equity in education* (Buckingham, Open University Press).

Gillborn, D. (1995) *Racism and exclusion from school.* Paper to European Conference on Educational Research (Bath, University of Bath).

Gillborn, D. & Mirza, H. (2000) *Educational inequalities: mapping race, class and gender* (London, Office for Standards in Education).

Gillborn, D. & Youdell, D. (2000) *Rationing Education* (London, Routledge).

Goring, B. (2004) *The perspectives of Caribbean parents on schooling and education: continuity and change* Unpublished PhD. (London, University of the South Bank).

Graham, D. (1993) *A lesson for us all: The making of the English national curriculum* (London, Routledge).

Hey, V., and Bradford, S. (2004) *Successful subjectivities? The beaconisation of class, ethnic and gender positions.* Paper to Conference on New Labour's Education Policy and Social Justice (Northampton, University College Northampton).

Home Office (2002) *Secure borders, safe haven: integration with diversity in modern Britain* (London, The Stationery Office, Cm. 5387).

House of Commons Education Committee (1995) *Performance in city schools, third report* (London, HMSO).

House of Commons Education Committee (2004) *Social cohesion: report of a select committee* (London, House of Commons).

Jesson, D. (2003) *Educational outcomes and value-added by specialist schools* (London, The Specialist Schools Trust).

Lepkowska, D. (2004) *Children's bill will cost billions,* Times Educational Supplement, 19 September.

London Development Agency. (2004) *Rampton revisited: the educational experiences and achievements of black boys in London schools* (London, London Development Agency Education Commission).

Major, J. (1997) Speech given at the Commonwealth Institute London, 18 January.

MacPherson, Sir W. (1999) *The Stephen Lawrence enquiry* (London, The Stationery Office, Cm. 4262).

Midgley, S. (2004) Three Year Rule is a Two-Edged Sword, *Times Educational Supplement* FE Focus. 3/9/04

Noden, P., West, A., David, M. & Edge, A. (1998) Choices and destinations at transfer to secondary schools in London, *Journal of Educational Policy,* 13, 221–236.

O'Connor, M., Hales, E., Davies, J. & Tomlinson, S. (1999) *Hackney Downs. The school that dared to fight* (London, Cassell).

OECD (1994) *Schools: a matter of choice* (Paris, Centre for Research and Innovation, OECD).

Office for National Statistics (2003) *The National Census 2001* (London, ONS).

Office for Standards in Education (1999) *Raising the attainment of minority ethnic pupils: school and LEA responses* (London, OFSTED).

Osler, A. & Morrison, M. (2000) *Inspecting schools for race equality: OFSTED's strengths and weaknesses* (Stoke-on-Trent, Trentham Books).

Osler, A. & Vincent, K. (2003) *Girls and exclusion: rethinking the agenda* (London, Routledge-Falmer).

Owen, D., Pritchard, A. & Maguire, A. (2000) *Ethnic minority participation and achievements in education, training and the labour market race for the future* (Warwick, DfEE/ University of Warwick, Paper 225).

Phillips, R. (1998) *History teaching, nationhood and the state* (London, Cassell).

Phillips, T. (2004) *Multiculturalisms' legacy is have a nice day racism,* The Guardian, 28 May.

Power, S., Whitty, G., Gewirtz, S., Halpin, D. & Dickson, M. (2003) *Paving a third way: A policy trajectory analysis of EAZs : final report to the ESRC* (London, Institute of Education, University of London).

Public Accounts Committee (2004) *Early years: progress in developing high quality child care and early education : report no 444* (London, House of Commons).

Qualifications and Curriculum Authority (1999) *Review of the National Curriculum in England* (London, QCA).

Rex, J. (1986) *Race and ethnicity* (Buckingham, Open University Press).

Rex, J. & Tomlinson, S. (1979) *Colonial immigrants in a British city: a class analysis* (London, Routledge).

Refugee Council (2000) *Helping refugee children in schools* (London, The Refugee Council).

Rutter, J. (2003) *Supporting refugee children in 21st century Britain (2nd edition)* (Stoke-on Trent, Trentham Books).

Shaw, M. (2004) School put up for internet auction, *Times Educational Supplement,* 3 September.

Shotte, G. (2002) *Education, migration and identities: relocated Montserratian Children in London schools.* Unpublished PhD thesis. (London, Institute of Education, University of London).

Shiner, M. & Modood, T. (2002) Help or hindrance? Higher education and the route to ethnic equality, *British Journal of Sociology of Education,* 23, 209–232.

Smith, D.J. & Tomlinson, S. (1989) *The school effect: A study of multiracial comprehensives* (London, Policy Studies Institute).

Smith, Z. (2004) *My* smart school still failed me, *The Observer,* 12 September, p. 18.

Social Exclusion Unit. (1998) *Truancy and exclusion from school* (London, The Stationery Office).

TTA. (2000) *Raising the attainment of minority ethnic pupils: guidance and resource materials* (London, Teacher Training Agency).

Thatcher, M. (1993) *The Downing Street years* (London, Harper-Collins).

Tomlinson, S. (1982) *A sociology of special education* (London, Routledge).

Tomlinson, S. (1983) *Ethnic minorities in British schools* (London, Heinemann).

Tomlinson, S. (1984) *Home and school in multicultural Britain* (London, Batsford).

Tomlinson S. (1988) Education and training: reports, *New Community,* 15(1), 103–109.

Tomlinson, S. (1993) The multicultural task group: the group that never was, in: A. King & M. Riess (Eds) *The Multicultural dimension of the national curriculum* (London, Falmer), 21–31.

Tomlinson, S. (1997) Diversity, choice and ethnicity, *Oxford Review of* Education, 23(1), 67–76.

Tomlinson, S. (2001) *Education in a post-welfare society* (Buckingham, Open University Press).

Tomlinson, S. (2004) Globalization, race and education: continuity and change, *Journal of Educational Change*, 4, 213–230.

Walford, G. & Miller, H. (1991) *City Technology Colleges* (Buckingham, Open University Press).

Ward, L. (2004) Parents told to buy their own school, *Guardian Education*, 11 June.

Warren, S. & Gillborn, D. (2004) *Race equality and education in Birmingham* (Birmingham, Equalities Division, Birmingham City Council).

West, A. & Hinds, A. (2003) *Secondary school admissions in England: exploring the extent of overt and covert selection* (London, Centre for Research and Information on State Education).

A reconstruction of the gender agenda: the contradictory gender dimensions in New Labour's educational and economic policy

Madeleine Arnot and Philip Miles

Introduction

> New Labour is a party of ideas and ideals but not of outdated ideology. What counts is what works. The objectives are radical. The means will be modern. (Labour Manifesto, 1997, p. 4)

In this paper, we consider how Labour's policy repertoire has re-interpreted gender politics for the twenty-first century. Sociologically speaking, we are interested in how gender relations are recontextualised, produced and reproduced through education (Arnot, 2000). Social reproduction theory suggests that in the 1980s and 1990s gender boundaries and identities were loosened as a consequence of, on the one hand, the processes of individualisation encouraged by Conservative educational policy which emphasised choice, standards and excellence and, on the other hand, the effects of vibrant feminist movements which were especially active in the education system and which encouraged girls especially to seek autonomy by breaking out of traditional gender moulds (Arnot, *et al.*, 1999). Gender codes within the educational system which in the past differentiated between the sexes had also shifted substantially by the time Labour came to power. In the late 1980s, the Conservative government's response had been to turn back the schooling system towards traditionally male educational forms of knowledge, pedagogy and evaluation systems whilst holding onto modernising economic agendas.

Our paper reviews the first phases of the Labour government's gender policy in relation to education. It draws upon the various critical interpretations of New Labourism which assess the ways in which egalitarian discourses (especially feminism) were aligned with the agendas of performativity in schooling. The tensions and contradictions associated with Labour reforms of schooling and the ways it tackled what is euphemistically called 'the gender gap' are exposed through these analyses, suggesting just how complex were New Labour's gender politics. For example, critics suggest that the first phase of the Labour government paradoxically promoted both an increased feminisation of schooling and the (re)masculinisation of schooling. At the same time, its schooling policy contributed to an aggravated hierarchy of masculinities and neglected the educational needs of lower achieving and excluded girls. Such policies arguably have added to the widening of social class inequalities within male and female categories (Gillborn & Mirza, 2000). The mix of *laissez-faire* and accountability politics used for schooling contrasts sharply with the rhetoric of social inclusion and equality politics associated with interventionist economic and welfare policies. Such is the complexity of Labour's gender politics that it is difficult to do more than offer an embryonic assessment of the impact of Labour's education policies on gender relations.

Influenced by feminist theorist Iris Marion Young, Sharon Gewirtz (1998) argued for the need to use a range of 'equality indicators' to make sense of this complexity. When assessing post-welfarist Labour policies, she considered whether such policies encouraged, for example: (a) exploitative relationships, marginalisation and inclusion within and beyond educational institutions; (b) the promotion of relationships based on recognition, respect, care and mutuality, or the production of powerlessness; (c) practices of cultural imperialism; (d) and/or violent practices within and beyond the educational system. Her preliminary audit of Labour education policies suggested a 'complex amalgam' of at least ten key discursive strands of which only some had 'both distributional and relational dimensions' (p. 61). Labour's commitment to *experimentation, redistribution, welfare integration, responsibilisation, associationalisation* and *professionalisation* implies egalitarian goals whilst the other four elements, *marketisation, managerialism, privatisation* and *pedagogic traditionalism* were antithetical ideologically and in practice to such goals. The key issue, she argued, was whether individuals would experience their marginality or feel empowered by Labour reforms. On first reading it seemed such reforms were more likely to 'perpetuate social injustice' and to shift blame for such injustice onto communities, parents, pupils and teachers rather than onto the state.

The much quoted 1997 Labour Manifesto was quite explicit about its goals for schools: 'standards not structures are the key to success' (p. 2). This neo-liberal ethic inherited from the Conservative government suggested that Tony Blair's agenda was unlikely to engage seriously in a modernist intervention educational project in the name of gender equality. Avoiding the traditional Labour emphases on universalism, consensus and material equality (Forbes, 2002, p. 34), concerns such as 'individuation, realisation of self, celebration of difference and the construction of identity' (p. 35) helped shaped the new agenda. This was a time when the concept of the Third Way inferred a new form of political relationship between the state and the populace—the gender agenda therefore would be reformulated within a 'refreshed' notion of educational governance. In our first section we consider this construction of the 'gender problem' through the policy focus on boys' underachievement. In the second section we discuss the critiques of Labour policy of those concerned about girls' education and the marginalisation of feminist expertise in this policy field. The consequences for gender politics in education are explored in the conclusion.

From equality to performativity: the emergent boys' education debate

Initially, Labour education policy was dominated by three major concerns—the need to raise standards, increase cost effectiveness, and respond to the demands of a changing and often unpredictable labour market (Orr, 2000). Although gender differences in attainment were an obstacle to the achievement of such national targets—the mechanisms for tackling them were not described. There were few or even no specific mentions of gender inequality in the plethora of policy documents produced by the new Labour government. Nor was there a celebration of the success of girls in closing many of the gaps in science and maths, and in school leaving examinations at 16 and at 18 years (Arnot *et al.*, 1999). The failure to address women's rights and gender equality in mainstream education policy suggested that gender redistribution or recognition were not major goals.

The problem associated with 'the gender gap' at 16 was defined as that of boys (particularly white, working-class boys) whose lack of educational motivation and achievement Chris Woodhead (as Chief Inspector at OFSTED) declared to be 'one of the most disturbing problems we face within the whole education system' (quoted in Raphael Reed, 1998, p. 57). This shift in emphasis drew different agents and agencies into the gender policy field. The agenda was worked on primarily by new groups of (predominantly male) gender consultants with an interest in performance agendas. They replaced feminist educationalists who were sidelined to the periphery of educational policy-making. The consequences of this strategy not only antagonised feminist educationalists but also lost for the government the possibility of drawing on the last twenty years of research and policy development in the UK which had been so successful in strengthening girls' educational achievement. Feminist academics who were co-opted into the QCA Gender Advisory Group quickly discovered that their role was to legitimate reforms that were already *fait accompli* (Mahony, 2003). Equally significant was the marginalisation of the Equal Opportunities Commission despite its legal powers to constrain sex discrimination in education and support schools (Madden, 2000). As a consequence, Labour education policies were likely to aggravate problems of differential patterns of male and female access to, for example, single sex and mixed schools, hide gender inequalities within National Curriculum subjects and sideline gender issues in relation to vocational courses (Madden, 2000).

The involvement of various educational quangos in gender issues was erratic and not fully committed. The Qualifications and Curriculum Agency (QCA) advised schools how to address the problems of boys' low achievement in English (QCA, 1998) as did the Office for Standards in Education (OFSTED, 1993, 1996). OFSTED and the Department for Education and Science (DES) commissioned research on boys' achievement (cf. Arnot *et al.*, 1998; Younger & Warrington, 2003). The DES also set up a rather limited website on gender issues (Orr, 2000). Some centralised attempts were made to encourage local education authorities and schools to record gender differences in achievement in line with their development plans. However, OFSTED inspectors were not pushed to take action on their failure to deliver gender equality even though, since 1993, it had equal opportunities built into its inspection criteria. Similarly, the small pilot schemes that were established by central government agencies in three Local Education Authorities (LEAs) and three Education Action Zones to develop specific strategies to raise boys' achievement, and the encouragement given to teacher training institutions to develop the awareness of young teachers in gender issues particularly in relation to post-16 choices (Orr, 2000) had little national impact. Not surprisingly, given this low level of support, school initiatives to improve boys' school performances were sporadic. In 1998, only 40 gender initiatives in England were found (only four of which specifically targeted girls (Arnot *et al.*, 1998)). Some local authorities and schools pulled up boys' performance by developing their own in-house strategies around targeting, pastoral care, organisation change and more structured teaching and learning (Arnot & Gubb, 2001; Younger & Warrington, 2003). However, if boys' underachievement was one of 'the most disturbing problems' in education, it clearly did not receive the priority in government policy or in schools that it deserved.

It is important to note that the boys' education debate did not just restrict the parameters of Labour's gender agenda in education, it significantly shifted gender from the terrain of social justice to that of performance. By the time Labour came to power, the problem of boys' achievement had already become public knowledge—a result of the publication of school league tables with GCSE /A-level results. The public knew that the average boy had lost ground to his female counterpart in terms of school achievement. Each year the statistical dossiers revealed major gender gaps in performance in a range of different national tests and examinations from age 7, 11, 14, 16 and at 18 (Arnot *et al.*, 1999). Of particular concern to Labour, especially in relation to its national literacy targets, was the relative failure of boys to keep up with girls in primary schools in reading and writing. For example, in 2000, the 10% gap in Key Stage 1 English level 2 reading, writing and spelling was disconcertingly large and even more worrying was the increase in this gap at level 3; at Key Stage 2, 10% more girls than boys reaching level 4 in English and 11% and 17% more girls achieved level 5 at KS2 and KS3 respectively (Lewis, 2003, p. 64). Girls pull ahead at English as they progress through secondary school (Arnot *et al.*, 1998) whilst closing the gaps in mathematics and science. Yet despite the introduction of the literacy targets and despite the best efforts of schools, boys still substantially lag behind girls in English at very young ages.

By 1989, even though nationally both boys and girls had increased their level of qualifications in examinations at 16 and 18, major gender gaps at GCSE in favour of girls had been established. Credential inflation was associated with girls' success at gaining 5+ GCSEs at higher grades and to a lesser extent with A-level passes and entry to university. Since then, Labour's policies appear to have made little difference. In 2003 for example, 58% of girls compared with 48% of boys achieved five or more GCSEs with A*–C grades. Boys had only closed this gap by 0.3%—in most intervening years the gap had widened (DfES, 2004a). And, although the proportion of pupils with no GCSE passes has been steadily falling for both sexes since 1993, in 2002/3 there was still a gender gap, with the proportion of boys exceeding that of girls (6.3% to 4.1%). (DfES, 2004b). Similarly the proportion of young women achieving two or more A Levels surpassed that of boys in 1989 (though these figures are tallied without figures from 6th form colleges and excluded GNVQ) (Social Trends 31, 2001, pp. 68–69). By 2001/2, 46% of girls achieved two or more A-level passes compared with 36.2% of boys. Two years into Labour's second term, 82% of girls compared with 76% of boys achieved three or more A levels. Labour educational policies appeared not to be successful in encouraging more boys to achieve the credentials necessary for university education—instead as the DfES (2004c) noted, this 'gender gap has widened noticeably over the last ten years'.

The ideological approach taken by the Labour government to gender relations has been to fit the problem of gender into discussions about school improvement, the re-organisation of teaching (i.e. managerialism) and the setting of targets. The underlying assumption about the gender gap was that boys' underachievement was related to their socialisation within families and schools. The focus of attention which was upon boys' attitudes, motivations, learning preferences and aspirations reflected 1980s' concerns about girl-friendly schooling and female underachievement, although little recourse was made to the wealth of feminist research in this area. This time, there were more biological/natural explanations of male 'failure' and female 'success' and only passing reference to male and female segregation in traditional forms of employment. The DFES standards website summed up official thinking on the reasons for boys' so-called 'underachievement'.

- girls' greater maturity and more effective learning strategies at all ages;
- the apparent success of equal opportunities programmes in schools;
- the emphasis amongst girls on collaboration, talk and sharing;
- (some) boys' disregard for authority, academic work and formal achievement, and the identification with concepts of masculinity which are frequently seen to be in direct conflict with the ethos of the school;

- differences in students' attitudes to work, and their goals and aspirations, linked to the wider social context of changing labour markets, de-industrialisation and male employment;
- differential gender interactions between pupils and teachers in the classroom, particularly as perceived by (some) boys;
- the influence of laddish behaviour, the bravado and noise as boys seek to define their masculinity;
- peer group pressure against the academic work ethic;
- boys' efforts to avoid the culture of failure—a 'can't do/can't win' insecurity leads to a 'won't try/won't play' culture.

(Department for Education and Skills: Standards Site http://www.standards.dfes. gov.uk/ genderandachievement)

The uncritical use by the Labour government of the Conservative bivariate national assessment and examination data also distorted the policy picture in ways that were detrimental to the disadvantaged. The Labour government fell into the binary trap— a form of categoricalism that relied heavily upon theories of sex-role socialisation. From this zero-sum perspective, girls' successes were interpreted as boys' failures and vice versa. The social-psychological implications of such a policy approach were considerable. Epstein *et al.* (1998) suggest that boys as well as their families and schools were not encouraged to address the social conditions of their own formation. The less successful male pupil was likely to see himself as a failure, internalising the discursive construction of masculinity in crisis and boys more generally were demonised as potential criminals, delinquents, as anti-social, and as law and order problems.

Also as a result of this approach, the state failed in its ability to discriminate between different categories of boys and girls. As Teese *et al.* (1995) argued, governments needed to focus on 'which boys' and 'which girls' achieve in different school subjects (cf. Arnot *et al.*, 1996). Rather than focus on the interconnections between ethnicity, social class and gender patterns, a simple statistical story is still constructed around the concept of gender (Gorard, 2001; Gorard *et al.*, 2004). In a recent meta-analysis of updated national examination and assessment data used by Labour in the boys' debate, Connolly (2004) concludes that the moral crisis around boys' under-achievement 'exaggerated and amplified public concern about the issue out of all proportion to the actual size of the problem' (p. 29). Although boys tend to perform less well across all social class and ethnic categories, the overall differences between the sexes at the level of the school, as Gillborn and Mirza (2000) discovered, was 'relatively small' and overshadowed by the differences created by these other social inequalities. The gap between the sexes in school achievement tends to differ *within* each social group and is largest amongst the working classes who are likely to be the lowest achievers. However, the pathologising particularly of working-class boys did not address the material and social inequalities between male pupils, not least the realities faced by African Caribbean boys who are eight times more likely than other pupils to be disciplined and excluded from school and to face discrimination in school and in the labour market (Arnot *et al.*, 1998). Generalisations about girls also hid the reality that particular groups of girls 'significantly underachieve' (Connolly, 2004, p. 30) whilst others achieve exceptionally well (Lewis, 2003).

This 'standards not structures' focus of Labour policy not surprisingly had contradictory spin-offs. For example, attention was focused on the problems associated with the so-called 'feminisation' of boys (Skelton, 1996, p. 186). Evidence for this 'feminisation' was that the majority of primary teaching staff were female. In 2002, women primary teachers outnumbered men by five to one (p. 85). The media, following suit, encouraged the view that primary teaching environments were characterised by 'feminine' teaching styles and interactions with pupils, by low teacher expectations of boys, and by the absence of male role models. Without evidence of such feminisation, there were rather half-hearted attempts by the Teacher Training Agency (TTA) to encourage teacher-training institutions to recruit more men into primary school teaching in order to tackle the problem of boys' underachievement. Meanwhile, the Labour government has been responsible for the appointment of some 132,000 teaching assistants (including nursery nurses and assistants) in England, the majority of whom are female—thus massively accelerating the alleged feminisation of schooling.

More crucially the emphasis on boys' underachievement, on standards not structures, failed to address the impact of a competitive performance-driven school system on boys themselves. Critics argue that the neo-liberal reforms of schooling themselves encourage a 'laddish' culture of resistance amongst a large group of boys, not just working-class boys. Although Labour politicians declared 'laddism' to be the cause of 'unacceptable' levels of educational underachievement (Raphael Reed, 1998), they failed to connect their educational (and economic) policy to such male youth cultural responses. Jackson (2002), for example, argues that competitive highly individualised schooling increases insecurity and pressure especially amongst boys whose gender identity needs to be based upon achieving power, status or superiority. Laddishness is about coping with the fear of academic failure in a dominant culture of performativity. Becky Francis (1999) found that boys associate 'laddishness' with procrastination, intentional withdrawal of effort, a rejection of academic work, the appearance of effortless achievement and disruptive behaviour. The discursive rhetoric around 'underachievement' fails to engage with the production of such male responses to the performance agenda.

Haywood and Mac an Ghaill (1996) read deeper social class implications in the 'standards not structures' ethos of New Labour—implications that were also embedded in the New Right agenda. The authority system, intensified surveillance, disciplinary codes, curriculum and testing, stratification technologies and the allocation and knowledge selection processes which Labour promoted in schools produced a new range of hierarchically ordered masculinities. By raising the stakes in terms of compliance to a school culture which was already class oriented, the sorting and selecting functions of schools became more visible whilst the new school ethos bore little relationship to the realities of economic dysfunction and community breakdown experienced by male working-class youth. In areas in which working-class youth were already marginalised, surveilled and excluded from the productive life of the society, the reconstruction of schooling according to market principles was likely to force confrontations between schoolboys and their teachers. The responses of the 'macho lads' to the new ethos of schooling involved celebrating alternative sources of gender power based on what Mac an Ghaill (1994) called a *hyper-masculinity*—an exaggerated concept of heterosexual masculinity. By 'behaving badly', they regained control of their lives. In Mac an Ghaill's analysis, the major difference from 'the lads' of the 1970s and 'the lads' of the 1990s therefore appeared to be in terms of the purposes/ significance of their counter school culture. Similarly Sewell (1998) found that male heterosexuality played a major role amongst African Caribbean boys in schools. In order to succeed, aspiring black youth assumed a form of 'racelessness' and tried to lose their community and ethnic identity to avoid the wrath of their teachers. A reaction to this racelessness was the counter-promotion of a new black identity which took the form of 'phallocentric masculinity' especially amongst those who found comfort from exclusion in hedonism and an anti-school black machismo.

Paradoxically, Labour's turn towards boys' schooling therefore appeared not to have had the desired consequences of significantly pulling up their achievement levels, nor did it encourage a critical engagement with masculinity *per se* that would promote gender equality. Also as we describe below, the masculinisation of education or its 're' masculinisation would mask serious concerns about girls' continuing social and economic disadvantages.

Feminist concerns and the (re)masculinisation of schooling

Some critics see both Labour's reconstruction of schooling through performativity and its construction of boys as the new victims of schooling as examples of what have been called in Australia the 'backlash blockbusters' (Mills, 2003). Rather than focus on the ways in which dominant forms of masculinity promoted through schooling may cause harm to some boys and to many girls (Mills, 2003, p. 57), the boys' education debate reflected 'the extent to which traditional forms of Western masculinities has been disrupted' (p. 57). The 'masculinity crisis' from this perspective signals the crisis in patriarchy already at play in the Thatcher era (Arnot, 2000). What new school projects for boys could be offering is a form of 'therapeutic politics' (Kenway, 1997) to cope with the effects of gender change—another way perhaps of unifying males through an antagonism to feminism (Kenway, 1997, p. 58).

These critical perspectives suggest that the standards discourse is not gender neutral. Bob Lingard (2003) associates contemporary shifts in policy discourse towards neo-liberal, globalised economic regimes with what he calls 'recuperative masculinity politics' that has little to do with egalitarianism. Here, neo-liberal government policy of the sort associated with the boys' education debate represents an increasing masculinisation of education and greater regulation of the female. For example, even though many more women are entering schools as teaching assistants, the masculine language of 'technical rationality' which privileges teacher accountability over professionalism has major consequences for gender reform movements (Kenway, 1997). In the 1980s, teachers were the 'insider reformers' of schooling in the UK, especially in their development of positive gender practice (Arnot *et al.*, 1999). Today, Mahony (2003) argues, in England teachers are made to feel powerless, teacher training neglects equity issues and management structures in schools are not conducive to the development of gender equality programmes. In 1995, a national review commissioned by the Equal Opportunities Commission (EOC) suggested that the language of equal opportunities had already been converted into performance discourses and that social justice elements of gender equality were sidelined (Arnot *et al.*, 1996). By 2000, the publication *Whatever Happened to Equal Opportunities in Schools?* (Myers, 2000) argued that the activism of the 1980s around gender equality and particularly girls' education had been lost.

Support for Lingard's thesis is found in Raphael Reed's (1998) analysis of the standards discourse found, for example, in *Excellence in Schools* (DfEE, 1997). She suggests that this discourse has been permeated by 'masculinist and bellicose language and imagery'. The new policy language offers to use ' tough love', ' hit squads', 'a name and shame approach', 'zero tolerance of failure', 'silencing the doubts of cynics and the corrosion of the perpetual sceptics' (Raphael Reed, 1998, p. 65). She argues that 'improving schools and boys' performance seems to be predicated on the restitution of hegemonic forms of masculinity and gender oppressive practices' (p. 73). Not only are 'empowering and powerful counter discourses' not available, but neither are broader curriculum approaches which could address the 'fears, anxieties, displacements' (p. 73) and the effects on gender relations of this new pedagogic and political context of education. There appears instead to be an inherent danger that girls' impression that the world is male dominated will be reinforced (Arnot & Gubb, 2001; Lewis, 2003). Associated with this masculinisation of school policies has been the lack of interest in assessing the impact of educational policy on girls' self esteem and in considering their particular needs, particularly in relation to the effects of a macho boys' culture.

In 1997, the setting up of the Social Exclusion Unit which Blair said would ensure 'social cohesion and not social division' (quoted in Raphael Reed, p. 64) created some optimism. However, new approaches to tackle youth crime and truancy focused especially on parental (especially female) responsibilities rather than societal structures and government economic policies.

> All this points to the discursive repositioning of family and state responsibilities but what is of real significance ... is the placing of gender at the heart of state actions: the 'out of control' and uneducable boy is in need of reigning in; the parent at home, oftentimes the single parent/mother, is made responsible for and penalised for his actions; at the same time, she is culpable in the production and sustenance of family poverty by not having a real job, and will be further penalised by changes to tax and benefit support. (Raphael Reed, 1998, pp. 64–65)

Even this discourse of social exclusion, although signalling a shift towards more social democratic agendas, has been found to be masculinised. Social exclusion tends to be defined as a boys' problem—either it is a problem for boys in general or for a particular group of boys. As a result, most of the practices dealing with exclusion are designed with boys in mind, even though girls constitute quite a significant minority of those excluded (Osler & Vincent, 2004). Between 1995 and 1999, over 10,000 secondary aged school girls were permanently excluded from school in England. As

Osler and Vincent (2004) comment—this amounts to the equivalent of the population of a small town (p. 11). Girls represent 'one in four of those subject to formal, permanent disciplinary exclusion from secondary school'—in 2000/1, this meant some 1,566 girls were permanently excluded from school (DfES, 2002). Many more girls are subject to fixed term disciplinary exclusion, are unofficially excluded (for example, when parents were asked to find alternative schooling for their daughters) or self exclude by truanting. Osler and Vincent argue that policy makers fail to take account of the systemic problems of feelings of isolation, personal, family and emotional problems, bullying, withdrawal or truancy, and the disciplinary action taken against girls. They comment:

> ... for many girls informal and unrecognised exclusion is as significant as formal disciplinary exclusion. It can restrict or deny girls their right to education and lead to more general social exclusion. (p. 3)

Given the level of female disadvantage in the labour market, girls' exclusion from schooling, they argue is, 'a particularly blatant injustice' (p. 13). The prioritising of boys' education and the assumptions about girls' success 'masks a reality where there are vast differences in educational experiences and opportunities among girls, as there are among boys' (p. 1). Yet as these authors point out, programmes, provision and resource allocation are targeted at boys (p. 169). Often the needs of pregnant young women, young mothers and young women involved in complex personal relations are not supported by adults and only recently have new ideas been developed to address girls' lives (for example: Cruddas & Haddock, 2003).

Arguably, not only has the (re)masculinisation of schooling failed to help working-class boys but it has also eclipsed the problems faced by working-class girls in the school system. Plummer (2000) documents the statistics of 'failing' working-class girls. In the 1980s, women in the manual working classes only had an eighth of 1% chance of getting to university and a 1.2 chance of any form of higher education. In 1993, the National Commission on Education (1993) set up by the Labour Party similarly reported that this group of women had the least chance of access to higher education. Only 1% of women whose fathers were in Social Class V (unskilled manual classes) had gained a degree—in contrast with 41% of men from the upper middle classes (Social Class 1) (p. 14).

Walkerdine, Lucy and Melody (2001) recently argued that so powerful are the 'discourses/rhetoric of internationalism and progressivism', that concerns about social inequalities associated with traditional forms of social democracy are offered little space within the Labour manifesto:

> The Blair government is fully committed to globalism and its attempts to reduce the welfare state are quite in line with monetarist practice. By and large it sees its job as the humane management of an inevitable global shift. In this context, for social democrats, the end of 'welfarist dependency' and words such as autonomy, grass roots organisation and social capital provide the basis for a mode of government with some element of personal control at a time of profound but inevitable change. (Walkerdine *et al.*, 2001, p. 2)

The production of girls in this context is now 'complex and problematic'—girls and women are being remade into the 'modern neo-liberal subject, the subject of self-invention and transformation who is capable of surviving within the new social, economic and political system' (Walkerdine *et al.*, 2001, p 3). However, the new concept of the autonomous, self managing ' new psychological subjects' (p. 2) is only applicable to middle-class girls, particularly from the professional middle classes.

> The terrible and central fact is this: it is social class that massively divides girls and young women in terms of their educational attainment and life trajectories. [...] Indeed we suspect that the situation is even worse than it had been in the 1960s and 1970s, despite the expansion of higher education. Via a hard and painful route, a small minority of [working class girls in their study] got to university and then to professional careers, but most did not succeed at school and entered the poorly paid labour market ... the gains of the 1960s and 1970s have been shown to be ephemeral and it is wishful thinking ... to pretend that class has disappeared either as a tool of analysis of as a concrete fact. (Walkerdine *et al.*, 2001, p. 4)

These authors challenge what they see as the triumphalist tone in the analysis by the think tank Demos of *Tomorrow's Women* (Wilkinson *et al.*, 1997) which celebrated the rise in women's participation in the labour market. They argue that 'women's position in the new economy is not comfortable' (p. 216). The future, rather than being 'rosy' is in fact distorted by the realities of widening social class differences.

The Labour government's response to women's issues (other than social disrupters such as teenage pregnancies) has been to locate them primarily in the economy and welfare. Here different political ideologies are at play. Paterson (2002) argues that in these spheres Labour politicians draw upon what he calls a form of weak 'developmentalism' to address the requirements of globalisation as well as a revamped European concept of social democracy which allows for state intervention in the name of both economic progress and redistribution. The Fourth PSI survey found that gender inequalities in the labour market 'may be stronger and more persistent than those associated with race and ethnicity'. They have particular importance therefore in the context of encouraging reskilling, modernisation, efficiency and competitive performance in the economy (Mason, 2002, p. 98). In the 1970s, shortages of skilled scientific labour were recognised as holding back economic progress. Yet despite the Equal Pay Act 1970, the then Labour government did not promote gender equity in its interventions into the corporate economy. When the Labour Party took office again in 1997, gender segregation of the work force and pay inequalities were substantial and embedded in traditional employment practices.

New Labour has encouraged the economic sector to create more diverse, less male-centric domains, improve the rights of access to all forms of employment, create more conducive 'micro-cultural' work conditions for men and women and ensure a better work-family balance. Various ministries, from the DTI, Health, the Treasury and the Home Office offer modernising policies to encourage women into productive work, and especially into science and engineering. The Women and Equality Unit (WEU) significantly was moved in 2003 into the Department of Trade and Industry bringing together the Cabinet Minister for Women, Patricia Hewitt and

Jacqui Smith, Minister for Women and Equality. DTI has taken on responsibility for the new single equality body, the Commission for Equality and Human Rights, which will assume the EOC's gender issues and include matters relating to race, disability, age and sexuality. A stream of reports and initiatives (for example the *SET Fair* report (DTI, 2002)), give employers incentives to modernise their gender profiles, to recruit women, engage women academics and foster female enterprise. However, the Equal Opportunities Commission reports that the problem of female low pay, part-time work and continuing correlations of motherhood with childcare has not been effectively tackled. Women still outnumber men in service industry employment, whilst men outnumber women in managerial and administrative positions. The 'mother gap' which disadvantages women with children is large by international standards, and badly affects teenage mothers and low skilled women (Rosenblatt & Rake, 2003, p. 2). The EOC (2001a) highlights the continuing 'life cycle of inequality' which faces many women because of their low pay.

Despite Labour's use of social democratic rhetoric around gender equity in post-16 training and employment, the modernisation of the economy is associated with increasing income differentials between the families of women of different social classes (Arnot, 2002). The ambition of raising national skill levels by New Labour has been thwarted to some extent by continuing patterns of gender differentiation in choices of academic and vocational courses and careers. By 1994, there was clear evidence that girls' success in mathematics and science did not continue after 16, with the result that these subjects became even more masculinised and training and careers in scientific and technical sectors were still male dominated (Arnot *et al.*, 1999; EOC, 2004). The gender skills gap is also embedded in young people's sex stereotypical choices of pre-vocational programmes and in GNVQs, NVQs, Modern Apprenticeships and further and higher education courses (EOC, 2001b). Twenty nine years after the Sex Discrimination Act 1975, large groups of girls still choose 'to train as hairdressers and boys as car mechanics and computer specialists' (EOC, 2001b). Care, childcare, hairdressing and beauty therapy courses are predominantly female whilst the overwhelming majority of students on construction, manufacturing, information technology, motor industry courses are male. Yet despite such extensive gender differentials, the Labour government is intent on pursuing a policy of uncoupling the National Curriculum, introducing a more flexible range of work related courses for 14–16 year olds. Increased flexibility in the school curriculum, as many gender experts have warned, will run counter to the desire to degender the work force and working practices in the UK economy.

Conclusions

The various strands within Labour education policy are complex and interwined. They generate a confusing plethora of reforms, initiatives in schools and in training agencies. The neo-liberal discourse which frames central government understandings of gender inequalities in schooling is in sharp contrast with its own awareness of sex segregation and discrimination in the economy and its understandings of family change and poverty. Gender policy within schools is different from that found in post-16 provision. As we have seen the messages are contradictory. At the school level, a *laissez-faire* approach is promoted and educational failure is explained by drawing on outmoded socialisation theories rather than on contemporary understandings of gender identities and subjectivities about the ways in which competitive school cultures aggravate gender differences and produce disaffected masculinities. Without tackling the cultures in which 'sexual, racial and class inequalities are still embedded it is unlikely that British masculinities will change' (Frosh *et al.*, 2002, p. 264). The outcomes for boys of Labour educational policies therefore may well turn out to be more socially divisive than successfully integrative.

The 'standards not structures' approach fundamentally failed to appreciate the outcomes for women which were highly divisive. Women's issues were assumed to lie outside the educational arena, with the resulting marginalisation of working-class girls' educational needs. Gender equality as an economic goal tends to benefit those most able to benefit—the professional middle classes—thus increasing the economic and social divisions between women and their families. The encouragement of a female scientific and technological labour force could not, of its own, lead to gender equality. Also, the new social policy framework which focuses on single mothers' and children's poverty and discrimination in the work place may reduce the obstacles which women face in bettering their lives. But, as David (2004, p. 48) points out, the 'ideological push for individuality, the adult worker model combining family–work balance ... may also distance women from the educational development of their children'.

Pat Mahony's (2003) biting attack on New Labour suggests that the gender agenda in the UK is 'morally bankrupt' not least because of its displacement of egalitarian agendas. She argues that long before Labour came to power, feminism was seen as part of the problem not part of the solution (p. 75). Thatcherism and the fragmentation of the women's movement contributed to this view. The allegedly more 'inclusive' policy making of Labour could have changed this view. However, in reality, Labour's commitment to policy continuity with the Conservative government meant that a similar aversion to feminist egalitarianism was hidden in the 'softer less aggressive and overtly threatening version of the politics of the Third Way'. Gender became part of the redistributionist discourse in which poverty is explained in cultural terms, in which inclusion means 'labour market attachment', in which inequality is redefined as social exclusion (Levitas, 1998 quoted in Mahony, 2003). Even when citizenship education is called into play to aid social inclusion, stronger egalitarian notions of social justice and rights are marginalised and traditional gendering of public and private spheres are reinforced (Garmarnikov & Green, 2000; Arnot, 2004).

This marginalisation of the women's movement, education feminism and female education by New Labour is not dissimilar to that found in Canada and Australia (Gaskell & Taylor, 2003). In Canada, 'the more developed politics of the women's movement was sidelined'—it occupied less 'public space, gender issues were mainstreamed or 'broadbanded' (p. 166). Whilst the Whitlam Labour Federal government brought femocrats into the policy bureaucracy, by the mid-1990s, concern about boys overrode public discourse about equality overseeing the end of 'state feminism'. Femocrats in Australia are also described as being on the defensive, of 'working a politics of non-decision making' (Lingard, 2003, p. 34).

> This defensive role is about keeping a feminist project on the state agenda, defending past policy aims, and resisting as far as possible a recuperative masculinist policy agenda, or at least the most repugnant aspects of it ... (p. 35)

Lingard (2003) sees the 'end game for national girls' educational policies' when 'gender' was in the title of policy documents (p. 34). Similarly Hayes (2003, p. 7) describes such government strategies as weak and feeble 'accommodations of gender concerns'. These commentators refer to a sense of loss, the 'dumbing down of what we know about how gender functions in schooling', a concentration on 'high stakes' school subjects, on unitary, stable and uncontested notions of identity. The new discursive regime in Australia, according to Foster (1994) offers a notion of 'presumptive equality' in which boys appear to be equally disadvantaged to girls, and men to women. There is 'no reference to power differentials' instead there is, as Lingard (2003, p. 36) points out, a shift 'from modernist hope to postmodernist performativity'. This 'evacuation of a national equity policy presence' (p. 36) is also found in the UK. The new 'educated' citizen, according to Garmanikov and Green (1999, p. 120) is called upon to take responsibility for economic renewal and building social cohesion over and above the state. There is now no 'notion of serious struggle for rights in relation to both the state and other structures of power' (p. 120).

The gender politics of the Labour government in education in relation to English schooling has been diversionary rather than focused—a contrast especially with the post-16 interventionism of Labour's economic policy. It has been both visible and invisible, proactive and *laissez-faire*, promising and disappointing. At best, it is neither coherent nor consistent in its commitment to transform gender relations in the name of gender equality. Gender relations within education reflect both continuities and social change. The spiralling differences between women and between men from different social classes and ethnic groups suggests that Labour's aims for 'education for all' might well be distorted in the long run by its poorly conceived gender politics.

Notes on contributors

Madeleine Arnot is a Professor of Sociology of Education and Fellow of Jesus College, Cambridge. She has published extensively on gender, race and class relations in education and has been actively involved in gender equality initiatives and research. Her recent publications include: *Challenging democracy: international perspectives on gender, education and citizenship* (ed. with J.Dillabough, RoutledgeFalmer, 2000); *Reproducing gender? Essays on educational theory and feminist politics* (RoutledgeFalmer, 2002).

Philip Miles is a lecturer in sociology of education at the University of Lancaster. His recent doctoral thesis focused upon processes of individualisation amongst working class male and female youth engaged in post-16 education in a de-industrialised valley of south Wales. Previous research has included popular music, youth cultures and the pervasive and complex power of producer/ audience relationships.

References

Arnot, M. (2002) *Reproducing gender? Essays on educational theory and feminist politics* (London, RoutledgeFalmer).
Arnot, M. (2004) Citizenship education and gender, in: A. Lockyer, B. Crick & J. Annette (Eds) *Education for democratic citizenship: issues of theory and practice* (Aldershot, Ashgate).
Arnot, M., David, M. & Weiner, G. (1996) *Educational reforms and gender equality* (Manchester, EOC).
Arnot, M., David, M. & Weiner, G. (1999) *Closing the gender gap: postwar social and educational reforms* (Cambridge, Polity Press).
Arnot, M., Gray, J., James, M. & Rudduck, J. (1998) *Recent research on gender and educational performance*, Ofsted Review of Research (London, The Stationery Office).
Arnot, M. & Gubb, J. (2001) *Adding value to boys' and girls' education: a gender and achievement project in West Sussex* (Chichester, West Sussex County Council).
Arnot, M., Millen, D. & Maton, K. (1998) *Current innovative practice in schools in the United Kingdom*, Final Report, Council of Europe.
Connell, R.W. (1987) *Gender and power: society, the person and sexual politics* (Cambridge, Polity Press).
Connolly, P. (2004) *Boys and schooling in the early years* (London, RoutledgeFalmer).
Commission for Social Justice (1993) *The justice gap* (London, IPRR).
Cruddas, L. & Haddock, L. (2003) *Girls' voices: supporting girls' learning and emotional development* (London, Trentham Books).
David, M.E. (2004) *Personal and political: feminisms, sociology and family lives* (London, Trentham).
Department for Education and Employment (DfEE) (1997) *Excellence in schools* (London, Stationery Office).
Department for Education and Science (DfES) (2002) *Permanent exclusions from school and exclusion appeals: England 2000/2001*, Provisional Estimates, 23 May (London, DfES).
Department for Education and Science (DfES) (2004a) *GCSE/GNVQ qualifications, Chart A: percentage of pupils aged 15 achieving 5 or more GCSE's at grades A* to C, England, 1992/3 to 2002/3*. Available online at: www.dfes.gov.uk/trends.
Department for Education and Science (DfES) (2004b) *GCSE/GNVQ qualifications, Chart D: percentage of 15 year old pupils achieving no GCSE passes, 1992/3 to 2002/3*. Available online at: www.dfes.gov.uk/trends.
Department for Education and Science (DfES) (2004c) *GCE/VCE A/AS qualifications, Chart A: Percentage of young people achieving 2 or more GCE A Level passes in schools and FE colleges, England, 1990/1 to 2001/2*. Available online at: www.dfes.gov.uk/trends.
Department for Trade and Industry (2002) SET Fair, the Greenfield Report (London, DTI).
Epstein, D., Elwood, J., Hey, V. & Maw, J. (Eds) (1998) *Failing boys: issues in gender and achievement* (Buckingham, Open University Press).
Equal Opportunities Commission (EOC) (2001a) *Women and men in Britain. The lifecycle of inequality* (Briefing Paper) (Manchester, EOC).
Equal Opportunities Commission (EOC) (2001b) *Women and men in Britain. Sex stereotyping: from school to work* (Manchester, EOC).
Equal Opportunities Commission (EOC) (2004a) *Breaking free from sex stereotyping* (Manchester, EOC). Available online at: www.eoc.org.uk/cseng/policyandcampaigns/sex_stereotyping_-_summary.asp?

Forbes, I. (2002) The political meanings of the Equal Opportunities Project, in E. Breitenbach, A. Brown, F. Mackay & J. Webb (Eds) *The changing politics of gender equality in Britain* (London, Palgrave).

Foster, V. (1994) What about the boys? Presumptive equality and the obfuscation of concerns about theory, research, resources and curriculum in the education of girls and boys, paper presented at the *AARE Annual Conference*, Newcastle, November

Francis, B. (1999) Lads, lasses and (new) Labour: 14–16 year-old students' responses to the 'laddish behaviour and boys' underachievement' debate, *British Journal of Sociology of Education*, 20, 355–371.

Frosh, S., Phoenix, A. & Pattman, R. (2002) *Young masculinities* (London, Palgrave).

Garmanikov, E. & Green, A. (1999) Social capital and the educated citizen, *The School Field*, 10, 103–126.

Gaskell, J. & Taylor, S. (2003) The women's movement in Canadian and Australian education: from liberation and sexism to boys and social justice, *Gender and Education* 15, 151–168.

Gewirtz, S. (1998) Post-welfarist schooling: a social justice audit, *Education and Social Justice*, 1(1), 52–64.

Gillborn, D. & Mirza, H. (2000) *Educational inequality: mapping race, class and gender* (London, OFSTED).

Gorard, S. (2001) Keeping a sense of proportion; the 'politician's error' in analysing school outcomes, *British Journal of Educational Studies*, 47, 235–246.

Gorard, S., Salisbury, J. & Rees, G. (2004) *Revisiting the apparent underachievement of boys: reflections on the implications for educational research*, Education-Line. Available online at: www.leeds.ac.uk (accessed 15 September 2004).

Hayes, D. (2003) Mapping transformation in educational subjectivities: working within and against discourse, *International Journal of Inclusive Education*, 7, 7–18.

Haywood, C. & Mac An Ghaill, M. (1996) What about the boys? Regendered local labour markets and the recomposition of working class masculinities, *British Journal of Education and Work*, 9, 19–30.

Jackson, C. (2002) 'Laddishness' as a self-worth protection strategy, *Gender and Education*, 14, 37–51.

Kenway, J. (1997) Taking stock of gender reform policies for Australian schools: past, present and future, *British Education Research Journal* 23, 329–344.

Levitas, R. (1998) *The inclusive society: social exclusion and New Labour* (London, Macmillan).

Lewis, C. (2003) Raising academic standards: are initiatives aimed at boys detrimental to girls' self esteem? *Education and Health*, 21, 64–67.

Lingard, B. (2003) Where to in gender policy in education after recuperative masculinity politics? *International Journal of Inclusive Education*, 7, 33–56.

Mac An Ghaill, M. (1994) *The making of men: masculinities, sexualities and schooling* (Buckingham, Open University Press).

Madden, A. (2000) Challenging inequalities in the classroom: the role and contribution of the Equal Opportunities Commission, in: K. Myers (Ed.) *Whatever happened to equal opportunities in schools? Gender equality initiatives in education* (Buckingham, Open University Press).

Mahony, P. (2003) Recapturing imaginations and the gender agenda; reflections on a progressive challenge from an English perspective, *International Journal of Inclusive Education*, 7, 75–81.

Mason, D. (2002) Equality, opportunity and difference, in: E. Breitenbach, A. Brown, F. Mackay & J. Webb (Eds) *The changing politics of gender equality in Britain* (London, Palgrave).

Mills, M. (2003) Shaping the boys' agenda: the backlash blockbusters, *International Journal of Inclusive Education*, 7, 57–73.

Myers, K. (Ed.) (2000) *Whatever happened to equal opportunities in schools? Gender equality initiatives in education* (Buckingham, Open University Press).

National Commission on Education (1993) *Learning to succeed after sixteen* (London, National Commission on Education).

Ofsted (1993) *Boys and English* (London, Ofsted).

Ofsted/EOC (1996) *The gender divide: performance differences between boys and girls at school* (London, HMSO).

Orr, P. (2000) Prudence and progress: national policy for equal opportunities (gender) in schools since 1975, in: K. Myers (Ed.) *Whatever happened to equal opportunities in schools? Gender equality initiatives in education* (Buckingham, Open University Press).

Osler, A. & Vincent, K. (2004) *Girls and exclusion: rethinking the agenda* (London, Routledge-Falmer).

Paterson, L. (2003) The three educational ideologies of the British Labour Party, 1997–2001, *Oxford Review of Education*, 29(2), 165–186.

Plummer, G. (2000) *Failing working class girls* (London, Trentham Books).

Qualifications and Curriculum Authority (QCA) (1998) *Can do better: raising boys' achievement in English* (London, QCA).

Raphael Reed, L. (1998) Zero tolerance: gender performance and school failure, in: D. Epstein, J. Elwood, V. Hey & J. Maw (Eds) (1998) *Failing boys: issues in gender and achievement* (Buckingham, Open University Press).

Rosenblatt, G. & Rake, K. (2003) *Gender and poverty* (London, Fawcett Society).

Sewell, T. (1998) Loose canons: exploding the myth of the 'black macho' lad, in: D. Epstein, J. Elwood, V. Hey & J. Maw (Eds) (1998) *Failing boys: issues in gender and achievement* (Buckingham, Open University Press).

Skelton C. (1996) Learning to be tough: the fostering of maleness in one primary school, *Gender and Education*, 8, 185–197.

Teese, R., Davies, M. Charlton, M. & Polesel, J. (1995) *Who wins at school? Boys and girls in Australian secondary education* (Melbourne, Department of Education Policy and Management, University of Melbourne).

Walkerdine, V., Lucey, H. & Melody, J. (2001) *Growing up girl: psychosocial explorations of gender and class* (London, Palgrave).

Wilkinson, H. & Howard, M. with Gregory, S., Hayes, H. & Young, R. (1997) *Tomorrow's women* (London, Demos).

Younger, M. & Warrington, M. (2003) *Raising boys' achievement: interim report* (Cambridge, University of Cambridge Faculty of Education).

INDEX